D0280955

THE CAVENDISH GUIDE TO MOOTING

Second Edition

Cavendish
Publishing
Limited

London • Sydney

THE CAVENDISH GUIDE TO MOOTING

Second Edition

John Snape, MA (Oxon)
Solicitor, Senior Lecturer in Law,
Nottingham Law School,
The Nottingham Trent University

Gary Watt, MA (Oxon)
Solicitor, Lecturer in Law,
School of Law,
The University of Warwick

Cavendish
Publishing
Limited

London • Sydney

Second edition first published in Great Britain 2000 by Cavendish Publishing Limited, The Glass House, Wharton Street, London WC1X 9PX, United Kingdom

Telephone: +44 (0) 20 7278 8000   Facsimile: +44 (0) 20 7278 8080

E-mail: info@cavendishpublishing.com

Visit our Home Page on http://www.cavendishpublishing.com

© Snape, J and Watt, G   2000

First edition   1997

Second edition   2000

All rights reserved. No part of this publication may be reproduced, stored in a retrieval system, or transmitted in any form or by any means, electronic, mechanical, photocopying, recording, scanning or otherwise, except under the terms of the Copyright, Designs and Patents Act 1988 or under the terms of a licence issued by the Copyright Licensing Agency, 90 Tottenham Court Road, London W1P 9HE, UK, without the prior permission in writing of the publisher.

British Library Cataloguing in Publication Data

Watt, Gary
The Cavendish Guide to Mooting – 2nd ed
1 Moot courts 2 Case method
I Title II Snape, John III Guide to mooting
348.4'1'04

ISBN   1 85941 549 0

Printed and bound in Great Britain

Dedication

To Edward and Elizabeth Snape

John Snape

To my parents

Gary Watt

Foreword

In the early days of the Inns of Court and of Chancery, as in the Inns of Court during this century, moots have been a most important part of the life and education of the student and the young barrister. Now, the practice of holding moots has grown far beyond the confines of the Inns. Most law schools either organise moots themselves, or provide facilities for students' law societies to do so. Any which do not, should. International mooting competitions have been established which bring great prestige to the winners, whether on a transatlantic, Commonwealth or European Community basis. National and international moots foster interest in particular areas of the law which might otherwise be left to classroom teaching. On a national level, the annual environmental law mooting competition organised by the United Kingdom Environmental Law Association (where The Nottingham Trent University has done particularly well) has covered some important topics at a high standard. On the international level, one of the most remarkable moots I have presided over was the final of the competition in a European Community law topic. This was held in English and constituted students from 12 universities from nine States in Central and Eastern Europe which were not Member States of the Community. I understand, also, that mooting is catching on in some continental countries, for example, France – another pointer that Community influences are not all in one direction.

So, mooting is alive and well. But, no one pretends that to moot successfully is an innate gift. Indeed, a first moot, without help, can be an ordeal; taking place before a distinguished panel of eight or 10 judges in a large hall with a big audience of experienced lawyers, younger rivals and, most difficult of all, friends and chambers colleagues, it can be an unnerving experience. My first certainly was. Even mooting before the, more or less, friendly face of a familiar professor demands more, or at least different, preparation and presentation skills from a weekly tutorial or annual viva.

The basic idea of what a moot is, can, of course, be picked up by observing moots and talking to others who have mooted. But, this is not nearly enough to ensure success and to avoid avoidable mistakes. There has been a real need for a book to give the sort of help to which I have referred. This is that book.

The authors are very conscious of the pressures on a first time mooter and, for that reason, they treat mooting as a sort of game – as it is in comparison with an actual case in court – by way of helping to reduce the tension. But, they do not underestimate the seriousness of the game, whether the object of the moot is to elucidate the answer to a difficult point of law (on which there may be no or only inconsistent authority, and on which students are interested enough to want to know the answer) or to test the prowess of those who seek to become advocates and to find the stars. In the former case, the judge's aim is to try to give the right answer, in the latter, to seek the best performance on the basis only of the arguments advanced before him, so that the judge should not be seen to be reading a fully prepared judgment.

The technique adopted by the authors is to ask 100 very down to earth questions; the answers are given lucidly and, it is clear, after the most careful thought and preparation. As a consequence, the mooter can quickly find the help he or she needs, at various stages, to deal with his or her weaknesses and doubts and does not have to plough through whole chapters in order to do so. The text is extremely readable and I did not have a boring moment in reading it. The advice and the rules are interspersed with anecdotes and reminiscences of great advocates and reportable judges which enliven the already interesting text.

Some of the material is necessarily basic. As well as not having too many points and not citing too many cases, the book has advice on how to choose and cite authorities; how to address the judge and deal with his interruptions; how to deal with a hopeless case and not be discouraged if the argument is lost (so long as the chance of winning the competition is still open); how to be ready to deal with the co-mooter's argument in case the judge asks about it and, not least, how to phrase the parts of a speech whilst coping with the time limits which begin by seeming too long and end by being too short. Some of these points may appear very elementary, but a breach of them can all too easily disturb the atmosphere in which the mooter speaks.

But, much of the material in this book has a long term value as well and includes advice on how to find one's way around the law library; how to look for cases (including those in the individual parts of the *English Reports*); how to winnow the *ratio decidendi* of a case and to appreciate the scope of *stare decisis*. Essentially, it demonstrates how to achieve a clear and compelling, or at least persuasive, statement of one's case, rather than insisting on producing an overload of irrelevant research material.

The appendices are very useful, not just the specimen moot, but others besides. The student will find many tips as to how to win a competition by studying the moot assessment sheet intended for the judges in Appendix 7.

This is a splendid book in every way, not only calculated (that is, intended) to give rules and advice but also calculated (that is, likely) to encourage young lawyers and law students to want to moot.

The regular mooter – and not only the ambitious advocate or politician – will want his own copy of this book. Every law school in the English-speaking world should have at least two copies or, preferably, since there are usually four mooters to a moot, four copies. They will quickly become well thumbed.

Lord Slynn of Hadley

Preface

To the authors' knowledge, this is the first book which is dedicated solely to the instruction and inspiration of mooters. This is surprising, since the history of mooting in England goes back more than 500 years. There have been a number of books of moots, but the greater part of these have been devoted to the reproduction of moot problems, rather than to mooting itself. Our overriding goal in this book is to be the student's guide.

With that goal in sight, we have set out to answer 100 questions which students have asked, might ask, or ought to ask, about the subject. The questions are loosely grouped under the following broad headings: (1) Preliminary; (2) Preparation; (3) Performance; and (4) Principles and Practice. We hope that a quick glance at the sort of questions appearing under each of the four headings will swiftly guide you, the mooter, to a solution to whatever mooting query you might have. If you do not immediately identify the precise wording of your own burning question in the list of 100, ask yourself whether the substance of your question might still be covered somewhere else on the list. There is a detailed index which enables you to see where related material is discussed in the answer to more than one question. Because of the approach we have taken, there is some overlap between the answers to some of the questions and, where appropriate, we have therefore cross-referenced them. You should, thus, be able to read the Guide from beginning to end, just as easily as refer to the answers to individual questions. If, despite your searching, you can still find no answer to your own question, please write to the authors. There is always room to consider one more. After all, it is an enduring oddity that 101 is taken to be a round number for the purposes of a question and answer book!

Throughout the Guide, we emphasise that mooting should be viewed as a game. Like all games, the details of its rules may differ slightly, depending on where it is played. We have made some reference to the rules of individual mooting competitions. However, we must emphasise strongly that, whether you are mooting competitively or as part of the assessment of your course, you should always check the rules of the relevant competition or assessment in order to ascertain whether the answers which we suggest are in any way modified by those rules.

Great though the emphasis is, throughout the Guide, on mooting being seen as a game, it must be stressed, most forcefully, that this fact makes the moot court a fundamentally different place from a real court which can be a terrifying place. Part of the benefit to be gained from the experience of mooting is to appreciate the difference of context and, in this sense alone, the emotional limitations of the mooting exercise. No lives are ruined or fortunes lost, it is to be hoped, through what happens in a moot court. In a real court, naturally, the position is quite different.

Throughout the Guide, we have tried to keep in mind the fact that not every mooter will be free from disability. Where possible, our writing has tried to reflect our appreciation of this fact.

The authors each bring a different experience of mooting to this guide. As a student, John Snape mooted both for his college, St Edmund Hall, and for Oxford University. He appeared, in turn, before Lord Templeman and Lord Justice Robert Goff, and was a member of the moot team which defeated Cambridge in the Varsity Moot of 1984. The *Cambridge Law Journal* for that year records that defeat for Cambridge came by the narrowest of margins! He is a mooting tutor on the LLB course at Nottingham Law School, The Nottingham Trent University, and an experienced moot judge. For a number of years, Gary Watt had responsibility for mooting on the law degree at Nottingham Law School, The Nottingham Trent University, where mooting has been a constituent part of the law degree course for a number of years. As a young student, his first experience of mooting was to sit as a moot judge with Lord Justice Henry, with whom he concurred. He has a special interest in the intellectual skills content in legal education and has written on that subject.

The authors would like to express their thanks to Cliff Atkins, Principal Lecturer in Law, The Nottingham Trent University, who has, for many years, supervised competitive mooting by students at Nottingham Law School. In this time, he has organised the Law School's participation in the English-Speaking Union National Mooting Competition and guided student teams to national victory in that competition, and to others in the Philip C Jessup International Law Moot Court Competition and the United Kingdom Environmental Law Association Moot. The contract, evidence and trusts law moot problems included in Appendix 2 were written and prepared by him. We are grateful to Mr Atkins for his support for this guide, and for his inspirational enthusiasm for mooting.

The authors would also like to thank Chris Garratt, Terry Hanstock and Angela Donaldson of the Library and Information Services, The Nottingham Trent University, for assistance in obtaining source materials; Professor Peter Kunzlik, for reading the Guide in manuscript; Professor Michael Gunn, Head of the Department of Academic Legal Studies, The Nottingham Trent University, for reading the Guide in typescript; and Professor Diane Birch of the University of Nottingham, for permission to use the criminal law moot problem in Appendix 2. For detailed advice on the effect of the Civil Procedure Rules 1998 on the material covered in the Guide, the authors are greatly indebted to Jane

Ching, Principal Lecturer in Law, The Nottingham Trent University. The impact of 'Woolf' in the mooting context is only gradually being assessed.

Finally, our thanks are due to Lord Slynn of Hadley, a long time supporter of student mooting, for his generous Foreword to this Guide.

John Snape
Gary Watt
April 2000

Acknowledgments

Grateful acknowledgment is made for permission to reproduce the extracts from the *Official Handbook for the English-Speaking Union National Mooting Competition 1999–2000*. In 2000–01, the competition will be sponsored by Essex Court Chambers.

Grateful acknowledgment is also made to the Incorporated Council of Law Reporting for England and Wales for permission to reproduce extracts from the *Weekly Law Reports*.

Every effort has been made to trace all the copyright holders but, if any have been inadvertently overlooked, the publishers will be pleased to make the necessary arrangement at the first opportunity.

Contents

Table of Cases

Table of Statutes

Table of Statutory Instruments and European Legislation

Statutory Instruments

European legislation

1   Preliminary

1   What is mooting?

We must begin this *Guide to Mooting* by explaining what the word *mooting* means. To do so, we need, first of all, to define the word *moot*. Each of these words may be used either as a verb or a noun.

As a noun, a *moot* is the argument of the legal issues raised by a hypothetical case which takes place in the imaginary setting of a court of law. This argument is highly stylised, since it follows the conventions of argument used in a real court as closely as possible. There are usually five participants in the moot. Two of the participants represent one party to the hypothetical case. Two more of them represent the other party to the case. The fifth participant acts as the *moot judge*. The two participants representing one party to the case are, together, one *moot team*, whilst the two participants representing the other party to the case are the other moot team. Each of the four participants representing the parties is usually a law student, while the fifth, the moot judge, is usually a more experienced lawyer, such as a member of staff at the law school where the moot is being held, a postgraduate law student, a legal practitioner or, very occasionally, a real judge.

The parties to the case are usually, although not always, referred to as *Appellant* and *Respondent*, respectively. Since the parties are fictional characters, being represented by each of the two moot teams, two of the four members of the teams are styled *Appellants*, and the other two *Respondents*. As we shall see in a moment, one of the Appellants is called the *Lead Appellant*, whilst the other is called the *Junior Appellant*. In the same way, one of the Respondents is styled the *Lead Respondent* and the other the *Junior Respondent*. Naturally, where a real judge occasionally sits as a moot judge, he or she is acting in the capacity of a moot judge, rather than as a judge of the court to which he or she belongs.

These, then, are the five participants usually involved in a moot. There may, occasionally, be one or more of three others also, as discussed in the answer to Question 11. These are, the *court clerk*; the *amicus curiae* and the *master/mistress of moots*. The number of participants may, in some cases, be less than five. In the authors' view, it is unwise for there to be more than two members of each moot team. It is something of a luxury to have more than one moot judge, although it is not unknown. Usually, the single moot judge is taking the place of what, in a real court, would be a panel of at least three judges, or possibly five, depending on the court in which the case was being heard. Moreover, when the moot forms part of a course of legal study, the Appellants and Respondents need not be divided into teams since moot problems can be designed to enable each of the participants to make autonomous submissions.

During the moot, the five participants argue the legal issues raised by the hypothetical case in a way which, as we have said, reflects the form and substance of the legal arguments in a real court as closely as possible. We refer to the contribution of each member of the two moot teams as his or her *moot presentation* or *moot performance*. Appendix 1 to this Guide is a transcript of a moot, illustrating typical moot presentations by each member of the two moot teams, with typical interjections by the moot judge. In fact, before reading any further, you may wish to read through the example moot in Appendix 1, in order to concretise the abstractions referred to above, by reference to that example.

The hypothetical case which raises the legal issues argued by the five participants is devised in order to highlight particular issues of doubt in the law. These issues of doubt may arise from case law or statute and, where the moot is set in an appellate court, are referred to as *grounds of appeal*. We make frequent references to this term throughout the Guide. Most moot problems contain two grounds of appeal. Each member of each team argues one side of each ground of appeal. In doing so, they are described as making *submissions* on the relevant ground of appeal. Thus, the Lead Appellant and the Lead Respondent make submissions on opposing sides of the *first ground of appeal*, whilst the Junior Appellant and the Junior Respondent make submissions on opposing sides of the *second ground of appeal*.

The hypothetical case, which we refer to as *the moot problem*, may require the participants to imagine, for example, a combination of facts which are subtly different from the leading case in the relevant area of law. The five participants will therefore be required, by the grounds of appeal, to argue whether the legal rule applicable to the facts of the moot problem is different from, or the same as, the rule which was applied by the judges in that leading case. To take a second example, doubt may have been expressed by legal commentators as to whether the provisions of a particular statute might apply to a particular set of facts. This type of issue of doubt is reflected in the first ground of appeal in the example moot in Appendix 1. In the example moot, the issue is whether *wilful default*, in s 30(1) of the Trustee Act 1925, covers what the Respondent, Mr Dearing, has done, as described in the facts of the moot problem (see Appendix 1, para 2(a)).

The *selection* of the grounds of appeal in the moot problem will have been the task of the author of the moot problem. This individual, who is not usually a participant in the moot, is often anonymous, although he or she may be identified by name where the moot problem is taken from a published collection of moot problems (see the answer to Question 99). In certain cases, the author of the moot problem may even be the moot judge, although he or she may not make the other four participants in the moot aware of this fact!

However, in other cases, the author of the moot problem may be prohibited from also being a participant in the moot.

Once the arguments have been completed, say after about an hour, the moot judge will usually give a short judgment, in which he or she will not only reach a conclusion as to the legal issues of doubt raised by the grounds of appeal, but will also decide which of the teams of participants has mooted better than the other. Thus, as a member of each moot team, you will need to have given careful attention, not only to the law, but also to the presentational and interpersonal skills involved in persuading the moot judge of the correctness of the submissions made by you.

Some moots are held on a competitive basis, according to competition rules. Others are held for fun, merely to air the arguments on particular issues of doubt in the law. With increasing frequency, however, others are assessed as part of a course of legal study, usually a law degree. Where a moot forms part of a law degree in this way, you may find that certain features of the moot described above are modified. For example, greater weight may be given in the assessment to the *law* in your submissions, than to your presentational and interpersonal skills. Again, you might not be mooting as a member of a moot team, but as an individual. In other words, because the moot is taking the place of a coursework assessment, your moot presentation will be assessed as an individual. Again, in this context, no judgment is likely to be given by the moot judge, an assessment being made afterwards as to whether you have given a satisfactory moot presentation.

It follows from the meaning of the noun *moot* that the verb *to moot* denotes what a participant in a moot is doing during the moot. Although, strictly perhaps, it denotes only what an individual does in the course of his or her moot presentation, it seems fair to use it as a verb to describe everything that an individual does, throughout the whole process of preparing and performing his or her presentation.

It should also be apparent, from everything we have discussed so far, that the verbal noun *mooting* is a word used to describe the whole process of participating in a moot, either as Appellant, Respondent or as the moot judge. As a verb, *mooting* is a present participle, meaning 'taking part in a moot'. Naturally enough, the word *mooter* is, therefore, used to describe each of the participants in the two moot teams. Surprisingly, perhaps, it is not often used to describe the moot judge.

The word 'moot' even appears as an adjective in some contexts. Thus, it has been said that 'a case is moot when the issues presented are no longer "live" or the parties lack a legally cognisable interest in the outcome'.[1] See, further, the answer to Question 3.

---

1   *Powell v McCormack* 395 US 486, p 496 (1969).

Finally, it is worth noting how old the words *moot, mooting* and *mooter* are. For instance, if you look at *The Oxford English Dictionary*, you will see that the earliest reference given there to the meaning of 'moot', as a noun meaning a formal legal discussion, is 1531. Other meanings are shown to go back to the late eighth century AD.

The origins and history of mooting are considered by us in the answer to Question 4.

2 How does a moot differ from a mock trial?

The skills which you need as a mooter are, to some extent, similar to those which you would need as a participant in a mock trial. There is, however, a fundamental difference between a moot and a mock trial.

A mock trial is an adversarial exercise intended to *test the evidence* in a hypothetical case set in a hypothetical court. In other words, a mock trial is designed to establish the *facts* of the case. By contrast with a mock trial, the participants in a *moot* have to assume that the evidence has already been tested, and that the facts of the case have been determined, as set out in the moot problem (see the answer to Question 1). Rather than being designed to test the participant's ability to argue a question of law, as in a moot, a mock trial is designed to test the participant's skills of *handling and presenting evidence*, and examining, cross-examining and re-examining witnesses.

We do not discuss the meaning of these terms in detail in this Guide. However, a brief explanation may be appropriate, since it may serve to clarify how different the skills employed in a moot are from those employed in a mock trial. Examination – examination-in-chief, as it is also known – is the questioning of a witness on oath by the advocate who has called that witness.[2] Cross-examination is the questioning of the same witness by the advocate on the other side in order to reduce the impact of the witness's evidence; and re-examination, which is confined to points arising out of the cross-examination, means questioning by the advocate originally calling the witness in order to explain any apparent inconsistencies shown up by the cross-examination. (The answer to Question 38 includes a summary of one of the most devastating real court cross-examinations on record, the one conducted by Norman Birkett QC of a defence witness, Mr Arthur Isaacs, in the so called 'burning car case'.)

One way of getting to understand the difference between a moot and a mock trial, is to note that moots are almost invariably set in appellate courts, where the judges are asked to dispose of an appeal on a question of law. Mock trials, on the other hand, are set in a court of first instance, where a judge or jury is

---

2   Following the introduction of the Civil Procedure Rules (CPR) 1998, examination-in-chief is now often dispensed with: see CPR, Part 32, r 32.5(2). See fn 38 below.

asked to make findings of fact on the evidence and to apply established law to those facts, in order to produce the verdict in the case. You can thus think of a mock trial as being, in one sense, the *reverse* of a moot. In a moot, the emphasis is on the *legal* argument and, in a mock trial, the emphasis is on the *factual* argument. Mock trials of civil actions taking place on and after 26 April 1999 need to take account of the Civil Procedure Rules 1998, the product of Lord Woolf's report of 1996, *Access to Justice*. Most noticeably, perhaps, the new rules replace 'plaintiff' with 'claimant', but there are other important changes of language, some of which are discussed at various points in this Guide.[3] (There have been no 'plaintiffs' in England and Wales since 25 April 1999!)

(See the answer to Question 90 for the distinction between a judge's finding of fact and his or her decision on the law.)

3   How does a moot court differ from a real court?

... it has never, so far as I know, been part of our system for the court to decide questions of law on facts which are, or have become, hypothetical. Ours is not a mooting system.[4]

In a comparatively recent edition of the *Columbia Law Review*,[5] there is an essay by an American appellate judge, Judge Alex Kozinski, entitled 'In praise of moot court – not!'. In this lengthy critique of mooting in American law schools, the judge highlights a number of ways in which the 'moot court' of American law schools fails to reflect the realities of American appellate court practice. The judge's criticisms flow from the fact that American moot courts claim, according to Judge Kozinski, 'to be the pre-eminent tool for teaching students the skills of courtroom advocacy'.

The fact is, of course, that US law degrees, unlike their English counterparts, are postgraduate studies designed to be a precursor to legal practice. English law degrees do not have, as their sole aim, preparation for legal practice, nor do they claim that mooting is the prime source of advocacy training for practice (see the answer to Question 2). Having thus drawn the sting from the American essay, as it appertains to mooting in an English law school, it is nevertheless worth extracting some parts of the essay in the answer to this question, since

---

3   See, generally, Grainger, I and Fealy, M, *An Introduction to the New Civil Procedure Rules*, 1999, London: Cavendish Publishing (2nd edn, 2000); Plant, C (ed), *Blackstone's Guide to the Civil Procedure Rules*, 2nd edn, 1999, London: Blackstone. See fn 38 below.

4   *Re Rowhook Mission Hall, Horsham* [1985] Ch 62, p 83H, *per* Nourse J. US cases also attest to the fact that courts generally '... do not sit to decide abstract questions of law'. See *Guinness plc v Ward* (1992) 955 F 2d 875, p 896 (1992).

5   (1997) 97 Col LR 178.

they indicate some basic differences between a moot court and a real court. Judge Kozinski writes, pp 182–83:

> In real court, the advocate's focus is on winning the case for the client. The client's and lawyer's interests almost always dovetail, so the lawyer isn't happy unless the client wins ...

> Moot court is much different: the advocate has no interest in the outcome of the case; his interest is entirely personal – winning praise for his performance ...

> Experienced lawyers do, of course, use their wit and charm to win the trust of the judge and jury. But this is not an end in itself; it is a means for winning the case for the client. Personal charm, the ability to give good answers to questions, the subtle art of intimidating judges with veiled warnings that they will look foolish or unprincipled if they reach a particular result – these are merely some of the tools in the advocate's arsenal of persuasion. But persuasion is an art quite distinct from any of the techniques used to persuade; ... What this means is that we can almost never tell how persuasive an advocate is, unless we actually let him try to persuade us.

> But this is precisely what moot court judges are told *not* to do: Judge not the merits of the case, they are told, but the effectiveness of the advocates.

Quite apart from the differences between American and English law degrees, even in a moot in an English law school, the importance attached to non-legal skills in that moot may vary, depending on the reason why the moot is being held. More importance may be attached, in a competitive moot, to non-legal skills than in a moot which forms part of a course of legal study (see the answer to Question 9). Mooting is essentially to be seen as a game, which is saved from pretentiousness by the fictitious nature of the grounds of appeal. In addition, as the passage above makes clear, the moot judge and the mooters have different objectives from real advocates and real judges. Moot judges are expected to pronounce on a different type of issue from those on which real judges pronounce. As Judge Kozinski states, moot judges usually pronounce on the moot rather than on the law (see, again, the answer to Question 9).

So much for differences of *objective* between a real court and a moot court. In terms of *physical appearance*, the moot court can hardly be expected to match the Victorian Gothic splendour of the Royal Courts of Justice in the Strand in London.[6] Professor William Twining, conducting a tour of the imaginary University of Rutland (his representation of the typical English law school), observes:[7]

> Returning to the ground floor, one finds ... an open area, known as 'reality checkpoint' (again a sign of American influence), which provides the main, rather limited social space for undergraduates; and perhaps the one feature of the new

---

6   *The Royal Courts of Justice – An Introduction for Visitors* (see fn 9 below) contains an engaging account of the design and building of the Royal Courts of Justice.

7   Twining, W, *Blackstone's Tower: The English Law School, The Hamlyn Lectures*, 1994, London: Stevens/Sweet & Maxwell, p 71.

extension that clearly identifies this as a House of Laws. This is the Moot Court, which was designed to look something like a courtroom, but doubles as the main lecture theatre and meeting room. This peculiar hybrid has an elevated bench, a fair imitation of a jury box and cramped uncomfortable pews for counsel; but the 'public' sits in the standard banked seats of a modern lecture theatre. Here students argue simulated appeals before real or simulated judges with some eagerness; much less frequently, they stage an occasional mock trial.

For a suggestion of how a moot court could be laid out, see Appendix 9.

Occasionally, in the authors' experience of mooting, we have witnessed moot judges and mooters attempt to lift, momentarily, the veil between the hypothetical moot court and the reality of legal practice. On one occasion, for instance, a moot judge asked one moot team why the case in the moot problem had been initiated in the High Court of Justice, when the damages claimed were so small that the action ought to have been brought in the county court.[8] On other occasions, students have tried to avoid tough questioning by asking the moot judge's permission to take their 'client's further instructions'. All such incursions into practical reality add interest to the moot and may lighten the proceedings, but they, typically, serve no useful purpose and, ideally, are to be avoided.

To see a real English appellate court, a visit to one of the sittings of the Court of Appeal in the Royal Courts of Justice – the only location where the Court of Appeal sits – is a very worthwhile experience. You will be familiar with the names of many of the judges hearing the appeals from your reading of recent reported cases.[9] As a law student, you may also be able to obtain access to sittings of the Law Lords and of the Judicial Committee of the Privy Council.

4 Where did mooting originate?

Mooting, today, continues a tradition which probably began in England about five centuries ago, in a relatively small geographical area of London. We say, *probably*, because recent research by Professor Baker indicates that, depending

---

8   Whether a moot judge would be inclined to ask the same or a similar question after 25 April 1999 is, as is said, a moot point. (The reasons for this are complex and beyond the scope of this Guide.)

9   The Court Service have produced helpful guides to and information about the Royal Courts of Justice, see, eg, Court Service, *The Royal Courts of Justice – Access and Facilities Information for People with Disabilities* (a useful pamphlet of a single sheet); *The Royal Courts of Justice – An Introduction for Visitors* (a 12 page booklet of historical notes, directions, notes on court dress, ceremonial occasions, etc); *Visitor Information for Hearings at the Royal Courts of Justice* (a four page booklet giving details of what to do on arrival, facilities for disabled visitors, etc). All of these publications are available free of charge from the Enquiry Desk just inside the main entrance to the Royal Courts of Justice. All of these lack publication details, which is surprising since they contain a great deal of useful and interesting information.

on how many types of legal discussion qualify as moots, mooting may be even older than this (see the footnotes to this question, below).

Be that as it may, mooting was a fundamental component in the system of education at the Inns of Court and the Inns of Chancery, at a time when printed materials were non-existent, or at least fairly scarce, and when the oral opinions of eminent lawyers outside court were just as important as those spoken by the judges in court. However, over the centuries, legal texts became more easily available and practical legal education came to be valued less, as the essence of legal science came to be seen as the digesting of written authorities rather than as the shared oral learning of the barristers. Consequently, mooting lost its pre-eminent place in legal education. Indeed, it is only in very modern times that law schools have given mooting at least some of the importance that it once enjoyed in the Inns of Court.

The heart of the system of education for aspiring barristers, which evolved in the Inns of Court and the Inns of Chancery between about 1400 and 1500, was a combination of lectures and verbal argument, rather than private study and written work. The system was, as Sir William Holdsworth said, 'a constant rehearsal and preparation for the life of the advocate and judge'.[10] Lincoln's Inn, Gray's Inn, the Middle Temple and the Inner Temple, the four Inns of Court which we know today, were already prestigious schools for barristers by 1400. On the other hand, the Inns of Chancery,[11] the buildings of only two of which survive today (those of Staple Inn and Barnard's Inn), were where younger law students were taught basic legal procedure, before they moved on to one of the Inns of Court. In all, there were nine Inns of Chancery by 1500, at about which time they came under the supervision of the four Inns of Court. Moots took place in both the Inns of Court and in the Inns of Chancery. The division between lectures (which were called 'readings') and oral argument in the Inns seems to have been similar in concept to the division between lectures, on the one hand, and seminars, tutorials and moots on the other, which is used by law schools today. Obviously, before the 1470s, when printing presses began to operate in England, readings and verbal argument, including moots, were central to the education of barristers at the Inns, because of the total absence of printed texts. Professor Baker estimates that, even by 1600, more than a century after the advent of printing in England, there were only about 100 law books in print!

---

10 Holdsworth, W (Sir), *A History of English Law 1903–72*, 1965, London: Methuen/Sweet & Maxwell, Vol 2, p 508.

11 The use of the word Chancery here is different from the modern usage: see Baker, JH, *An Introduction to English Legal History*, 3rd edn, 1990, London: Butterworths, p 184. The authors would like to record their indebtedness to this fine work, which has been of great assistance to them throughout the preparation of this book.

In the heyday of mooting at the Inns of Court, between the late 15th century and about 1550, moots would be held in the great halls of the Inns, with the *Benchers of the Inn* or, depending on the time of year, *Utter Barristers*, acting as the judges, and with two Inner Barristers and two Utter Barristers acting as counsel. These terms, as used in this period, require explanation. An *Inner Barrister* was one who was still engaged in his seven years' training, attending readings and keeping commons with his fellows, prior to being called to the bar. *Inner Barristers* were so called because they sat within the bar at moots. *Utter* (that is, 'Outer') Barristers were ones who had already been called to the bar, having completed this period of training. These stood outside the bar. *Benchers* were barristers of at least 10 years' standing who had previously been *Readers*, but became Benchers subsequent to giving a series of readings on a statute. The main task of the Benchers was to sit on the bench and take the part of moot judges. Because of the relative seniority of the Benchers and the Utter Barristers, and because of the importance of oral opinions in the tradition of the bar before about 1550, it was not unknown for opinions given in moots actually to be cited in the courts in Westminster Hall.

You can see examples of 15th and 16th century moot problems in the Selden Society's *Readings and Moots in the Inns of Court*, edited by Professor Baker.[12] These moot problems will strike you as being rather odd, to say the least. First, they seem to be intended to raise a profusion of points, rather than just two grounds of appeal. Secondly, most 15th and 16th century moot problems seem to end with the instruction *Ceux que droit*, instead of containing the equivalents of grounds of appeal. According to Professor Baker, these three words are a telescoping of the law-French *Ceux que droit en ount sont a lour recoverie*, which he translates as 'The parties with the right wish to be advised how to go about their recovery'.[13] This indicates that the emphasis in these 15th century moots seems to have been on the niceties of pleading and procedure rather than on what would look to the modern lawyer like substantive law. These moot problems have wonderful names, like *The Brewer* and *Le Leverer* (law-French for *The Greyhound*, the modern French being *Le Lévrier*) and, famously and tortuously, the moot problem known as *Cat in the Pan*, a strange expression which 'may have been associated with the kind of subtle reasoning which led to

---

12 Baker, JH (ed), *Readings and Moots at the Inns of Court in the Fifteenth Century*, 1989, London: Selden Society, Vol 2. The source of the material in this part is the introductory essay to that volume by Professor JH Baker (especially pp xlv–xlvii), which is a wonderfully informative window on this lost world.

13 *Op cit*, Holdsworth, fn 10, Vol 2, p 507, note 2, quotes a text from the time of King Henry VI (1422–61) referring to the inferior standard of pleading in the Inns of Chancery. The quotation is in law-French: *'Ceo este la forme de pleading en Inns de Chancery; mes la forme n'est bon.'*

a surprise conclusion'.[14] The beginning and very end of the involved moot problem called *Cat in the Pan* is as follows:[15]

> A villein purchases a carucate of land unto him and his lord and their heirs; the lord has issue three daughters; the eldest releases to the villein [all the right that she has], with warranty; the villein aliens a moiety [of the carucate by metes and bounds] to the youngest daughter and her heirs begotten on the body of the villein, and the other half to the same person for the term of the life of B and of his heirs and assigns ... *Ceux que droit.*

We have obviously not set the moot problem out in full here, but even this extract shows how the complexities are heaped up one by one. The word *villein* is probably deliberately used here to denote a low-born, base-minded rustic, and the word *carucate* means as much land as could be ploughed with one plough in a year, in other words, quite a lot!

Having reached its heyday between about 1500 and 1550, mooting began to decline in the Inns of Court in the latter half of the 16th century. Holdsworth attributed this decline both to the growing availability of printed texts and to a growing indifference to legal education in the Inns of Court, whilst there was money to be made by the would-be educators in Westminster Hall. Selfishness on the part of the educators and laziness on the part of the students, in other words. Holdsworth illustrated this point by reference to two sets of judges' orders, one from 1557 and one from 1591. The former, which indicates a flourishing mooting culture in the Inns of Court, was obviously issued by the judges in response to excessive enthusiasm in mooting on the part of the Readers and Benchers. The orders basically said that no moot judges were to argue more than two points (presumably so as to give the student barristers a chance) and that moot problems were to contain no more than two arguable points.[16] By contrast, the second set of judges' orders, those from 1591, expressed concern that moots, which were 'very profitable for study' were being cut short because the readings which preceded them were finishing too early in the legal terms. Growing indifference on the part of the students was shown by the fact that, in Lincoln's Inn at least, a system of deputising had grown up, which was countered at least once in 1615 by the Benchers threatening to record the *deputies'* names, rather than those of their principals in the record book of mooting exercises.[17]

That mooting had not died out completely by the early part of the 17th century is shown in the reminiscences of the antiquary, Sir Simonds D'Ewes (1602–50),

---

14   *Op cit*, Baker, fn 12, pp xlii–xliii.

15   *Op cit*, Baker, fn 12, pp 33–34, where the full text of the *Cat in the Pan* is set out in parallel law-French and modern English. There is also a contemporary drawing of the figurative feline, sitting rather disconsolately in the pan, complete with a rather gratuitous spatula!

16   *Op cit*, Holdsworth, fn 10, Vol 6, pp 481–82.

17   *Op cit*, Holdsworth, fn 10, Vol 6, p 483.

of the Middle Temple, who recorded his experiences of mooting, both as a student and as an Utter Barrister, in the early decades of the 17th century:[18]

> I had ... twice mooted myself in law-French before I was called to the bar, and several times after I was made an Utter Barrister in our open hall ... And then also, being an utter barrister, I had twice argued our Middle Temple readers' case at the cupboard ... and sat nine times in our Temple Hall at the bench, and argued such cases in English as had been before argued by young gentlemen or utter barristers themselves ... For which latter exercises I had but usually a day and a half's study at the most, everpenning my arguments before I uttered them, and seldom speaking less than half an hour in the pronouncing of them.

By the end of the 17th century, however, mooting was all but dead as part of any organised educational system of the Inns of Court. Although it is a generalisation, it seems that, from the latter half of the 17th century, right up to the middle of the 19th century, students were generally left to their own resources in educational terms, and this included mooting.

There were exceptions, of course, where mooting was done on a voluntary basis, rather than as part of the formal training of a barrister. Lord Mansfield (1705–93), the Chief Justice of the King's Bench for 32 years from 1756, for example, organised a mooting club while still a student, and it was recorded that, 'they prepared their arguments with great care ... [Lord Mansfield] afterwards [finding] ... many of them useful to him, not only at the bar, but upon the bench'.[19] Sir Samuel Romilly (1757–1818), briefly Solicitor General from 1806–07, also organised a mooting club as a student, with three friends. The four of them divided up the roles of judges and counsel unusually, by modern standards, but presumably this was done in order to take account of there being only four participants in all:[20]

> One argued on each side as counsel, the other two acted the part of judges, and were obliged to give at length the reasons of their decisions.

These seem to have been very much the exceptions, however. In the late 19th century, Sir William Holdsworth, who had spent so much time researching the educational systems of the Inns of Court when mooting was in its heyday, deplored the fact that not enough attention was paid in his own time in university law schools to practical exercises such as mooting:[21]

> The sacrifice of the old system destroyed to a large extent that organised discussion which prepared the students for actual practice. In our modern system, it does not take the place which it once took, unless, as at Oxford and at one or two other places, the pupils are wiser than their teachers, and set up for themselves a moot club, which

---

18   *Op cit*, Holdsworth, fn 10, Vol 6, pp 485–86.

19   *Op cit*, Holdsworth, fn 10, Vol 12, pp 86–87, note 1, p 87.

20   *Op cit*, Holdsworth, fn 10, Vol 12, p 86, citing Sir Samuel Romilly's *Memoirs*, Vol 1, pp 48–49.

21   *Op cit*, Holdsworth, fn 10, Vol 6, p 497.

reproduces some of the advantages of that old system which the Benchers of this period were too selfish to maintain.

The picture in the Inns of Court was slightly different by the late 19th century. In 1875, Gray's Inn formed a 'moot society', its moots being attended by members of the other Inns of Court and formal moots began to be held in the hall of the Inner Temple in 1926.[22] Nowadays, when mooting sometimes forms part of a course of legal study in many university law schools, we can see that the importance attached to mooting has, in one sense, resumed its rightful place.

5 Why should law students moot today?

As a student reading this Guide, you will probably either be a student on an undergraduate law course, or you will be a graduate student reading for the postgraduate diploma in law. Whichever of these two you are, the question of why you should moot at all will have some prominence in your mind. This will either be because you have no choice at all as to whether to moot or not, the moot forming part of your course of legal study, and you are questioning the reasons for the imposition of the task on you or, as someone wondering whether to moot voluntarily or not, you doubt whether the moot will be worth the considerable effort it will certainly involve. Undergraduate students at an increasing number of law schools are now in the former position. Indeed, it is increasingly common to see mooting employed, not only to teach students, but to assess them as part of a degree course. In the past, as has been observed by S Sheppard, 'the moot argument was an essential tool not only of student instruction in the Inns and at Oxbridge but also of student evaluation'.[23] Recent attempts to incorporate mooting as part of law degree courses, therefore, represent the re-discovery of an ancient treasure of legal education.

At the risk of being contentious, we assert that most lawyers would acknowledge the presence of a certain nebulousness at the heart of their skills as lawyers. This indefinable quality is what enables the specialist, a corporate tax lawyer, for example – not you might think an advocate at all – to be able to explain, clearly and persuasively, the practical effect of an enormously complex piece of tax legislation to a client or to another non-specialist lawyer. Mooting nurtures this indescribable ability to explain what may be very complex legal

---

22 *Op cit*, Baker, fn 12, p lxxvi.

23 Sheppard, S, 'An informal history of how law schools evaluate students, with a predictable emphasis on law school final exams' (1997) 65 UMKCL Rev 657, p 689. Sheppard attests to a similar significance being attached to mooting within the US tradition: '[The] pattern of hypothetical essay examinations being the sole record of the students' performance is a recent stage in the evolution of US legal education. Once exams were only one form of evaluation to judge fitness, used in conjunction with class recitations, notebook inspections, and moot court performance [p 658].'

material simply and clearly. The background preparation to the explanation of the law by the corporate tax lawyer, say, can be the most minute trawl through the relevant statutory provisions or case law. By itself, the ability to carry out this minute trawl is only one part of the job of any lawyer, however. Being able to put your conclusions into a clear written form is, again, only part of the job, for it goes without saying that you must be able to explain your conclusions. Fundamental, though, is that mercurial quality of being able, orally, to explain, concisely and persuasively, the meaning of complexities understood only by specialists such as yourself, eliminating all irrelevant material. This ability to interpret and present complex legal material is a skill which can be acquired by practice. This Guide aims to give you the tools to acquire this skill through mooting. It is a skill which all lawyers – not just advocates – will require. The advocate specialising in family law requires it no less than the corporate tax lawyer. This is because being a lawyer, *in its very essentials*, involves being able to justify and explain any course of action that you propose to take on behalf of your client.

This task of explanation and justification also involves the ability to withstand interruptions from the individual or individuals to whom you are speaking. In WS Gilbert's play, *Patience*, one of the characters exclaims that 'life is made up of interruptions!'.[24] This may be true in ways which we can scarcely even imagine, especially perhaps in the professional life of the lawyer. Moots, being dialogues, albeit highly formal ones, between the mooter and the moot judge, involve the ability to deal with interruptions and challenges. Such interruptions and challenges, not necessarily ill natured, however politely and good humouredly put by a first class moot judge, will seem threatening enough to you, and will require you to respond effectively to them. Like the skills required for research and presentation, these skills can be acquired by the mooter, with practice. The great advantage of making a presentation before a moot judge – or a real judge – over discussions conducted in other environments in which you may have to explain and justify your conclusions, is that the environment in which you work is regulated by courtroom etiquette.[25]

Teamwork is also an essential skill of the lawyer. Not all mooting encourages this and there is no doubt a fine line between academic discussion and plagiarism. As a leader, say, on one side of the argument in a moot, you will discuss the issues raised by the moot problem with your junior. As a junior, you will inevitably do the same, but with your leader. In so doing, you will tend to get to

---

24 Gilbert, WS, *Patience*, Act 1, line 426, in Bradley, I (ed), *The Complete Annotated Gilbert and Sullivan*, 1996, Oxford: OUP, p 295.

25 There is an interesting discussion of the contrast between the cross-examination (see the answer to Question 2) of politicians and that of witnesses in court, by the keenest of political interrogators and former practising barrister, Sir Robin Day. (See Day, R (Sir), *The Grand Inquisitor*, 1990, London: Pan, pp 164–66.)

the essence of the issues with which you have to deal. No stone will be left unturned. Both Appellants and Respondents will wish to persuade the moot judge of the correctness of their submissions. Karl Llewellyn, the American jurist, was thinking of this in his emotive description:[26]

> Moot court work will bring you into quick contact with a group. And in groups of students lies your hope of education ... In group work lies the deepening of thought. In group work lie ideas, cross-lights; dispute, and practice in dispute; co-operative thinking and practice in consultation; spur for the weary, pleasure for the strong. A threefold cord is not quickly broken: in group work lies salvation.

The authors cannot improve on this exhortation. After reading it, you should be able to moot till you drop.

So, mooting can give you skills of interpretation and presentation, along with the ability to counter interruption and to work in teams. As a mooter, you learn to disguise the most detailed examination of the most technical of material in the most persuasive way. Skills of research and presentation are absolutely interdependent. You may argue that people made very good livings as lawyers, in times gone by, without the experience of the moot court as students. Well, this is true up to a point, but do not be fooled. Nineteenth century barristers were known to take lessons from famous stage actors of the day on voice projection and in the cultivation of the ability to work on the emotions of a jury.[27] What they couldn't get in law school, they got elsewhere! Even earlier, mooting was a compulsory element in the educational system of the Inns of Court and Inns of Chancery (see the answer to Question 4). When you stand up to address a moot court, you are doing one of the few things that a 16th century student barrister would recognise in the life of a modern law student. No doubt, these are the reasons, also, why prospective solicitor employers, no less than potential pupil masters, are usually impressed by the fact that a would-be trainee or pupil has mooted as a student. In a 1991 academic survey, half of the respondents to the survey felt that mooting should be at least an optional part of a law degree.[28] Again, practitioner respondents to a 1996 survey conducted by final year students at the University of Warwick were unanimous in the view that mooting is beneficial to potential solicitors, particularly in the interviewing process.[29] Even if you have no desire to practise law, the many skills which we have considered here, including skills of research, reasoning, persuasion,

---

26   Llewellyn, KN, *The Bramble Bush – On Our Law and Its Study*, 1930, New York: Oceana, p 96.

27   Lewis, JR, *The Victorian Bar*, 1982, London: Robert Hale, p 13. However, note that, in modern mooting, acting ability is unnecessary (see the answer to Question 78).

28   Bright, S, 'What, and how, should we be teaching?' (1991) 25 Law Teacher 11, p 18.

29   Calder, K, and Sacranie, S, 'Is mooting useful in degree level education, and if so, how should it be integrated into a degree programme?', unpublished LLB dissertation, 1996, University of Warwick.

interpretation and presentation, all skills which mooting develops, will be important to you whatever your chosen career.

Of course, most of the benefits of mooting referred to in this answer have been highly instrumental and it should not be forgotten that the attraction of mooting for most students is the simple fun of taking part!

6 How does mooting differ from participating in tutorials and seminars?

There are significant differences between answering a tutorial problem and presenting arguments for a moot.

First, in tutorials, all the legal issues raised by the problem can be discussed, whereas only the legal issues raised by the identified grounds of appeal can be argued in a moot. There may be other issues which could have been argued but, if they are not within the grounds of appeal, the moot judge will not permit you to argue them. When you are preparing your arguments, keep referring back to the moot problem, to ensure that you are dealing with the legal issues raised in the grounds of appeal (see the answer to Question 42). For instance, in the example moot in Appendix 1, para 2(b), the second ground of appeal is stated to be: 'It is possible for the agent of a trust to commit the tort of procurement of a breach of trust, and Mr Holmes committed such a tort when he advised Mr Dearing to make unauthorised investments.' Mr Neil Wright, junior counsel for the Appellant, may well have wished that he had been permitted to advance arguments, not on a common law action based on tort, but rather in equity, in an action for dishonest assistance in a breach of trust. He is, however, prohibited from doing so because he would be going outside the grounds of appeal in doing so.

If it is any consolation, arguments outside the grounds of appeal would, in any case, usually have been unsuccessful. This is, often, precisely the reason why they were not chosen as grounds of appeal in the first place. It has to be acknowledged, however, that sometimes a clearly winning argument might have been raised, had it not been excluded from the grounds of appeal. One of the authors' colleagues (Cliff Atkins), drafted the criminal law moot which was used in the final of what is now the English-Speaking Union National Mooting Competition in 1991.[30] The moot concerned manslaughter charges against a mother who had refused permission for a life-saving operation to be performed on her child and against the surgeon who failed to carry out the operation. An argument, on behalf of the mother, based on causation, would inevitably have

---

30 This moot problem is not reproduced in the Appendices because the subsequent case of *Airedale NHS Trust v Bland* [1993] AC 789 has made one of the grounds of appeal effectively unarguable.

been successful, since the ultimate responsibility lay with the surgeon, who had accepted the mother's refusal to grant permission and had allowed the child to die. His failure to apply to the court for an order overruling the mother's refusal of consent was the *causa causans* (see Appendix 8) of the death of the child. In fact, one of the mooters attempted to raise the causation point but Dame Elizabeth Butler-Sloss, who was judging the moot, disallowed the argument because it was outside the ground of appeal.

A second point that is partially related to the first, is that, in a moot problem, you are often told that a concession has been made on a legal issue that you bitterly wish had not been made. You are bound by that concession and you are not allowed to say that your side is withdrawing the concession. The reason for this is that, sometimes, the author of the moot is merely attempting to make it easier for the mooter to keep to his or her ground of appeal. For instance, the example moot (see Appendix 1) could have included the words: '... the beneficiaries have conceded that there would be no equitable remedy against the broker for dishonest assistance in a breach of trust.'

For the author of a moot problem, it is sometimes easier and clearer to have a broader ground, coupled with concessions, than to draft a moot with a narrower ground of appeal. Thus, in a tort moot, the issue could be whether the victim of a self-inflicted injury owed a duty of care to avoid causing nervous shock to a third party. A mooter could easily argue that, whether or not it was a self-inflicted injury, on the facts of the moot problem, there was no duty of care owed because there was insufficient proximity in time and space and the presence of the third party was not reasonably foreseeable. If these were not the points which the author of the moot wished to be argued, the problem could have been drafted to read: 'Mr Smith concedes that there was sufficient proximity in time and space and the presence of Mrs Jones was reasonably foreseeable but he claims that he did not owe her a duty of care because he, Mr Smith, was the victim of a self-inflicted injury.'

Thirdly, sometimes, in tutorials or seminars, the class will agree about the relevant law but may disagree about how that law must be applied to the facts of the tutorial or seminar problem. Very rarely will a ground of appeal be concerned with a contest as to how undisputed law applies to facts. Rather, a moot is generally a contest as to the proper law to be applied to undisputed facts.

There are, however, many similarities between moots and tutorials. To do well in the academic part of your legal education requires you to do a great deal more than understand the basic concepts of the area of law that you are studying and apply that law to a straightforward factual situation. You must also demonstrate your ability to learn and argue controversial issues of law. You are expected to recognise uncertain areas of law and, within the constraints of English legal methodology, to be able to formulate tenable arguments to resolve this uncertainty.

Like moots, most tutorial, seminar, written coursework or examination questions focus on areas of debate or uncertainty in the law, and are drafted in order to make the solving of these 'debatable issues' vital to attaining a good mark. Many of you will have seized, with relish, the opportunities presented by tutorials and seminars. If you are such a student, then mooting is simply a different forum, albeit a more formal one, in which to advance your arguments.

7 I sometimes don't prepare for tutorials – is it always necessary to prepare my moot presentation?

Unfortunately, some students do not capitalise on the advantages of the tutorial system. Instead of thoroughly preparing the required work and coming to the tutorial bristling with possible solutions to the difficult problems that have been set, they decide to wait for the tutorial, in the hope that their tutor will explain the controversial points to them and supply them with the elusive 'correct answers'. They are invariably disappointed because, although they hear the various arguments being advanced by fellow students, they have not carried out sufficient background work to understand them. Not only that, but, most irritatingly of all for them, their tutor does not provide 'correct answers' but provides, at the very most, an assessment of the tenability of the assorted arguments put forward in the tutorial.

For such students, tutorials will prove to have been of very limited value and mooting will constitute a serious shock to their nervous systems because, perhaps for the first time, they will not have the option of saying: 'I did not understand the point I was supposed to be arguing and therefore I have not prepared it at all.' We cannot hide the fact that avoiding looking foolish in public, that is, before your moot judge and fellow mooters, provides a powerful incentive for hard work.

The fact remains that, for whatever reason, most students put a lot of effort into their mooting research and preparation and end up thoroughly enjoying it, often surprising themselves at the high standard which they have achieved in their moot presentation.

8 How is the moot judge's assessment divided between the moot and the law?

The answer to this question depends on who is assessing your moot presentation and whether the moot is a competitive one, forms part of a course of legal study or is held merely for fun. Like Question 9, this question is directed at the fact that a moot judge does not simply adjudicate on matters of law. He or she also adjudicates on the range of presentational and interpersonal skills which a mooter must display in order to moot successfully.

17

As mentioned in the answer to Question 1, after the submissions of the two moot teams have been completed, the moot judge will usually give a short judgment. In the judgment, unlike in a real court, the moot judge will not only reach a conclusion as to the legal issues of doubt raised by the grounds of appeal. He or she will also decide which of the teams of participants has mooted the best. However, although this is *usually* how a moot is structured, where a moot forms part of a course of legal study, it may be the case that no judgment is given by the moot judge, an assessment being made by him or her after the moot, as to whether the participants have demonstrated the legal skills necessary in order to moot satisfactorily. Whichever of these possibilities applies to the moot in which you are taking part, the question of how the judge's assessment is divided between the moot and the law is equally important.

To give you, the mooter, a general indication of the range of legal skills which a moot judge considers when judging a moot, we have included a specimen Moot Assessment Sheet in Appendix 7. This has been designed not for competitive mooting or mooting for fun, but for the situation where a moot forms part of a course of legal study. It is not, of course, intended to be definitive. If you turn to Appendix 7, you will see that the specimen Moot Assessment Sheet contains 20 moot performance criteria, ranging from purely legal matters (for example, the ability of the mooter to understand and apply English legal method), through presentational matters (for example, posture, eye contact with the moot judge), to interpersonal skills (for example, courtesy to the moot judge, confidence, persuasiveness, etc). You will also see that each of these is given a grading on the sheet from F, a fail, through to 1, meaning first class. This reflects the fact that this specimen Moot Assessment Sheet is designed for use in a moot forming part of a course of legal study. In competitive mooting, the performance criteria might not be so detailed. The authors would suggest that each of these 20 performance criteria is given a mark allocation of 5%; in other words, that each of the legal, presentational and interpersonal criteria identified are accorded equal weight. On this basis, just under half of the 20 performance criteria are purely legal, with the others being presentational and interpersonal. The weighting here, therefore, is in favour of the law. Again, this reflects the fact that the sheet is designed for use in an *assessment* context, where it is appropriate to attach greater weight to purely legal skills. The Moot Assessment Sheet is designed, also, to show a student exactly where he or she has gone wrong, and equally where his or her strengths lie. It could, of course, easily be adapted for use in a competitive moot, possibly with the weighting of the performance criteria adjusted.

The assessment sheet used by moot judges in the English-Speaking Union National Mooting Competition, is reproduced in Appendix 6. The function of this Assessment Sheet is obviously different from the specimen Moot Assessment Sheet in Appendix 7, since it is for use in the particular competition to which it relates. You will notice that it is far simpler to have only three performance criteria for each of the four mooters, who are divided into the two teams of Appellants and Respondents. The three performance criteria, namely, (1) 'Content'; (2) 'Strategy'; and (3) 'Style', are weighted in favour of the first two.[31] Notice, also, that no separate marks are allocated in the sheet to the Appellants' right to reply, which is a feature of this competition (see the answer to Question 13). The three performance criteria shown here are, in fact, one category less than was previously the case. Until recently, there were four performance criteria in what was formerly *The Observer* Moot, namely, (1) 'Presentation and Clarity of Argument'; (2) 'Use of Authorities'; (3) 'Ability to Answer Questions'; and (4) 'Courtroom Manner'.

To be sure of the correct answer to this question, in relation to the moot in which you are a participant, therefore, you should always seek to obtain a copy of the assessment sheet (if available), showing how the performance criteria are weighted in the particular moot in which you are taking part.

9 Is it possible to lose on the law and win on the moot?

The answer to this question is a definite 'yes'.

The fact is that the legal authorities on both sides of a moot problem should be of roughly equal strength, so whichever decision the moot judge reaches on the law will not necessarily reflect the judge's view as to the skills of the mooters who presented those authorities. In fact, the opposite is often true. The judge of a competitive moot between two law schools will, not infrequently, judge in favour of one law school on the issues of law as a way of softening the blow before he or she then awards the moot to the other law school. This practice is apparently so common that mooters are sometimes heard to whisper, as they await the judgment, 'I hope we lose this case'.[32] The practice of law is different, of course. There, we assume that the judge awards no prize to the most persuasive advocate, and that victory in a case before an appellate court follows the law!

It follows, from the above, that you should not be too downhearted if you are ever presented with an apparently unarguable ground of appeal. The weight of legal authority may well be stacked against you, but you can still win the moot if you are skilful and persuasive enough in the way you develop what little authority, persuasive or binding, is on your side. The judge may not agree

---

31 In the 'Guidance for judges' set out in the extracts from the English-Speaking Union National Mooting Competition (see Appendix 5), these three performance criteria are further sub-divided and a detailed explanation is given of their precise meaning.

32 For avoidance of doubt on this point, the rules of most mooting competitions include a rule to the effect that a team may win the moot, even if they lose on the law (see the answers to Questions 95 to 98 and Appendix 5).

with your arguments as to the law, but he or she is well aware that you did not choose to argue the particular ground of appeal and will give you special credit for making the most of a difficult legal argument.[33]

10   In which courts are moots set?

The moots in which you are most likely to take part will be based on English law. That being the case, the courts in which the moot is set will usually either be the Court of Appeal or House of Lords.

With rare exceptions (see below), a moot must take place in an appellate court because the mooters will be arguing points of law rather than questions of fact (see the answer to Question 2). Indeed, the facts are imagined to have been decided by the trial judge or jury, as appropriate, and those findings of fact will not be in dispute. Authors of moot problems usually set their moots in the Court of Appeal because it forces you, the mooter, to be very disciplined in your legal methodology. Generally, unless you can distinguish apparently binding cases which have been cited against you, you will lose the legal argument. If the moot is set in the House of Lords, then virtually all arguments are permissible. This is because, by virtue of its *Practice Statement* of 1966 (see Appendix 4), the House of Lords will depart from its own previous decisions, when it appears right to do so. Accordingly, although authoritative cases in support of your argument are helpful in the House of Lords, they will not guarantee legal victory. You must, at House of Lords level, always have policy arguments as to why the law should either remain as it is or be changed (see the answer to Question 74). Indeed, one of the rules of the English-Speaking Union Moot is that the moot has to take place in either the Court of Appeal or the House of Lords.

Despite all that has already been said, the House of Lords and Court of Appeal are not the only appellate courts for England and Wales.

Other courts in which moots are frequently set, include the International Court of Justice and the Court of Justice of the European Communities. The former will be the setting for a public international law moot, and the latter for an EC law moot.

The International Court of Justice does not actually hear appeals, and so this is one of the rare occasions when a moot is not set in an appellate court. However, in such moots, the moot proceeds on a hypothetical compromise between the parties, in other words there is an agreement about the factual basis of the legal dispute, so allowing the mooters to concentrate on the legal issues which appear from those agreed facts. The same may be true, depending on the

---

33   See the answer to Question 60 and the specimen Moot Assessment Sheet in Appendix 7, which specifically rewards ingenuity of legal argument.

procedure which is imagined to have been followed, for a moot set in the Court of Justice of the European Communities.

11 Who takes part in a moot and what functions do they perform?

If mooting were a board game, it would say on the side of the box, 'a game for three or more players'. For an effective moot, you must have at least one mooter on each side and a neutral moot judge. In fact, it is unusual for a moot to have fewer than five players. These are: Lead and Junior Appellant, Lead and Junior Respondent, and the moot judge. A moot heard in an appellate tribunal, for example, the Court of Appeal or the House of Lords, will ideally have more than one judge presiding, but this is a luxury usually reserved for a few of the international mooting competitions.

Moot judges will usually be legal academics or legal practitioners and it is best to know which type you will be appearing before. If we can indulge ourselves in a little stereotyping, we should say that they each display certain general characteristics. Practitioners have often spent so long locked up in that ivory tower they call the real world that they sometimes take an altogether too realistic approach to mooting. We have even heard practitioner moot judges complain to a mooter, on account of the lowly sums involved in the moot problem, that the case in the moot problem was started in the High Court instead of the county court.[34] Academics, on the other hand, might occasionally see a moot as an opportunity to trap the mooters with obtuse points, or to test their own pet theories or the, as yet untried, theses of their colleagues on the mooters. Neither approach is particularly helpful to the nervous and inexperienced mooter. However, the more experienced, competitive mooter can have no cause to complain at either approach (see, further, the answers to Questions 64–66). A good mooter must take the moot judges as he or she finds them. Very occasionally, a moot judge will deliberately put a mooter to the sword – to this there can be no objection provided the judge also remembers to employ the scales of justice!

Judges, Appellants and Respondents are not the only persons who take part in a moot. There are three others who may have significant roles to play: the court clerk, the *amicus curiae* and the master/mistress of moots.

---

34 For current restrictions on values in the High Court and county courts, see CPR Practice Direction 7.

The court clerk (or clerk of the court)

He or she should sit at a separate table in front of the moot judge and, like the judge, should face the mooters. The court clerk has many functions to perform which are all designed to facilitate the smooth and proper execution of the moot. First, and perhaps foremost, the clerk is ultimately responsible for ensuring that the judge will have ready access to originals (or photocopies as a last resort) of every authority intended to be relied upon by the mooters. The clerk's desk should be as near as possible to that of the judge because, during the moot, the clerk will hand each authority to the judge at the moment that it is first referred to by the mooter relying on it. It is sensible for the court clerk to have inserted a bookmark at the relevant part of the authority, for example, at the first page of a law report or at a particular section of a statute. Secondly, the clerk should announce the imminent arrival of the judge with the shout, 'court rise!', at which point everybody in the moot court who is able to do so, audience included, should stand up. Thirdly, another of the clerk's functions is to act as timekeeper (see the answer to Question 29), so, if you are the clerk, don't forget to bring a watch with a seconds hand.

The *amicus curiae*[35]

This person is the 'friend of the court', to give the literal translation of the Latin. His or her role is to assist the court on specialist questions of law, or to alert the court as to the public policy implications of the possible outcomes in a case. The *amicus curiae* does not represent the adversarial interests of either party.

It is not often that *amici curiae* are used in moots. If they are, it is usual to restrict their speeches from the floor to a maximum of five minutes. They are most unlikely to need more time than that, as what they have to say is not a matter for dispute.

The master or mistress of moots

The staff or student member responsible for organising the moot should also be present at the moot to ensure that it runs smoothly. The tasks of the master or mistress of moots before, during and after the moot are as follows.

Well in advance of the moot

- In the case of a national or international competitive moot, pay any fee. Where required by the rules, select a workable moot problem. (In fact, this is often a requirement of competitive moots.)

---

35 At the time of writing and despite the CPR 1998, this term still seems to be applicable.

- Choose your mooters, appoint a date and time for the moot, invite a moot judge (the judge will appreciate it if the moot problem is in an area of his or her expertise) and book a venue for the moot.

- Exchange authorities with the other side.

- Make arrangements for providing refreshments for the moot judge and the mooters.

- Book a venue for taking refreshments.

Just before the moot

- Photocopy the moot problem for distribution to the audience.

- Set out the moot court (see Appendix 9), complete with lecterns.

- Provide drinking water for the mooters and the moot judge.

- Provide the mooters with gowns, if appropriate (see the answer to Question 50).

- Provide the moot judge with any guidelines and a moot assessment sheet, for judging the moot.

- Place a *Moot In Progress* notice on the door to the moot court.

During the moot

- Introduce the moot and welcome the moot judge and the audience.

- Deal with any emergencies, for example, obtrusive noise outside the moot court.

After the moot

- In a national or international competition, inform the organiser of the result of the moot as soon as possible.

- Put up a notice in the law school thanking the mooters, and any other participants in the moot, and congratulating or commiserating with the mooters over the result.

- Thank the moot judge by letter. This will be appreciated by him or her far more than you may realise.

12   How is a moot structured?

There are two levels of answer to this question. The first is that of the moot problem itself. It is almost universally the case that this is divided up into two entirely self-contained grounds of appeal, from the judgment of an imaginary judge at first instance, the intention being that one person on each side will argue each one. As mentioned in the answer to Question 2, the grounds of appeal always raise questions of law, rather than questions of fact.

The second level is that of the proceedings in the moot court. The most basic division in moot proceedings is between the presentations of the mooters and the judgment of the moot judge or judges, once those presentations have been made. So far as the judgment is concerned, you may find that this is dispensed with, where the moot is forming part of a course of legal study. We consider the functions of the moot judge in the answer to Question 100.

The presentations of the mooters fall in a particular order, which may vary slightly, according to the rules of the moot in which you are taking part. The order of the proceedings with which the authors are familiar is as follows. (The conventions of standing and bowing, and so on, are obviously inapplicable where any of the participants, judges or mooters, are prevented from doing so through disability.)

Before the moot presentations take place, the moot judge will have come into the moot court, bowed and sat down. (This bow is no more than a nod.) Bowing in return, the mooters sit down, until the first to speak, as noted below, is called upon to do so by the judge.

(1) *Lead Appellant*: As elsewhere in this Guide, the Lead Appellant is to be taken to refer to *leading counsel for the Appellants*. Once standing up, the Lead Appellant makes his or her submissions on his or her ground of appeal and, having done so, will sit down again at the judge's invitation, in order for the judge to invite the Junior Appellant to make his or her presentation.

(2) *Junior Appellant*: As above, this is in fact the *junior counsel for the Appellants*. Again, he or she will sit down at the end of his or her presentation, in order for the judge to invite the Lead Respondent to make his or her presentation.

(3) *Lead Respondent*: As above, this is in fact the *leading counsel for the Respondents*. As above, after having made his or her presentation, the Lead Respondent will sit down, in order for the judge to invite the Junior Respondent to make his or her presentation.

(4) *Junior Respondent*: Again, this is the *junior counsel for the Respondents*. After having made his or her presentation, the Junior Respondent will sit down, to allow the judge to do one of the following:

(a) in some moots only (see the answer to Question 13), to invite the Appellants to reply to the Respondents' submissions; *or*

(b) to allow the judge to deliver a judgment immediately; *or*

(c) to allow the judge to announce that he or she will adjourn the moot for a few moments to compose a judgment; *or*

(d) as mentioned above, simply to bring the proceedings to a close, where the moot is taking the place of a coursework assessment.

We would make a number of points regarding each of these. First, the timing of the presentations of each of the mooters can vary, again according to the rules of the moot. This point is discussed elsewhere in this Guide (see the answer to Question 29). In principle, the timings should not include the time that the judge takes in asking, and the relevant mooter takes in answering, questions. However, there are special considerations in these areas in certain competition moots (see the answer to Question 29). Secondly, the rules of the moot may provide for the order of presentations to be varied. It could be, for example, in the order of, Lead Appellant, Lead Respondent, Junior Appellant, Junior Respondent. Or again, Lead Appellant, Lead Respondent, Junior Respondent, Junior Appellant.

Thirdly, especially when the moot is forming part of a course of legal study, there might not be a full complement of four mooters. This is only practicable if, as mentioned in the answer to Question 1, each ground of appeal is entirely self-contained. Fourthly, while you are actually making your presentation, the moot judge may call upon another of the mooters appearing before him or her and ask him or her for their opinion on the point which you have just made. If this happens, sit down immediately. Equally, if you are the other mooter asked to comment in this way, make sure that you do so standing up. The golden rule is that, if you can physically do so, you stand to address the moot court.

Bearing these points in mind, our final point would be this. Avoid interrupting another mooter's presentation at all costs. If, however, it is absolutely necessary, for example, because of illness (see the answer to Question 59) make sure that you stand up to do so, bringing all your powers of charm to bear and observing the rules of etiquette discussed elsewhere in this Guide, to a fault.

In some moots, where there is no element of competition or assessment, certain further variations to the above may be permitted. There might be an audience, for example, in which case the judge might invite comments from the audience regarding the law. In the authors' experience, this is fairly rare.

13 As Appellant, do I get a right of reply?

The answer to this question depends entirely upon the rules of the competition or assessment. If, as an Appellant, you have a right of reply to the Respondents' arguments, it goes without saying that, when the Respondents are making their own presentations, you should annotate the points to which you may wish to make reply.

However, do not feel obliged to exercise your right to reply if you are content that there is nothing in the Respondents' presentation to cast doubt upon your main submissions. If the moot judge offers you the opportunity to reply (which he or she generally will where the rules allow), it can leave a positive impression to reply 'My Lord/Lady, I am content to rest on my earlier submissions', or words to that effect. On the other hand, if you suspect that the judge would prefer it, the wisest course may be to use your right of reply and thereby ensure for yourself the last word on the matter.

The Biblical proverb warns: 'He who states his case first seems right, until the other comes and questions him.'[36] Even if the Respondent has made no strong points to which you feel compelled to reply, exercising your right of reply gives you an opportunity to point out the weaknesses in the Respondents' case and/or to reiterate the strengths of your own.

14   How are the roles of Appellants and Respondents chosen?

These roles may either be allocated by the rules of the competition or by the rules of the assessment. If there is no element of competition or assessment in the moot, some procedure *neutral to the moot teams* must be adopted, such as the drawing of straws for roles.

One of the points we reiterate in this Guide, is our contention that mooting shares many features in common with a team game. Mooting is, therefore, subject to certain rules of fair play, which we discuss in some detail in the answer to Question 18, and this question is directed at an important aspect of how those rules of fair play should work in relation to the allocation of mooters to their roles.

Where you are participating in a moot which is taking the place of a coursework assessment, the master or mistress of moots (see the answer to Question 11), in other words, the member of staff responsible for mooting at your law school, will allocate the roles among the participators. In that situation, the question of fair play in the selection of the participants and the roles they play does not arise. However, where the moot is being held for fun, or as part of a competition, it does arise and is a matter which is likely to be covered in the rules of the competition. If the moot problem is distributed centrally, under the rules of the competition, then the mooters' roles should be allocated centrally.

In the absence of a specific rule, fair play demands that, if one team, or one law school, chooses the moot problem, then they, or it, should offer the opposing team or law school, as the case may be, the choice as to which side of the argument to take.

---

36   *Proverbs*, 18: 17.

15 If I am a Respondent, how do I balance the need to make a case and to challenge points made by the Appellants?

Owing to the limited amount of time available for argument, it is not generally advisable for you to spend time at the beginning of your presentation replying, in debating style, to the submissions put forward by the Appellants. Instead, your submissions should be made, and brief responses to the points raised by the Appellants should be incorporated into your submissions as your presentation progresses.

If you were to act for the respondent on a real appeal in a real court, there would, in theory at least, be no need to make out a positive case of your own, as such. The appeal brought by the other side would be dismissed, were you able successfully to discredit every one of the points on which the appeal had been brought. However, in practice, submissions are unlikely to persuade the court unless they go beyond the somewhat negative process of merely gainsaying every one of the Appellants' arguments. A real appellate judge, and a moot judge, no less, will be far more likely to be persuaded by your submissions and to dismiss the appeal if there are positive reasons for preferring the Respondents' arguments.

In other words, the hearing of an appeal gives the Respondents another opportunity to put forward the strengths of their case and should not be viewed restrictively as a mere technical exercise in reacting to the Appellants' arguments.

(See the answers to Questions 88 and 89 for advice on how to challenge the authorities relied upon by the Appellants.)

16 Should I liaise with colleagues and should I know their arguments?

As a member of each moot team, you need to be acquainted with the submissions that your colleague is going to make, particularly if they are controversial. It is certainly not unusual for the moot judge to discuss, for example, the submissions of the Junior Appellant with the Lead Appellant.

An illustration of this is the exchange between Scales LJ and Felicity Fowler in Appendix 1, paras 7.4–7.6:

> *Scales LJ*: Yes, thank you Miss Fowler. Before you proceed, I must tell you that the second ground of appeal intrigues me. This tort, the existence and application of which you claim, has never, until the instant case, been argued before any court, has it?

Lead Appellant: My Lord, my learned junior will be contending that the issue has been before the courts on a number of occasions. Indeed, he will also be arguing that the existence of such a tort is consistent with principle.

Scales LJ: I am always open to persuasion. In practice, I very much doubt that such an argument would be advanced very often but I realise that you are bound by the moot problem. But, anyway, please continue.

This is almost at the beginning of the moot. We think you would agree that it would have been a very bad start to Felicity Fowler's presentation for her to have had to admit that she had no idea what her colleague's submissions were going to be. In fact, she coped well by showing that she knew that Neil Wright was going to rely on cases which supported the existence of a tort of procuring a breach of trust. She was, therefore, able, very diplomatically, to correct the moot judge's assertion that the issue in Neil Wright's ground of appeal had never previously been before a court, and to suggest that the argument was not as novel and unorthodox as the judge appeared to believe it was. Nevertheless, it would have been very unusual, and no doubt unfair, for the moot judge to have asked her to develop her colleague's submissions on the second ground of appeal any further.

Having said that, in a number of mooting competitions, such as the Philip C Jessup International Law Moot Court Competition and the Telders International Law Moot Court Competition, there is no rule to prevent the moot judge from doing precisely that. Many mooters in these competitions have, thus, found themselves having to deal with points that their colleagues have researched and prepared, but of which they knew very little. Obviously, it is not going to be possible to know your colleague's submissions as well as your own, but you should know at least the substance of their submissions. You would be extremely unfortunate were the moot judge or judges to insist that you dealt with these submissions in detail. The chances are that your colleague, who is probably sitting there wondering what on earth he or she is going to say if you are forced to cover all of his or her arguments, can then breathe a sigh of relief.

Even in a competition or assessment where you only have to assume responsibility for the submissions on one ground of appeal, it is still, of course, important to liaise with your colleague, so that you do not say anything which *conflicts* with their submissions. There are few things worse, in the context of a moot presentation, than to be half way through your submissions and to hear the moot judge say, 'Miss Smith, isn't this submission inconsistent with the ones just made by your Leader?'. The moral is to give your presentation a trial run with your colleague, in order to discover whether either of you are arguing inconsistently on any point. Obviously, if you are, then one of you is going to have to alter his or her submissions.[37]

---

37 The dangers of these problems are often avoided by the use of skeleton arguments: this is no doubt one reason for their use in 'real life'.

17 Why can't I argue points outside the ground of appeal?

There is a general understanding that mooters may not advance arguments outside the grounds of appeal in the moot problem (or, for competitive moots concerned with international law, outside the questions presented: see the answers to Questions 95–97). It is perhaps surprising, however, that (with the exception of the Philip C Jessup International Law Moot Court Competition), this general understanding is not expressly reflected in the rules of the various competitions.

The unwritten rule is, however, essential to both mooting and to litigation in practice. Thus, we find that the Civil Procedure Rules 1998[38] require that notice be given of the precise grounds of appeal and also make the permission of the court prerequisite to any amendment of the notice of appeal. Similarly, in competitive mooting, the participants are not at liberty to alter the wording of the grounds of appeal appearing in the moot problem, without first obtaining the leave of the national organiser (see the answer to Question 97).

The corollary to the unwritten rule is that a judge can only base his or her judgment on issues raised in the statements of case (formerly 'pleadings'). The classic illustration of this is to be found in *Dann v Hamilton*.[39] In this case, a claimant had accepted a ride in a car driven by the defendant, whom the claimant knew to be under the influence of drink. An accident ensued, in which the claimant was injured, and she brought an action against the driver for negligence. Counsel for the defendant pleaded the defence of *volenti non fit injuria*, but this was rejected by Asquith J, who gave judgment for the claimant. The decision attracted adverse academic criticism,[40] since the learned judge should have disposed of the case on the basis of contributory negligence and not of *volenti*. Had his Lordship done so, contributory negligence would, at that date, have provided the defendant with a complete defence. In the event, this criticism proved to have been completely ill founded, as is shown by the following extra-judicial note, written by the trial judge, who was by then Lord Asquith:[41]

---

38 SI 1998/3132 (L17), introduced by the Civil Procedure Act 1997, s 1(1). Lord Woolf was appointed in 1994 by the then Lord Chancellor, Lord Mackay of Clashfern, to review civil procedure in England and Wales. Lord Woolf's interim report, *Access to Justice*, appeared in July 1995, and the final report, with the draft CPR, in 1996.

39 [1939] 1 KB 509.

40 See Goodhart, AL, 'Contributory negligence and *volenti non fit injuria*' (1939) 55 LQR 184, pp 184–88. And see, further, Baker, RW, 'Guest passengers and drunken drivers' (1949) 65 LQR 20, pp 20–22.

41 An untitled note (1957) 69 LQR 317.

The criticisms ... were to the effect that even if the *volenti* doctrine did not apply there was here a cast iron defence on the ground of contributory negligence.

I have since had the pleadings and my notes exhumed, and they very clearly confirm my recollection that contributory negligence was not pleaded. Not merely so, but my notes show that I encouraged counsel for the defence to ask for leave to amend by adding this plea, but he would not be drawn: why, I have no idea.

There are a number of lessons to be learned from this example, not least of which is, perhaps, that even practitioners sometimes fail to take advantage of a helpful comment from the bench! Another, is that if a moot were based on similar facts to *Dann v Hamilton* and the two grounds of appeal were, let us say, on the issues of *volenti non fit injuria* and *ex turpi causa non oritur actio*, you would not be permitted to argue contributory negligence, for to do so would be outside the grounds of appeal. A further lesson, and one which would apply to competitive moots in which skeleton arguments are permitted, is for you expressly to plead any matter upon which you later intend to make submissions in your presentation.

18   Are there any rules of fair play to be observed in mooting?

One of the important differences between mooting and the harsh reality of litigation, on one level at least, is that mooting is to be seen as a game. Since the characters in a moot problem are entirely fictional, no liberty will be lost or lives ruined as a consequence of the quality of a moot presentation.

It follows from this proposition, that there are certain rules of fair play, which it is, perhaps, especially important to observe when you are participating in a moot held in a competitive context. It goes without saying that any game must be conducted by the players in as generous a spirit as possible and with dignity. If your participation is not in this spirit then, although you may not suffer tangible consequences, you may incur the censure of your friends and neighbours. Sportsmanship, not gamesmanship, is the watchword. We are not addressing clear infractions of the rules of mooting in answering this question. The consequences of such infractions will be obvious enough. We are, instead, addressing forms of behaviour which, although perhaps within the letter of the rules of the competition or assessment, are nonetheless not within its *spirit*. Since this is the case, it is not possible for us to describe every form which unacceptable behaviour could take. There is, no doubt, a fine line between acceptable cunning and conduct which most people, perhaps, would categorise as underhandedness. A little cunning never goes amiss in any forensic setting, but in the moot court you must never cross the fine line between cunning and deviousness. By way of illustration, we shall look at two practices which the authors would regard as falling into the latter category.

First, imagine you are a participant in a moot. You have devised an argument of astonishing simplicity. Nonetheless, you are convinced that it has a touch of brilliance about it. Indeed, so brilliant is this argument that it requires either the citation of no authority or, at the most, one short case only. You are confident that the opposing team in the moot will have no idea of what it is that you are going to argue. Just to make sure of this, however, you decide to throw them off the scent completely and to waste their time by exchanging a list of lengthy authorities with them which is roughly in point but upon which, at the time you exchange the authorities, you have not the slightest intention of relying. There may be nothing in the rules of the competition or of the assessment to prevent you doing this. Nonetheless, we would submit that to do this is to ignore the spirit of the exercise. It is, of course, quite unacceptable to disclose an authority which runs to over 100 pages, which is entirely off the point and upon which you have no intention of relying. If you attempt this, in the context of a mooting competition, you should not be surprised to receive, at the very least, an irate telephone call from the opposing team!

Secondly, think about a number of permutations of the following. Imagine now that you are about to participate in a competitive moot. The argument in the moot presentation which you have prepared is mundane, to say the least. You realise that, if you cite your authorities in the order in which you intend to refer to them, the banal simplicity of your argument will be plain for all to see. You have a bright idea, which is designed to get the opposing team worrying. You jumble the authorities up on exchange. It is a low bowl by you, but desperate measures are called for. Again, we submit that to do this is to ignore the spirit of the exercise. This is why, in our contention, it is good practice to agree to exchange authorities with the opposing team *alphabetically*, provided, as ever, that this is not prohibited by the rules. This will avoid any suggestion that you have acted outside the spirit of the mooting competition in which you are taking part.

An important aspect of the sportsmanship of mooting is to accept the moot judge's conclusion graciously, whether you win or lose. It may be difficult to do this if you are fighting back tears of rage and disappointment! Nevertheless, to complain or, still worse, to appeal to the national organiser, can only serve to add embarrassment to your defeat. Ironically, perhaps, in relation to a moot, even where the moot judge has fallen into some error of law, it is still inappropriate to appeal or protest, not least because the award of the moot need not necessarily follow the law (see the answer to Question 9).[42] What if you suspect the judge of bias? This is a most serious accusation and should not even

---

42 Francis Bacon, First Baron Verulam and Viscount St Albans (1561–1626), wrote: 'And let not the counsel at the bar chop with the judge, nor wind himself into the handling of the cause anew after the judge hath declared his sentence' (Bacon, F, 'Of judicature', in Hawkins, M (ed), *Essays*, 2nd edn, 1973, London: JM Dent, p 164).

be raised unless you have evidence with which you can clearly demonstrate that your suspicions are well founded. Cases of bias are likely to be extremely rare. Nevertheless, it is good practice to choose as objectively neutral a moot judge as possible. If your choice of judge might raise the merest suspicion of bias (for example, the choice of a judge who is a former student of your law school), disclose that fact and give the other side the opportunity to object to your choice in advance of the moot. Another method by which fairness can be fostered, is to offer your opponents the option to be Appellants rather than Respondents in any situation where you have selected the moot problem.

Remember, you want your mooting to be a positive experience for you. If you win and have played foul, then your victory will be a hollow one indeed. Equally, if you lose and have played foul, then to the pangs of defeat will be added the odium of disgrace.

2   Preparation

19 What is 'exchange of authorities' and is it appropriate to rely on my opponents' authorities?

In the English-Speaking Union Moot, as for most moots, only *cases* count as authorities. However, statutes, textbooks, or other legal literature on which one moot team intends to rely, must also be disclosed to the other side and to the moot judge. To 'exchange authorities' simply means to give the list of cases and other legal literature on which you intend to rely to the moot judge and to your opponents. One of the crucial things to remember about mooting is that it is your responsibility to give a list of your authorities to the judge and to your opponents at the time specified in the rules of the competition or assessment. (Don't forget to ensure that your name appears on your list of authorities.)

The rationale behind the exchange of authorities is that, in the interests of a fair debate, neither side is permitted to take the other totally by surprise (see the answer to Question 18). Each side must have the opportunity to read the other side's authorities in order to be able to prepare arguments to rebut them. The exchange of authorities also enables the judge to refresh his or her memory (or to read the cases for the first time) and to prepare testing questions on them.

Failure to exchange lists by the stated time is a serious breach of the rules of competitive mooting and could well be punished by disqualification. In moots which take place within your law school, especially if they form part of your course, such a breach is virtually certain to attract severe marking penalties.

Every competition, apart from those which require full skeleton arguments (formerly written pleadings), imposes a maximum number of authorities which may be exchanged. For example, the English-Speaking Union Moot restricts the number to eight cases per moot team. If you are taking part in a moot, possibly as part of your course within your own law school, there will also be a maximum number imposed by the rules of the assessment and you must find out what it is. You are not restricted to using a *minimum* number of cases. Do not think that your submissions will fail if you do not cite all your permitted number of authorities. It is always better to base your argument on principle and policy, rather than to cite authorities which are clearly distinguishable.

Generally, cases cited in the moot problem do not count towards your permitted number of authorities.

The English-Speaking Union Moot rules are that a single case which has been decided in more than one court (for example, a case that started in the High Court and then went to the Court of Appeal and finally to the House of Lords) counts as one authority. However, the citation for each judgment or speech being relied upon must be referred to separately. Once again, it is likely that, for internal moots, your law school will follow this rule.

Remember, you are entitled to use your opponents' authorities during the moot! For example, the English-Speaking Union Moot rules now state that: 'All authorities cited may be used by either the Appellants or the Respondents for any purpose.' Prior to the incorporation of this rule, it was thought that using your opponents' authorities was somehow improper or, to be more exact, using your opponents' authorities to support your initial submissions was a dubious tactic. Indeed, on one occasion some years ago, one of our students, when competing in the English-Speaking Union Moot, somewhat unimaginatively, based her arguments squarely on the other side's authorities, but was nevertheless awarded the moot. The national organiser, when appraised of these facts, said that he thought that such a tactic was within the rules of the competition but outside its spirit. Accordingly, our students graciously withdrew from the competition for that year.

In deciding how many authorities to exchange, you should remember the following contrasting points:

- The more authorities you cite, the more material you will need to read, understand and remember. As you refer to more authorities, the more questions can be asked by the moot judge about those authorities.

- The fewer authorities you cite, by contrast, the more the moot judge will be able to question you about the minute details of those authorities. If you choose to cite very few authorities, therefore, you should be prepared to answer questions even on the reported arguments of counsel in the case, where the case is reported in the semi-official law reports (see the answer to Question 51).

20   How do I read and choose my authorities?

Mr Haddock: My Lord, with great respect, there is a case – it is in the Law Reports –

The judge: I never read the Law Reports ...[1]

In the answer to this question, we consider the answers to two further questions. First, we consider what technique you should employ in reading authorities by way of preparation for a moot. In the process of considering this question, we

---

1   Herbert, AP, *Uncommon Law*, 4th edn, 1942, London: Methuen, p 415.

look at the difference between the *ratio decidendi* of a case and any *obiter dicta* which it may contain. Secondly, we consider, albeit, fairly briefly, the question of how to decide *which* authorities to refer to in your submissions. The second question may seem an obvious one. There are, however, a number of basic 'rules' which are worth observing (see, also, the answer to Question 42).

As mentioned in the *Practice Direction for the Court of Appeal, Civil Division* [1999] 2 All ER 490 (set out in the answer to Question 21),[2] the ideal choice of law report for any authority after 1865 is the report, if any, contained in the semi-official law reports published by the Incorporated Council of Law Reporting. In this discussion, we shall, therefore, follow the format of a report selected entirely at random from the law reports. In order to make life easy for ourselves and, incidentally, to illustrate the points made here most clearly, we have chosen the judgment of the House of Lords in the land law case of *Midland Bank Trust Co Ltd v Green* [1981] AC 513. We shall not be concentrating on the land law in the case, however. Instead, we shall describe a technique for reading it, before going on to look at the terms *ratio decidendi* and *obiter dicta* in relation to it.

If you take *Midland Bank v Green* off the shelf in your law library, you will see that the report can be divided into the 12 parts set out below. They are not numbered as such in the report. We use them for ease of reference. We should also mention that each page of the report has letters (A–H) down one side of the page, so that if you have to refer to a passage in a case, you can draw the attention of the moot judge to it easily.

Here, then, are the 12 parts of the report:

(1) At the very top of [1981] AC 513 is the court, the House of Lords in this case, where the case was decided.

(2) Underneath (1) are the full names of the parties to the case.

(3) Underneath (2) are the *dates* on which the case was heard, together with the *names of the judges* – Law Lords in this case – who heard it, that is, Lord Wilberforce, Lord Edmund-Davies, Lord Fraser of Tullybelton, Lord Russell of Killowen and Lord Bridge of Harwich.

(4) Underneath (3) are the *catchwords*, which are designed to provide a summary of what the case is about. This report tells you that the case is about 'Land Charge – Charges registrable – Estate contract ...' and so on.

---

2   At the time of writing, it is anticipated that the 1999 Practice Direction will be subject to further amendment in May 2000, when a further section will be added to the CPR (in which, *inter alia*, 'notice of appeal' will become 'appeal notice').

(5) Underneath (4) is the *headnote*, which is divided into a summary of the facts and, following on from the italicised word *held*, a summary of the decision in the case. Turning over the page, you can see from the summary of the decision that the Law Lords considered the case of *Re Monolithic Building Co* [1915] 1 Ch 643, the letters 'CA' indicating that that was a decision of the Court of Appeal.

(6) Underneath (5) is a list of eight *cases referred to in their Lordships' opinions*. In fact, as we shall see shortly, there was only one speech in the case, that of Lord Wilberforce, with whom the other four Law Lords agreed.

(7) Underneath (6) is a list of eight *additional cases cited in argument*.

(8) Underneath (7) is a *Summary of the Proceedings*. From this, you learn (see p 515C), that the case involved an appeal by the surviving personal representative of Evelyne Green (the appellant) against a decision of the Court of Appeal (Lord Denning MR, Eveleigh LJ with Sir Stanley Rees dissenting).

(9) Underneath (8), namely from pp 515D–26A, is a fairly full summary of the arguments of counsel in the case: Leonard Hoffman QC and Gavin Lightman QC, for the appellant, and Jonathan Parker QC and Malcolm Waters, for the respondents. The *Law Reports* are almost unique in containing full summaries of the arguments put in the cases reported in them. If you look at p 525B, you will see how Hoffman QC replied on behalf of the respondents to the appellant's submissions.

(10) Underneath (9), from pp 526B–32C, is a verbatim report of Lord Wilberforce's speech, with which (see p 532D–F) the other four Law Lords agreed.

(11) Underneath (10), p 532F–G, there is a note that the appeal was allowed.

(12) Underneath (11), p 532G, the names of the *solicitors* to the parties are given.

Although there are minor variations between the various series of modern law reports, these 12 parts are basically replicated, whichever the set of reports in which the case you are reading is located.

Each of the 12 parts may be of interest to the mooter in different ways. Of primary concern is (10), the verbatim report of Lord Wilberforce's speech. It is the task of the mooter, as of any lawyer, to distil the *ratio decidendi* of the case from this speech (since all the Law Lords were in agreement with it). In doing so, he or she must also note any relevant *obiter dicta* from the case.

Whether *obiter dicta* are relevant to your case depends on the reason why you are reading the case. Any *dicta* from this case may be very persuasive in other cases if relevant, since they are *dicta* of an eminent Law Lord in a relatively recent case. *Obiter dicta* in *Midland Bank v Green*, as in any case, are sayings by the judge 'by the way'. They must be contrasted with the *ratio decidendi*, the *ratio decidendi* being the legal reason why their Lordships reached their decision on the particular facts of the case.

A case may have only one *ratio* if there is only one judge, but the judgment or speech of each judge may have its own *ratio* if there is more than one judge in the case. It is always up to you to find the *ratio* of a case. The headnote will not always contain the *ratio* and you will find that no two lawyers will agree on exactly what the *ratio* of many cases is. The case of *Midland Bank v Green* is unusual in that the *ratio* of the case is so clear and simple, as we shall see, that most lawyers would agree as to what it was. Other cases pose much more complex questions, particularly where more than one judgment or speech is involved.

The first question, therefore, is what the *material facts* of the case are. These are the facts which are legally relevant (see the answers to Questions 88 and 89). By reading the headnote (p 513), together with Lord Wilberforce's summary of the facts (pp 526B–27B), you could come up with the following, or something similar:

> A father granted to his son an option to purchase his farm. The option was not registered as a land charge under the Land Charges Act 1925. Wishing to deprive the son of the option, the father conveyed the farm, worth £40,000, to the mother for £500. After the conveyance of the farm from the father to the mother, the son purported to exercise the option.

Thus, it is not legally relevant in this case that, for example, the farm was a 300 acre farm called Gravel Hill Farm; that the father's name was Walter Stanley Green, that the mother was called Evelyne, or that she had five children (as to all of which, see p 526).

The question in the case was whether what is now s 4(5) of the Land Charges Act 1972 meant that the purported exercise of the option by the son was invalid. Allowing the appeal of the mother's estate, the House of Lords held that it was, indeed, invalid. At the time, the relevant statutory provision was s 13(2) of the Land Charges Act 1925, which is set out in the headnote. It provided as follows:

> A land charge of ... class C ... shall ... be void as against a purchaser of the land charged therewith ..., unless the land charge is registered in the appropriate register before completion of the purchase: Provided that, as respects ... an estate contract created or entered into after the commencement of this Act, this sub-section only applies in favour of a purchaser of a legal estate for money or money's worth.

The issue with which Lord Wilberforce is concerned in his speech is whether the words 'in good faith' should be read into the section, so that the purchaser, the mother, must purchase in good faith before the section applies and whether the words 'money or money's worth' include the payment of £500, when the farm is worth £40,000. His Lordship held that the words were not to be read in and that £500, in these circumstances, *was* money or money's worth.

Going back to the facts, we find that they can be cut down even further in order to state the *ratio* of the case, thus:

> One person granted to another person an option to purchase his land. The option was not registered as a land charge under the Land Charges Act 1925. Wishing to deprive the grantee of the option, the grantor conveyed the land to a third party for an 80th of its value. After the conveyance of the land from the grantor to the third party, the grantee purported to exercise the option.

Taking into account Lord Wilberforce's decision, summarised above, the most obvious *ratio* of the case is that failure to register an option under the Act as a land charge means that it is void against a purchaser of the property for money or money's worth, including a purchaser at an undervalue and regardless of the state of mind of the grantor of the option.

As mentioned above, comments not within this *ratio* are *obiter dicta*. For example, Lord Wilberforce's decision as described above, made it *unnecessary* for him to decide whether £500 was in fact a nominal sum of money or not. Nonetheless, his Lordship goes on to say, 'I must say that for my part I should have great difficulty in so holding' (see p 532C).

Finding the *ratio decidendi* of *Midland Bank v Green* is a fairly simple process. In some measure, this is because of the fact that the case involved the interpretation of a statutory provision, namely, what is now s 4(5) of the Land Charges Act 1972. However, the process of determining the *ratio decidendi* of a case becomes a more complex one when, rather than involving statutory interpretation, the case you are reading involves the formulation of a rule of common law or equity from some, or even from no, previous case law. Determining the *ratio decidendi* when reading such a case is a process capable of attaining the level of high art!

Elsewhere in this Guide, we make the point that, with the exception of a moot set in the House of Lords, a moot court is bound by the *rationes decidendi* of indistinguishable cases at the same or a higher level in the hierarchy of courts. As a mooter, therefore, you will need to determine the *ratio decidendi* of a case and to use any *obiter dicta* it may contain for a number of purposes. One is to show that the material facts of the moot problem are indistinguishable from the material facts of the cases on which you rely. Another, is to show that the material facts of the cases on which your opponent relies are distinguishable from either, or both, of the cases on which you rely and the moot problem itself. The two methods of distinguishing cases are given in the answers to Questions 88 and 89. We should, however, stress that, if you accept the approach of Professor Goodhart, discussed below, then there is no scope for the concept of restrictive distinguishing discussed in the answer to Question 88.

We consider, below, two approaches to determining the *ratio decidendi* of a case suggested by eminent academic lawyers. Which one you choose is largely a personal decision. However, you will see that one approach could be more useful in some situations than the other. Professor Goodhart's approach to determining the *ratio decidendi* of a case is the first one.[3] The second one is that of Professor Glanville Williams in his well known book, *Learning the Law*.[4] It is perhaps true to say that the second approach is more clearly borne out in reported case law.

Although Goodhart and Williams are basically in agreement that the *ratio decidendi* of a case is 'the *material facts* of the case plus the decision thereon', it is necessary to be extremely careful as to what exactly is implied by the term the *material facts* of a case. As far as Professor Goodhart is concerned, it is clear that the material facts of a case are the material facts *as seen by the judge*:[5]

> It is on these facts that he bases his judgment, and not on any others. It follows that our task in analysing a case is not to state the facts and the conclusion, but to state the material facts as seen by the judge and his conclusion based on them. *It is by his choice of the material facts that the judge creates law.*

Using the Goodhart approach, you, the reader of a case, must:

(a) eliminate all facts of person, time, place, kind and amount as immaterial, *unless* they are stated to be material by the judge;

(b) consider to be *immaterial* all those facts which the judge expressly or *impliedly* says are immaterial;

(c) consider to be *material* all those facts which the judge expressly says are *material*.

If the judge says nothing about which facts are to be considered material and which are to be considered immaterial, then *all* the facts set out in the judgment are material. If a case contains more than one judgment, each of which agrees as to the result, but in each of which the relevant judge sees different material facts, the *ratio* of the case is limited to the facts seen as being material by all of the judges agreeing in the result.

Williams's approach is somewhat different. In his view, the judge does not have an unlimited discretion to decide which facts of a case are material facts. It is up to you, the reader, to decide what the material facts of a case are, as part of a process of abstraction from all of the facts that occurred in the case. This process of abstraction is guided by a number of factors, including what a judge says in his judgment; by knowledge of the law in general; by common sense; and by a feeling for what the law ought to be.

---

3   Goodhart, AL, 'Determining the *ratio decidendi* of a case', in *Essays in Jurisprudence and the Common Law*, 1931, Cambridge: CUP, p 1. See, also Goodhart, AL, 'The *ratio decidendi* of a case' (1959) 22 MLR 117.

4   Williams, G, *Learning The Law*, 11th edn, 1982, London: Stevens, Chapter 6.

5   *Ibid*, Goodhart, 1931, p 10.

Having decided what are the material facts of the case we are reading, we are a good part of the way to determining the *ratio decidendi* of that case. The next stage is to work out the judge's decision on those material facts. Again, there is a divergence of approach between Goodhart and Williams and it is necessary to keep the two approaches separate. According to Goodhart, it is essential to keep in mind that the *ratio decidendi* is not to be found in the reasons given by the judge in his or her judgment, since these reasons may be wrong, or the reasons given by the judge may be too widely stated, or (rarely) no reasons at all may be given by the judge. In Williams's view, however, this point contradicts Goodhart's assertion that it is the judge who determines what facts are material. Williams, therefore, contents himself with saying that the *ratio decidendi* is not necessarily the rule of law stated by the judge, because that may be too wide.

If you take the Williams approach, then you are free to adopt both forms of distinguishing discussed in the answers to Questions 88 and 89. However, because the Goodhart approach treats the material facts as seen by the judge as sacrosanct, you cannot logically use the process of restrictive distinguishing discussed in the answer to Question 88.

Consider that you have a number of cases, all with *ratios* and/or *dicta* which are favourable to the submissions you intend to make. How do you choose between them? With discretion, is our unhesitating reply. Keep the number of cases down to the minimum. Choose a 'Jessel' rather than a 'Kekewich' (see the answer to Question 92), if you can!

21   How should I cite authorities?

Your list of authorities should state the name of each case you wish to refer to in your moot presentation, together with the citation for each case, for example, *Carlill v Carbolic Smoke Ball Co* [1893] 1 QB 256.

If your case is not reported in the *Law Reports*, then you must use the *Weekly Law Reports* or the *All England Law Reports*. The *Practice Direction for the Court of Appeal, Civil Division* [1999] 2 All ER 490 makes this obligatory in practice for case citations in the Court of Appeal and, equally, one of the rules of the English-Speaking Union Moot is that reports should be cited in the following descending order of priority (placing the *Weekly Law Reports* above the *All England Law Reports*):

- *Law Reports*;

- *Weekly Law Reports*;

- *All England Law Reports*;

- others.

The full text of the relevant part of the *Practice Direction* is as follows (see [1999] 2 All ER 490, pp 520j–21h):

10.1.1 When authority is cited, whether in written or oral submissions, the following practice should in general be followed.

10.1.2 If a case is reported in the official *Law Reports* published by the Incorporated Council of Law Reporting for England and Wales, that report should be cited. These are the most authoritative reports; they contain a summary of argument; and they are the most readily available. If a case is not (or not yet) reported in the official *Law Reports*, but is reported in the *Weekly Law Reports* or the *All England Law Reports*, that report should be cited. If a case is not reported in any of these series of reports, a report in any of the specialist series of reports may be cited. Such reports may not be readily available: photostat copies of the leading authorities or the relevant parts of such authorities should be annexed to written submissions; and it is helpful if photostat copies of the less frequently used series are made available in court. It is recognised that occasions arise when one report is fuller than another, or when there are discrepancies between reports. On such occasions, the practice outlined above need not be followed. It is always helpful if alternative references are given.

10.1.3 Where a reserved written judgment has not been reported, reference should be made to the official transcript (if this is available) and not the handed-down text of the judgment.[6] If the judgment under appeal has been reported before the hearing and counsel wish to argue from the published report rather than from the official transcript, the court should be provided with photocopies of the report for the use of the judges in order that they may be able to annotate it as the argument proceeds.

10.1.4 Advocates are reminded that lists of authorities, including text, to which they wish to refer should be delivered to the Head Usher's office not later than 5.30 pm on the working day before the day when the hearing of the application or appeal is due to commence. Advocates should also seek confirmation that an adequate number of copies are available for the use of the court and, if this is not the case, should themselves provide an appropriate number of photocopies.

10.1.5 Where, as is often the case, one or other party chooses to provide photocopies of the principal authorities (including textbook extracts and academic articles) relied on, the benefit to the court is greatly enhanced if: (i) a list of those authorities, and the photocopies, are lodged with the skeleton argument so that they can be used by the members of the court when preparing for the hearing; (ii) counsel liaise with each other so as to ensure, so far as possible, that the authorities provided are not duplicated. The photocopies need only include, for each law report, the headnote and the pages containing the particular passages relied on and, for each textbook and article, the title pages and the pages containing the particular passages relied on.

---

6   See *Bromley v Bromley* [1964] 3 WLR 666, where the appellants accused the judge, at first instance, of having substantially altered his judgment between the handing down of judgment and its appearance in the official transcript.

10.1.6 Permission to cite unreported cases will not usually be granted unless advocates are able to assure the court that the transcript in question contains a relevant statement of legal principle not found in reported authority and that the authority is not cited because of the phraseology used or as an illustration of the application of an established legal principle.

Moving on, it is worth noting that you must avoid multiple citation of cases in your moot presentation. Therefore, when you are taking part in a moot, agree with your opponents which report of a case should be produced to the moot court, for example, *Commonwealth Law Reports* or *Australian Law Reports*? This will reduce the number of reports required for a moot and will ensure that both you and your opponent will be citing from the same law report.

Where a case is reported in the nominate reports (see the answers to Questions 39 and 40), you should give the name of the case and the citation of the case in the *English Reports*, for example, cite *Stilk v Myrick* as (1809) 170 ER 1168, rather than as *Stilk v Myrick* (1809) 2 Camp 317.

22 Should I delegate my research to others?

This question is only relevant to competitive moots.

It is common practice in competitive moots to separate the moot performance function from the research function and for the mooters to delegate the research function to other students. The other students will frequently be postgraduate law students with a particular interest in the areas of law on which the moot problem is set. For reasons which we shall shortly state, this common practice is not one that we would recommend. Nevertheless, there are certain time saving and energy conserving benefits to the mooters in delegating the research function where possible.

The disadvantages are, however, obvious and ought usually to be decisive in avoiding the delegation route. The main drawback is, of course, that the moot performance is liable to suffer if the mooter has only a very selective awareness of the relevant authorities. There is something in the research process itself, the creative search, the distilling of relevant *dicta*, and so on, which focuses the mind and is good training in creativity, clarity and conciseness, all of which are prime skills in the moot itself. In addition, research assistants can only truly assist if they filter out what they deem to be irrelevant or peripheral issues, although this very process may lend the mooter a somewhat false sense of security. There is every risk that the moot judge will make inroads into apparently peripheral matters, with a view to testing the mooter's flexibility and depth of knowledge.

23 May I use other people's (for example, textbook writers'/other students') ideas?

Don't go to the court without books![7]

It used to be said, for the purposes of argument in real courts, that a textbook writer only became an authority when he or she was dead. The quite reasonable justification for this was that they might otherwise change their mind; death lends finality to an argument.

In recent years, however, the courts have tended to allow citations from leading textbooks and articles, the authors having been very much alive at the time. Two examples, chosen entirely at random, are the passages in the Privy Council decision of *Royal Brunei Airlines Sdn Bhd v Tan Kok Ming* [1995] 2 AC 378, where Lord Nicholls makes extensive reference to academic writing on dishonest assistance in a breach of trust and *Spiliada Maritime Corporation v Cansulex Ltd* [1987] 1 AC 460, p 488B–D, where warm tribute is paid by Lord Goff to the work of Adrian Briggs and Rhona Schuz on the conflict of laws. There is an unwritten canon of superior texts for the purpose of making submissions before real judges. A clue to identifying members of the canon is the appearance of the author's name as part of the title of the work.[8]

From the point of view of good mooting technique you are advised, in the absence of contrary requirements imposed by the rules of the competition or assessment, merely to adopt the arguments of academic writers where they are favourable to your client's case, rather than to cite the author by name. Of course, if the judge asks you whether your argument is the same as, for example, the one propounded by Professor Sir John Smith in his *Law of Theft*, then do not be afraid to admit that it is.[9] Note also, that, in some moots, particularly where the moot forms part of a course of legal studies, you might be obliged to state the author's work as an authority.

As regards discussion with your colleagues, this is, to some degree, encouraged. It is certainly helpful to discuss the legal issues in a moot with your friends. Indeed, different viewpoints can give you a new idea, or assist you in

---

7   McLaren, I (QC), 'Advocacy before superior appellate courts', lecture given at Nottingham Law School, 23 March 1999.

8   A clue provided by the authors of *Mooting Net* (see http://www.mootingnet.org.uk). Examples they cite include *Snell on Equity*, *Chitty on Contract* and *McGregor on Damages*. Harvey McGregor QC is a rare example of an author who has been accepted into the canon during his lifetime. *Goff and Jones on Restitution* instances another two such authors. The citation of textbooks and articles is expressly envisaged by *Practice Direction for the Court of Appeal, Civil Division* [1999] 2 All ER 490 (see the answer to Question 21).

9   Smith, JC (Sir), *The Law of Theft*, 7th edn, 1993, London: Butterworths.

understanding your opponents' arguments. However, the moot judge will penalise you if there is any evidence of direct adoption of another student's arguments. Such evidence might include your limited or nominal understanding of the questions put to you by the judge (see the answer to Question 65).

24 May I seek help from tutors?

To this question, we could not resist quoting the following reply:[10]

> You recognise that before each of the teaching staff there floats a dream – a reputation as a scholar to win or sustain. You feel compunction then at breaking in upon his work. And that is good. Yet still I say – let him protect himself. And still I say, there is no stimulus like that of eager students. If you come not to milk the cow, but for help in a problem you have struggled with, and hard, then what you bring is worth the time you cost.

As this quotation makes clear, your tutors will not appreciate your request for a ready solution to a problem if the solution is readily obtainable from some other source and by your own efforts. Having said that, however, a good tutor will respond generously to a student who has obviously grappled with a question and wishes merely to discuss it in greater depth.

Be on your guard, however, when adopting advice given by your tutors. Moot points are usually on very narrow issues and should, by definition, be points that are arguable in more than one way. If your tutor's guidance is expressed in very general terms, or if your tutor is overly confident that the answer is 'such and such', you can be fairly confident that your tutor has lacked either the time or inclination to wrestle fully with the niceties of the debate. In such a case, you might be advised to take your own counsel!

25 Do I have to produce the original law reports to the moot court?

In competitive moots, it is usually the host team's responsibility to produce the original law reports for the judge, but in moots within a law school, this is unlikely to be a requirement.

In many law schools, it may not be feasible for students to take law reports out of the law library. You must therefore check the rules that apply to the provision of authorities for moots held in your own law school. These rules might not require you to produce anything other than your list of authorities to

---

10   Llewellyn, KN, *The Bramble Bush – On Our Law and Its Study*, 1930, New York: Oceana, p 96.

the moot court. It is, however, possible that your law school adopts the rules that apply for moots held at Lincoln's Inn. These rules require you, in respect of all cases that you have cited, to produce for the moot judge a photocopy of the headnote of the report of the case and a photocopy of the passage to which you intend to refer.

If you do photocopy material, do be aware that there are copyright restrictions which may limit your right to photocopy. For most materials, up to 10% of the work in question may be photocopied for personal use. However, in some cases, any photocopying is *prima facie* a breach of copyright and should not be embarked upon without the publisher's prior written consent. Most photocopiers in law libraries will sit in the shadow of a warning notice detailing which materials may be photocopied and which may not.

26   What are the regnal years of British sovereigns and do I need to know them?

The regnal years of British kings and queens, the dates between which they actually reigned, or are deemed to have reigned, are far more important in the context of the type of research involved in preparing a moot problem than you might imagine.

For example, particularly in an old case, you might have the following statute citation: 28 & 29 Vict Chapter 30. If so, it is very unlikely you will have a title of the Act – this used to be the standard method of citation, before 1963. This means that this Act was passed in the parliamentary session beginning in the 28th year of the reign of Queen Victoria and ending in the 29th year of her reign. As you can see, it was the 30th Act to receive the royal assent in that session.

There is certainly no need to remember them by heart. However, we hope that the list set out below may serve as a useful *aide memoire*:

William I	1066–87
William II	1087–1100
Henry I	1100–35
Stephen	1135–54
Henry II	1154–89
Richard I	1189–99
John	1199–1216
Henry III	1216–72
Edward I	1272–1307
Edward II	1307–27

Edward III	1327–77
Richard II	1377–99
Henry IV	1399–1413
Henry V	1413–22
Henry VI	1422–61
Edward IV	1461–83
Edward V	1483
Richard III	1483–85
Henry VII	1485–1509
Henry VIII	1509–47
Edward VI	1547–53
Mary	1553–58
Elizabeth I	1558–1603
James I	1603–25
Charles I	1625–49
Charles II	1649–85 [in fact, Lord Protector Cromwell ruled between 1649 and 1660]
James II	1685–88 [the 'Glorious Revolution']
William III and Mary	1689–1702
Anne	1702–14
George I	1714–27
George II	1727–60
George III	1760–1820
George IV	1820–30
William IV	1830–37
Victoria	1837–1901
Edward VII	1901–10
George V	1910–36
Edward VIII	1936 [the Abdication Crisis]
George VI	1936–52
Elizabeth II	1952–

In addition to being of use in relation to pre-1963 statute citations, we hope this list will be helpful in reading the nominate reports gathered in the *English Reports* (see the answer to Question 39), since the cases are often arranged in these reports by the legal terms in the regnal years in which they were decided.

27 What form should my presentation take?

You should commence your moot presentation with a concise and clear statement of the propositions of law and principle upon which your submissions are based (see the answer to Question 83). Great care needs to be taken in formulating these submissions. In particular, make sure that you:

- keep your submissions as brief as possible;

- limit the number of your submissions. It is doubtful that you will have time to do adequate justice to more than two submissions. We recommend three submissions as the absolute upper limit for most moots;

- make sure that your submissions are based upon sound legal principle (but note that it is not necessary, at the initial stage, to refer to the authorities supporting the principle for which you contend);

- state your submissions slowly, clearly and sufficiently loudly to enable them to be written down by the moot judge. If you can, watch the judge's pen, or wait for him or her to indicate that you should continue with your presentation. Pause whilst the judge makes a note of each of them.

Here are some examples which you might consider adapting for use in your moot presentations:

- My Lady, I have only one submission. It is that $X = Y$ and that there is authority binding on this court to that effect.

- My Lady, I wish to make two submissions in support of the first ground of appeal. First, that $X = Y$ and that the preponderance of authorities, albeit not binding, are in the Appellants' favour. If your Ladyship does not accept my first submission, it is my alternative submission that, in the absence of authority, there are compelling arguments of legal principle for declaring the law to be as I suggest it to be.

- My Lady, I wish to make two submissions in response to the first ground of appeal. First, that $X = Y$ and that the preponderance of authorities, albeit not binding, are in the Appellants' favour. If your Ladyship does not accept my first submission, it is my alternative submission that, the state of the authorities being in doubt, there are compelling arguments of public policy for declaring the law to be as I suggest it to be.

You might like to examine the example moot in Appendix 1 to this Guide to see how the mooters in that case formulate their submissions. You will notice that the submissions of the Lead Appellant, Ms Felicity Fowler, follow a form not dissimilar to that outlined above.

Submissions of the type appearing above, perhaps need some further explanation. They are known, not surprisingly, as alternative submissions, or arguments in the alternative. It is a peculiarity of English forensic methodology that counsel are permitted not one, but two or more, bites at the proverbial cherry. Indeed, they might argue that there is no cherry and, if they fail in that argument, they might still argue that they should be permitted to bite it. Glanville Williams tells the tale from *Punch* of the son of King's Counsel who was brought before the head of his school charged with breaking a schoolroom window.[11] The boy raised his defence as follows: '... In the first place, sir, the schoolroom has no window; in the second place, the schoolroom window is not broken; in the third place, if it is broken, I did not do it; in the fourth place it was an accident'.[12]

28 When is a submission outside the ground of appeal?

Perhaps the worst mistake that can be made in a moot presentation is to argue outside the deliberately narrow confines of the relevant ground of appeal (see the answer to Question 17). It is, however, an all too common error and the one most likely to lose you the moot. Sometimes a submission is clearly outside the ground of appeal, although, at other times, this is not immediately clear.

Submissions clearly outside the ground of appeal

If a first submission repeats verbatim the wording of a ground of appeal, a second submission, which is made in the alternative to such a first submission, will always, *a fortiori*, fall outside that ground of appeal. Therefore, if you have more than one submission to make on a ground of appeal, particularly where those submissions are in the alternative to each other, you must ensure that neither of them is worded so as merely to repeat or rephrase the ground of appeal in the moot problem. In order to avoid the error of arguing outside the ground of appeal, we suggest that you take the general wording of the ground of appeal and repeat or rephrase it in such a way as to ensure that your submission is within this general wording, but not co-extensive with it. So, for instance, where the ground of appeal is X, a submission will be within the ground of appeal if it takes the form 'X is true according to authority' or 'as a matter of public policy, X is true' (see the answer to Question 74).

---

11 *Op cit*, Williams, fn 4, p 20, note 36.

12 Jane Ching, Principal Lecturer at Nottingham Law School, points out that there is a problem with the boy's defence under the new CPR. Under these, statements of case (previously pleadings) must contain a statement that facts are true: can you, she says, in effect, swear both that there is no window and that it is not broken?

Submissions which may be outside the ground of appeal

These are sometimes hard to identify categorically. Consider the following exchange between judge and mooter taken from the example moot in Appendix 1 to this Guide:

> *Lead Respondent* [*Quoting*]: 'You are to endeavour as far as possible, having regard to the whole transaction, to avoid making an honest man who is not paid for the performance of an unthankful office liable for the failure of other people from whom he receives no benefit.'

> *Scales LJ*: Yes, Mr Khan, but as I understand it your opponent would not disagree with that statement. She relies upon the argument that honesty alone is not enough to exonerate the trustee and, upon the finding of fact at first instance, that Mr Dearing did not act prudently in relation to his dealings with Mr Holmes.

> *Lead Respondent*: My Lord, I am grateful. I merely intend to respectfully submit that if your Lordship were to allow the appeal today the report of this case may sit somewhat uneasily with *Speight v Gaunt*, the facts of both cases being so similar.

> *Scales LJ*: I thank you for your concerns, but I am inclined to think that the two cases are quite different. In the present case, it is not disputed that Mr Dearing acted imprudently; in *Speight v Gaunt,* the question whether Mr Gaunt had acted imprudently was the very essence of the case. The question before us today is a narrower one, it is whether, on the basis of mere imprudence, Mr Dearing can be said to be in 'wilful default' for the purposes of s 30, sub-s (1) of the Trustee Act 1925.

Here, the Lead Respondent attempted to show that the facts of the moot problem were indistinguishable from those of *Speight v Gaunt* (1883) 22 Ch D 727, intending thereby to persuade the moot court with certain dicta from that case. The moot judge was not drawn by this submission and hinted that it was outside the ground of appeal. The Lead Respondent may have thought twice about making that submission, had he realised, as did the judge (see above), that the Lead Appellant was unlikely to dispute the submission. So, although there are no hard and fast rules for determining whether a submission is within or outside the ground of appeal, a useful rule of thumb may be to ask, before making a submission, whether that legal issue is *in dispute* according to the narrow wording of the moot problem.

29   How long should my presentation be?

In practice, you may, one day, be involved in cases which drag on for weeks, months or even years. You will be relieved to discover that your moot performance, on the other hand, is subject to strict time limits. The time limits will depend on the context in which you are mooting.

For the English-Speaking Union National Mooting Competition, the rules allow 20 minutes to the leading mooters on each side, 15 minutes to the Junior Appellant and 20 minutes to the Junior Respondent. The Leading Appellant is permitted a five minute right of reply (see Appendix 5, under the heading 'Moot format').

When mooting at Lincoln's Inn, mooters have slightly different time limits. For the leading mooters on each side, the time limit is 20 minutes, whilst for the juniors, it is 15 minutes each. The Leading Appellant has a longer right to reply than in the English-Speaking Union Moot, that is, 10 minutes. For the Philip C Jessup International Law Moot Court Competition, the rules provide that each team has a total of 45 minutes to speak, which may be allocated between the team members at their discretion.

For the Telders International Law Moot Court Competition, the time limits are 40 minutes per team.

For the United Kingdom Environmental Law Association Moot, each mooter speaks for 10 minutes.

When taking part in a moot which takes the place of a coursework assessment, the time limits may be even more constraining than those above. The setting for such moots is generally a one hour tutorial or seminar slot. It is possible to fit a moot into such a one hour slot, especially if each side has only one mooter, but ideally more than an hour is required, in order to allow time for proper judicial questioning and a judgment from the moot judge at the end (see the answer to Question 1).

Whatever the time limit for your submissions may be, the crucial thing is to adhere to it, since the time limit is there to help you display one of the hallmarks of great advocacy which is concision. One stereotypical image of the persuasive advocate is that of the orator who is fluent in florid and circumlocutory periphrasis. All too often, however, verbosity serves only to obscure. Concision, on the other hand, clarifies. Clarity in communication of arguments is the principal aim of a moot, therefore plan and practise your submissions until you are sure that they are not overlong. As one great Victorian advocate and judge, Henry Hawkins (1817–1907) reminisced:[13]

> To show how we learn by steady and persistent study of the art of advocacy, I laid it down very early in my career that *an advocate should never have too many points.* Concentration is the art of argument. If you are diffuse you will be cut up in detail; if you advance with compactness and precision you will be irresistible.

If you do not use up the entirety of the time allotted to your presentation, you might use the spare time to reiterate your main points as part of your conclusion. It is better to re-emphasise a good point in a number of different ways than to weaken your one good argument with a number of lesser points. A rifle is generally more deadly than a blunderbuss! Another way of making constructive use of time is to exploit the power of the well placed pause. A brief pause after an important point has been made will serve to emphasise its importance and will allow the judge to make a mental or, indeed, written note of it.

---

13 Hawkins, H, *The Reminiscences of Sir Henry Hawkins, Baron Brampton*, Harris, R (ed), 1904, London: Edward Arnold, Vol 1, p 49.

In competitive moots, the clerk of the court (see the answer to Question 11) will assist you with your time-keeping. It is part of the clerk's role to display timing cards to the mooters and to the moot judge at certain intervals, for example, '10 minutes to go'; 'two minutes to go'; 'time'. Conversely, the judge will often appear to be doing his or her best to disrupt your time-keeping. In the English-Speaking Union Moot, the rules used to instruct the clerk to ignore time spent by the judge asking questions and time spent by the mooter responding to them. In fact, this is frequently an unrealistic instruction, which is why the rules have been changed. It is not always a straightforward matter to identify where judicial digression ends and moot argument resumes. All the mooting competitions listed in the answer to Question 96 require either a skeleton argument, as in the United Kingdom Environmental Law Association Prize Moot, or full written pleadings, as in the European, Jessup and Telders moots. Accordingly, the time limit for those competitions includes questions because, in effect, what the mooter is doing is fielding questions on arguments that the judge has already read.

Judicial interventions are often such that the mooter's pre-prepared sequence of argument will often have to be set to one side in favour of a more flexible mooting style (see, generally, Appendix 1). For this reason, mooters are advised not to approach a moot in the same way as they might approach the delivery of a speech in a debating competition (see the answer to Question 49).

If you should ever fail to complete your submissions within the allotted time, the judge has a discretion to allow you extra time. He or she may offer this time on his or her own initiative. If not, it is open to you to say: 'My Lady, I notice that my time has expired. I would respectfully request the court's permission to conclude briefly my submissions.' If the judge says 'Very well, put it in a nutshell', don't ramble on and put it in a coconut shell!

30 When, if at all, may I use skeleton arguments and what form should skeleton arguments, if permitted, take?

You may only use skeleton arguments if the rules of the moot in which you are taking part permit or oblige you to do so. The truth of the matter is, that it will almost never be a matter of choice as to whether you do so or not. You will either be obliged by the rules to submit skeleton arguments, or the rules will prohibit the use of such materials. An example of the former is to be found in the rules of the English-Speaking Union Moot.[14]

---

14   See Appendix 5 under the heading 'Skeleton arguments'.

If the competition does require skeleton arguments, then your first step is to check the precise wording of the rules very carefully. There will almost certainly be a word limit applicable to the skeleton arguments which you must keep within. Incidentally, for a number of years, the higher courts in England and Wales have required litigants to submit skeleton arguments prior to civil appeal hearings.[15]

All the international and EC law moots require full skeleton arguments (sometimes known as 'written pleadings'). In the case of the Philip C Jessup International Law Moot Court Competition and the Telders International Law Moot Court Competition, they are 25 pages long and have to be written on behalf of both the applicant and respondent countries. The winning *memorials* (that is, the name given to the skeleton arguments in the Jessup Moot) have all been published and are worth studying. They will assist you to model your own memorials on a style that has previously found favour with the judges.

There are, however, a number of common errors to avoid when you are preparing your skeleton argument or written pleadings.

First, you are not writing an essay or academic article. You are representing, for example, a fictional country in the International Court of Justice. It follows that you should never argue that the law in the area on which the moot problem is based is uncertain (of course it is, otherwise you would not be mooting it!). Instead, take a view on what you claim the law to be and how it applies to the facts.

Secondly, the temptation to do ever more research must be resisted. Instead, you should conclude your research at quite an early stage and concentrate on drafting and re-drafting your skeleton argument or memorial until you are absolutely satisfied with them.

Thirdly, it is easy to become embroiled in abstract legal issues and to lose sight of, or even to forget, the precise facts of the moot problem. You must, therefore, keep re-reading the facts, to make sure that your arguments do relate to them precisely (see, also, the answer to Question 42).

Fourthly, you are invariably tempted to write far more than the word limit allows. One way to avoid having to completely restructure your skeleton argument or written pleadings at a late stage, is to put your peripheral arguments in footnotes at the outset. (They cannot stay there, because only citations may be footnoted in the pleadings in their final form.) If you find, when you have completed your final draft, that you are within the word limit, you may simply

---

15 *Practice Direction for the Court of Appeal, Civil Division* [1999] 2 All ER 490, p 499f. See Roch LJ in *Manson v Vooght and Others* (1999) unreported, 13 October, CA, who was effusive in his praise for counsel who had prepared a skeleton argument for the purposes of the appeal: 'It would be difficult to conceive of the arguments available to the appellant being set out either more attractively or more clearly than Mr Kitchener has done [Smith Bernal transcript].' The 1999 Practice Direction contains a useful description of skeleton arguments; when they are necessary; their form and content; their length, etc (see [1999] 2 All ER 490, pp 499f–502f).

lift those peripheral arguments into the text. If, however, you are over the word limit (as is much more likely), you may simply jettison as many footnotes as necessary in order to bring the skeleton argument within the word limit. The text will not have been altered and will, therefore, read perfectly fluently.

Finally, be scrupulous in keeping a note of your citations. There is nothing more frustrating than having a wonderful quotation which directly supports your submission, only to discover at a late stage that you are unable to locate its source.

31   How can I express my submissions logically?

A great philosopher once summed up the whole meaning of a book, with the words: 'What can be said at all can be said clearly; and whereof one cannot speak thereof one must be silent.'[16] If you struggle to make yourself understood orally, you may find little comfort in the great philosopher's statement, but hopefully you will at least be inspired by the simplicity and clarity of it.

It teaches us the fundamental lesson that, in order to be understood, you must say precisely what you mean to say and you must say it without embellishment. In the same way that art students are often instructed to transfer an image from eye to hand by drawing 'what they *actually* see and not what they *think* they see', so too you must examine what you have actually said, to ensure that it is precisely what you had intended to say. Simplicity is hard to achieve, but in simplicity lies the mastery of clear logical expression.

Some logicians and psychologists describe logical reasoning as having two basic forms, the *deductive form* and the *inductive form*, although opinion is divided as to whether there is a true theoretical distinction between them, as opposed merely to a different practical utility.[17] The deductive process reasons out to specific propositions from core assumptions. As for the inductive process, the following definition may be helpful:[18]

> [It is where] one proposition (taken as established), a *factum probans*, makes another proposition in the case, a *factum probandum*, more or less probable than it otherwise would be.

An illustration of *inductive* reasoning is the proposition: 'It is warm outside because the sun is shining.' The deductive version of this is: 'When the sun shines it is always warm, the sun is shining, therefore, it is warm.'

---

16   Wittgenstein, L, *Tractatus Logico-Philosophicus*, Ogden, CK (trans), 1922, London: Routledge, p 27. ('*Was sich überhaupt sagen lässt, lässt sich klar sagen; und wovon man nicht reden kann, darüber muss man schweigen.*')

17   In fact, Wittgenstein himself denies that the inductive process is a logical process at all. It is, he says, 'the simplest law that can be made to harmonise with our experience' and has only a 'psychological' foundation, as opposed to a logical foundation (see *ibid*, paras 6.363 and 6.3631).

18   Anderson, T and Twining, W, *Analysis of Evidence*, 1991, London: Weidenfeld & Nicolson, p 446.

This example of deductive reasoning is called a *syllogism*. A syllogism comprises three main elements – a major premise, a minor premise and a conclusion. This is illustrated in the following example:

(1) all Romans are men;

(2) Caesar is a Roman; *therefore,*

(3) Caesar is a man.

The conclusion (3) is a logically valid one, as deduced from (1) and (2). Note that the factual inaccuracy of premise (1) does not detract from the internal logic of the conclusion.

However, beware the invalid syllogism:

(1) all dogs are male;

(2) Caesar is male; *therefore,*

(3) Caesar is a dog.

The point is, of course, that syllogistic reasoning has its semantic limitations. For one thing, a syllogism is a statement of what is, rather than what ought to be. JW Harris gives the following example of a syllogism which is arguably invalid for this reason:[19]

(1) all animals rear their young;

(2) men are animals; *therefore,*

(3) men ought to rear their young.

The reason why many philosophers would regard this syllogism as invalid is that the 'ought' copular does not appear in, or necessarily arise from, the premises.

Attempt to use deductive or inductive processes to solve the following logic problem.

Contemplate the following cards:

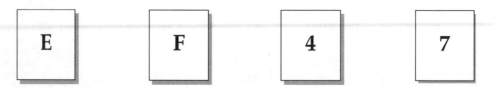

Your job is to test the following hypothesis: 'If a card has a vowel on one side, it has an even number on the other side.' To test the hypothesis, you are required to flip over one or more of the cards, but no more than it is necessary to flip over in order to test the hypothesis. Which cards will you choose to flip over?

If you chose to flip over the 4 card, you have made a mistake. The 4 card may, for instance, have been blank on its reverse side. Even if the 4 card had a consonant on the other side it would neither prove nor disprove the hypothesis.

---

19 Harris, JW, *Legal Philosophies*, 2nd edn, 1997, London: Butterworths.

Accordingly, to flip over the 4 card may prove nothing. If you omitted to flip over the 7 card, you were also in error. If the 7 card had a vowel on its reverse, the hypothesis would have been disproved. Most readers will have chosen to flip over the E card. That is, of course, correct. If you flipped over the 4 card or failed to turn over the 7 card, your error most probably results from a 'confirmation bias' common to human thought processes.[20] This is to say that you sought out evidence to prove the hypothesis, but failed to eliminate evidence to disprove the hypothesis. Returning to our metaphor of representative drawing, it is notable that confirmation bias is largely responsible for inaccurate representation of this sort. Indeed, art tutors will often tell their students that an accurate line drawing of an object results not from drawing the object alone but by drawing the significant shapes of the space not occupied by the object. This instruction is designed to counter the students' confirmation bias, that tendency to draw what they think they see as opposed to what they actually see.

Where does all this lead us in our search to enhance the logic of a mooter's submissions? The following guidance should emerge. You should think hard about what precisely it is that you wish to communicate. Do not assume that your first attempt at expressing an argument has been successful. Instead, you should reflect upon whether your expression has the clarity which the great philosopher with whom we began our answer describes as the hallmark of any worthwhile communication. It will assist you to write down your submissions and to set them to one side for a little while. Returning to your paper, somewhat later, imagine now that you are the moot judge, hearing the submission for the first time. Better still, imagine that you are your own opponent, desiring to demonstrate that what you have written is incorrect. Now re-draft your submissions until they flow logically and clearly and are less vulnerable to contradiction, taking care never to confuse statements of what is, with statements of what ought to be. An exercise such as this will serve to offset your natural 'confirmation bias'.

32   How do I use a law library in preparing my moot presentation?

The law library is crucially important to the mooter. If you don't know the law library in your law school very well, wait until a quiet moment, and have a good look round it. You will find many catalogues, usually on computer terminals, indices, works of reference (bibliographies, dictionaries and so on), various series of law reports and statutes and law journals. So where do you start?

---

20   This experiment is a paraphrase of one appearing in Gleitman, H, *Psychology*, 2nd edn, 1986, New York: WW Norton, p 288.

When you are presented with a moot problem, you will very quickly realise the general area of law involved, for example, crime, trusts or land. Look at the grounds of appeal and you will see the area of doubt in the law identified in them. Sometimes, you will be even luckier still and a case will be identified by name in the ground of appeal on which you are making your submissions. In any event, you will have enough information to go to the library and begin your research. In this answer, we are concerned with the research sources in the typical law school library and how to locate what you are looking for in it.

The process of researching a typical ground of appeal is discussed in the answer to Question 42. Having looked up the area of doubt in the law in a leading textbook, as described in that answer, it is always worth checking *Halsbury's Laws of England*, the vast brown-backed legal encyclopedia, in most law school libraries, before moving on to look at the materials under A and B below. *Halsbury's Laws* (not to be confused with *Halsbury's Statutes*, see below) is particularly useful for the mooter, since the relevant authority is given for most points of law in it and the annotations are very detailed indeed. The text is divided into numbered paragraphs and each volume deals with one or more areas of the law, covering not only the domestic legal position on these areas, but also the EC angle, where relevant. There is a monthly current service (see, also, below) as well as an annual *Cumulative Supplement*. Periodically, when a volume is made obsolete by large scale changes in the law, a new edition of the volume may be published. Besides having individual volume indices, like textbooks, the encyclopedia as a whole has a *Consolidated Index* and *Table of Cases*.

The next stage is to find the cases and/or the statutes you have located in these texts.

Finding law reports

As you may know, not all decisions of the courts contain new points of law and, as a consequence, are not reported. Cases which are reported are a very small proportion, comparatively speaking, of those decided every year. There is, therefore, a vast proliferation of reported case law.

As discussed in the answer to Question 42, you will tend to begin your research by looking for other cases on the area of doubt in the law specified by the ground of appeal. The ground of appeal may itself carry a reference to a case or a statutory provision, even. Besides beginning with the leading textbooks in the field, you will want to consult one of the standard case law indices. Examples of these are the *Current Law Case Citators*, currently in three volumes (1947–76, 1977–88 and 1989–95), which have full indices for all cases decided from 1947 onwards and contain references to some even earlier, where they have been considered in cases later than 1947. The publishers, Sweet & Maxwell, claim of the *Current Law Case Citators* that 'together, they provide a comprehensive guide to case law after 1946' (see 'Preface', in 1989–95 volume, p v). Also useful is *The Digest*: it contains listings of Scottish, Irish, Commonwealth and European cases, as well as English law ones. The *Law Reports Index* is also useful, containing, as it does, not only cases reported in the semi-official law reports, but also the *Weekly Law Reports* and a number of other series.

If, for example, you consulted the *Current Law Case Citator* for 1989–95, you would see the following entry for *Lloyds Bank v Rosset* [1991] 1 AC 107:

> *Digested, 90/706: Approved, 90/707: Considered, 89/467; 92/2031: Followed, 90/707; 93/572.*

This shows, among other things, that *Lloyds Bank v Rosset* was considered by the Court of Appeal in *Springette v Defoe* (1992) 24 HLR 552 (that is, 92/2031, above: para 2031 of the *Current Law Yearbook* of 1992) and followed in *Ivin v Blake* [1993] NPC 87 (that is, 93/572, above: para 572 of the *Current Law Yearbook* of 1993). *Current Law* will thus give you the references for cases reported in all the major series of law reports, together with cases decided on that case, but, in addition, you would need to check subsequent *Monthly Digests* to check that you are up to date.

Once you have found and assimilated the cases, you might want to see whether there are any articles dealing with the area of doubt identified by the relevant ground of appeal. The *Current Law Yearbooks* are useful for this and, since 1986, there has been the *Legal Journals Index*. This lists, at the front, the law journals included in the index and classifies articles according to subject matter and continues to be updated month by month. There is also the Monthly Current Service to *Halsbury's Laws of England* (see below). Specialist indices dealing with EC law developments are *European Access*, a bi-monthly publication, and the *European Current Law Monthly Digest*, not to mention the *European Legal Journals Index*.

Problems are caused, either where a case is from before 1865, or is so recent as not yet to have been reported. The latter you will have found out about from *The Times* daily law reports, say, or from your reading of journals such as the *Law Society Gazette* or the *Solicitors Journal* or *Legal Action*. Reports in each of these sources will tend not to be verbatim ones, so you will need to get a full transcript. These are available from the sources listed in the answer to Question 52. Your final port of call will be LEXIS, although its use by students is subject to severe restrictions (see, also, the answer to Question 34).

So far as cases earlier than 1865 are concerned, you should be able to obtain an English Reports citation from the huge index to that series or from the *All England Reports Reprint* (abbreviated to All ER Rep). The latter contains only the most famous of cases decided before the *All England* series began in the 1930s (see the answers to Questions 39 and 40). It is, therefore, not very likely to contain the case you are looking for, unless it is a very famous one, such as *Tulk v Moxhay* [1843–60] All ER Rep 9.

Finding an Act of Parliament

There are both official and unofficial editions of Acts of Parliament, that is, public general Acts. The unofficial publications are of vastly more use to a mooter, indeed any lawyer, than the official ones. The two official sources are: *Statutes at Large*, containing Acts from 1225–1865, in 44 volumes, and *Statutes in Force*, a series of loose-leaf binders. Of far more use are two excellent unofficial sources: *Current Law Statutes Annotated* and *Halsbury's Statutes of England and Wales*. The former contains all Acts of Parliament, from 1948 onwards. Acts from 1950 are accompanied by detailed specialists' annotations. If you are arguing a ground of appeal on a question of statutory interpretation, *Current Law Statutes Annotated* is, therefore, an excellent source of reference. *Halsbury's Statutes* contains statutes divided up by subject matter, rather than by reference to date. Provisions of certain Acts are, therefore, sometimes distributed among various volumes, depending on the subject area to which certain provisions most closely relate.

In certain areas, such as property law, company law and tax, there are commercially produced handbooks, which aim to present up to date texts of legislation in these areas. Examples are *Butterworths' Company Law Handbook*, *Butterworths' Intellectual Property Law Handbook* and *CCH Editions' Tax Statutes and Statutory Instruments*.

With statutes, no less than with case law, it is vital to keep up to date with developments, in this case new enactments and repeals. *Halsbury's Statutes* has a looseleaf noter-up and an annual cumulative supplement. For EC law developments, see the EC law sources referred to above.

The *Current Law Legislation Citators* so far comprise three volumes covering 1947–71, 1972–88 and 1989–95. The publishers, Sweet & Maxwell, state that 'The Citators list all amendments, modifications, repeals, etc, to primary and secondary legislation made in the years indicated' (see 'Preface', in 1989–95 volume, p v). Monthly updates are produced, to be found in *Current Law Monthly Digest*.

There are a number of specialist textbooks on using law libraries, including Peter Clinch's *Using a Law Library – A Student's Guide to Legal Research Skills*, 1992, London: Blackstone and Thomas, PA and Cope, C, *How to Use a Law Library: An Introduction to Legal Skills*, 3rd edn, 1996, London: Sweet & Maxwell. Both of these texts cover the avenues of research you might follow in some detail.

A booklet, entitled *Current Law User Guide*, is available from Sweet & Maxwell.

33 What is the difference between square and round brackets in a case citation?

The answer to this question depends on three factors. The first is the year in which the relevant case was reported; the second is the year in which judgment in the case was given; and the third is whether the volume in which the case was reported is part of a series numbered sequentially from volume 1. These three factors interact as follows.

Of the first two factors, the more important is the year in which the case was *reported*. This, rather than the date on which judgment was given, is taken to be the date of the case. Where a case is reported both in the *Law Reports* and some other series of reports, the year of the report in the *Law Reports* is conventionally taken to be the date of the case.

The year in which the case is reported is conventionally shown in all case citations in *square* brackets. However, this convention does not apply where the volume in which the case is reported is one which goes back sequentially to a volume 1, as distinct from being reported in a volume which is one of three, say, for the year in which the case was reported.

Thus, for example, *Re West Sussex Constabulary's Benevolent Fund Trusts*, judgment in which was given by Goff, J in 1970, is conventionally taken to have been decided in 1971, since its correct citation is [1971] Ch 1. The brackets shown are square brackets because the volume of the Chancery Division reports for 1970 is *not* one of a series which goes back sequentially to a volume 1. Thus, the other citations for the case are also shown in square brackets, according to the same convention: [1970] 2 WLR 848 and [1970] 1 All ER 544.

A contrasting example would be *Speight v Gaunt* (1883) 22 Ch D 727. At the time this case was reported in the law reports, a sequential numbering to a volume 1 was adopted, a system later abandoned by the publishers. This was the case at the time, not only for Chancery Division reports, but also, for example, for Appeal Cases (for example, see the appeal to the House of Lords in *Speight v Gaunt*, which is reported at 9 App Cas 1).

You will, of course, encounter anomalous exceptions to these conventions. For example, a case from the *Tax Cases* series of reports is conventionally cited without any date. Equally, in a particular case, there may be pressing reasons why the date of decision of the relevant case must be taken as the date of the decision rather than the date of the report.

(An interesting anonymous article on the question of 'Square or round brackets?' appears at (1993) 49 EG 110, pp 110–11.)

34   When and how should I use electronic information resources?

The brief answer to this question is: rarely and with caution.[21] Electronic information resources, or electronic databases, are generally available in three forms: CD-ROM, the world wide web and on-line. What follows is an attempt to provide a discussion of the typical ways in which each of these three forms are made available to students in a typical educational institution.

The principal value of electronic information resources to the mooter is that, in one or other of the forms in which they are encountered, they may contain transcripts or even full reports of relevant cases which are not reported in any of the main series of law reports. That said, it is important to emphasise that they also contain a vast range of materials other than transcripts and reports of cases, for instance, statutes and statutory instruments, many of which are reported in another form. This is one reason why caution is required but, as we shall discover shortly, there are also other reasons for caution.

Electronic information resources usually provide information in one of three formats: full text, citation and abstract and bibliographic. The first of these gives you the complete text of the original document. The second yields much less than this, giving full publication details only, but including a summary of the original document. The third gives only the publication details of the document in question. In order to avail yourself of any of these formats, you, the student, may need to have been allocated a username, a password and, possibly, a domain by the institution library. Usernames, passwords and domains may be allocated to students on enrolment at the institution in question.[22]

The three forms of electronic information resources are supplied in different ways within many, if not most, institutions. Resources on CD-ROMs, for instance, may be either networked or non-networked. Networked CD-ROMs are generally available via the institution's main academic computing network and can be accessed from any personal computer connected to that network. Other CD-ROM databases, however, can often only be accessed in certain areas and on special terms. In addition, the latter are sometimes loaded on specific workstations, in which case it is often necessary for students to book to use them in advance. Equally, on-line services may either be networked, or again available only via dedicated workstations. Some of the latter may not be directly

---

21   The answer to Question 34 is based closely on a pamphlet entitled 'Electronic information sources in law: a brief guide', prepared by Terry Hanstock and Angela Donaldson of Library and Information Services, The Nottingham Trent University. The authors extend their grateful thanks to the authors of the pamphlet for their permission to make such extensive use of its contents in their preparation of this answer.

22   It should be noted that every institution has different practices and the 'mechanics' of access will differ from institution to institution.

accessible by students. In other words, it may be necessary for you to contact the appropriate member of the library staff, should you wish to carry out a search of an on-line database. Finally, although access to the world wide web is generally available from most PCs connected to an institution's main academic computing network, the databases which it contains are sometimes accessible only by a password specific to the database in question.[23]

Common examples of each of the three forms of database discussed above are as follows. Obviously, what is available to the student varies from institution to institution. On CD-ROM, for instance, you may find the full text of *The Times* law reports from 1990. Similarly, on-line services famously include LEXIS (or LEXIS-NEXIS, as it is now known) and, less famously, perhaps, Textline. LEXIS-NEXIS has been described by Peter Clinch, a notable student of law reporting, in the following terms:

> Loaded in a computer in Dayton, Ohio, USA is the full text of a very large body of law from a number of different jurisdictions including all public general Acts and statutory instruments currently in force in England and Wales, virtually all cases reported since 1945 plus Tax Cases reports since 1875, and a large number of unreported cases of the Court of Appeal (Civil Division) and some of the High Court. It also contains a large body of European Communities law.[24]

Although LEXIS-NEXIS is probably the major database (on-line or otherwise) for law, Textline gives worldwide coverage of newspapers, trade journals and other periodicals. In addition, Sweet & Maxwell launched WestlawUK in 2000. As to the world wide web, this contains a growing number of relevant databases, including Butterworths Direct, Current Legal Information, Lawtel, Eurolaw and many more. A number of world wide web resources are freely available, for example:

- http://www.parliament.the-stationery-office.co.uk/pa/1d/1djudinf.htm

  (House of Lords decisions); and

- http://www.courtservice.gov.uk/cs_home.htm (the court service website).

In terms of electronic information resources, there is, therefore, an embarrassment of riches. One is tempted to ask: what price *stare decisis*? Indeed, the same commentator notes that, long before the advent of electronic information resources, the 1940 *Report of the Law Reporting Committee* had stated that, once the editors of the main series of law reports have selected the cases of genuine interest, what remains 'is less likely to be a treasure house than a rubbish heap in which a jewel will rarely, if ever, be found'.[25] This raises the

---

23   Again, it should be noted that every institution has different practices.

24   Clinch, P, *Using a Law Library – A Student's Guide to Legal Research Skills*, 1992, London: Blackstone, p 224. Appendix 6 of that book usefully contains 'An introduction to LEXIS'.

25   *Ibid*, p 91.

question of when, as a mooter, you should begin to look for the jewel in the rubbish heap, if we may be pardoned the expression. If you find that jewel of a case, should you cite it? We would suggest that you consult electronic information resources for cases unreported elsewhere only when you can find no case which even suggests the possibility of extending the law in the way that you contend. Even if you find a case which you think may be the jewel you seek, ask yourself whether it *really does* extend the law beyond the reported cases. If it does, then the second question, in a sense, answers itself, subject to the points made below. If it does *not* extend the law beyond the reported cases then, not being a jewel, you should not use it.[26]

Whatever your finding, however, you must bear two points in mind. First, the rules of the competition or assessment in the context of which the moot is taking place may actually *forbid* the use of unreported cases, whether from electronic information resources or otherwise. Secondly, the answer to this question highlights one of the main differences between arguing a point of law in practice and arguing it in a moot presentation. In practice, although you will tend to refer to everything which assists your case, you will have to note the stricture of the House of Lords in *Roberts Petroleum Ltd v Kenny (Bernard) Ltd* [1983] 2 AC 192. In mooting, either the rules of the competition or the type of assessment we suggest in this answer will determine your own answer to this question. We think the following may be useful generally. In *Roberts Petroleum*, Lord Diplock said, with the concurrence of the other members of the House of Lords sitting in that case (see [1983] 2 AC 192, p 202D–E):

> My Lords, in my opinion the time has come when your Lordships should adopt the practice of declining to allow transcripts of unreported judgments of the Civil Division of the Court of Appeal to be cited upon the hearing of appeals to this House unless leave is given to do so; and that such leave should only be granted upon counsel giving an assurance that the transcript contains a statement of some principle of law, relevant to an issue in the appeal to this House, that is *binding upon the Court of Appeal* and of which the substance, as distinct from the mere choice of phraseology, *is not to be found in any judgment of that court that has appeared in one of the generalised or specialised series of reports.* [Emphasis added.]

Obviously, it is important to note carefully the exact parameters of this admonition: (a) it applies to cases cited before the House of Lords; (b) it applies

---

26 There is a useful general discussion of the status of unreported cases in Bailey, SH and Gunn, MJ, *The Modern English Legal System*, 3rd edn, 1996, London: Sweet & Maxwell, pp 450–51 (see also *Practice Direction for the Court of Appeal, Civil Division* [1999] 2 All ER 490, extracted in the answer to Question 21). Readers might be interested to know that a conference sponsored by the Incorporated Council of Law Reporting (http://www.lawreports.co.uk) with support from Smith Bernal Official Court Transcribers (http://www.smithbernal.com), was hosted by the Cambridge University Law Faculty on Friday 17 March 2000. The conference title was 'Law reporting, legal information and electronic media in the new millennium'. The keynote speaker was the Lord Chief Justice of England, the Right Honourable Lord Bingham of Cornhill.

to unreported cases in the Court of Appeal (Civil Division); (c) leave must be given for the citation of such a case by the Law Lords; (d) such leave will be given only if counsel seeking to rely on it assures the House that the transcript satisfies the criteria set out in the extract and emphasised above.

(The fact that the extract is limited to cases in the civil division of the Court of Appeal may be quite significant, in the light of the finding of a study that, in 1985, 70% of the decisions of the Court of Appeal (Civil Division) were reported, as against under 10% of the decisions of the Court of Appeal (Criminal Division).)[27]

Finally, note that even electronic information resources are subject to a short delay between judgment being given in a case and the case finding its way onto the database in question.[28]

35 When and how may I refer to overseas authorities?

Overseas authorities fall into a number of broad categories for citation purposes. Which of these categories a particular case falls into determines the answer to this question.

Overseas authorities are authorities in any jurisdiction other than that of England and Wales. For this purpose, decisions of the European Court of Justice *are* part, obviously, of the case law of England and Wales. The basic principle is that overseas authorities may be *persuasive* authorities in the English courts. Overseas authorities will include decisions of, especially, Scottish, Irish and Commonwealth courts and those in other Member States of the EC. In fact, it has been stressed that, in areas such as revenue law (for example, in *Abbott v Philbin (Inspector of Taxes)* [1961] AC 352), it is desirable for English law to be the same as Scots law.

An interesting possibility has been raised by the implementation in English law of the Unfair Contract Terms Directive (93/13/EEC). The Directive has been implemented by the Unfair Terms in Consumer Contracts Regulations 1999 (SI 2083/1999), which came into effect on 1 October 1999. A term in a contract which has been drafted in advance by a business without influence on its substance by the consumer can be challenged as unfair where 'contrary to the requirement of good faith it causes a significant imbalance in the parties' rights and obligations under the contract to the detriment of the consumer'. It is modelled on the German Unfair Contract Terms Act (*Gesetz zur Regelung des Rechts der Allgemeinen Geschäftsbedingungen*, the AGB-Gesetz) of 1976. It,

---

27 See generally Clinch, P, 'Systems of reporting judicial decision making', unpublished PhD thesis, 1989, University of Sheffield.

28 That said, the House of Lords website (http://www.parliament.uk) generally contains full transcripts of decisions after 4 pm on the day the judgment is handed down!

therefore, raises the possibility that German case law may be used in English courts as persuasive authority on what is fair for these purposes.

Technically, advices of the Judicial Committee of the Privy Council to the Queen are not strictly binding on English judges. They are, however, highly persuasive, the Judicial Committee's personnel being drawn largely from the judicial House of Lords. An example of the potential standing of the Judicial Committee's advices is demonstrated by the fact that in *Doughty v Turner Manufacturing Co Ltd* [1964] 1 QB 518, the Court of Appeal said *obiter* that the Privy Council's decision in *Overseas Tankship (UK) Ltd v Morts Dock and Engineering Co Ltd (The Wagon Mound)* [1961] AC 388 had supplanted the decision of the Court of Appeal in *Re Polemis* [1921] 3 KB 560.

36   What does the Latin mean in a law report?

'And, as Jim Timson's counsel,' I told his Lordship, 'I might know a little more about his case than counsel for the prosecution.'

To which Mr Justice Everglade trotted out his favourite bit of Latin. 'I imagine,' he said loftily, 'your client says he was not *ejusdem generis* with the other lads.'

'*Ejusdem generis*? Oh yes, my Lord. He's always saying that. *Ejusdem generis* is a phrase in constant use in his particular part of Brixton.'[29]

We have included a glossary of Latin and law-French words and phrases as Appendix 8. Whilst generally avoiding the use of Latin yourself (see the answer to Question 37), you need to be aware of the meaning of at least the Latin words and expressions set out in Appendix 8. This is because they are still very commonly encountered, especially in the context of mooting.

In a law report, the Latin abbreviation which you will most commonly encounter is *cur adv vult* or *cur ad vult* (see Appendix 8), which occurs in many law reports, just under the headnote, and the words *per curiam*, which often occur in the headnote itself. *Per curiam*, sometimes abbreviated to *per cur*, simply means 'by the court'.

You may wonder why Latin words and phrases crop up so often in English law. It may seem odd that large parts of such an ancient language are still in use today. What we are seeing as lawyers is, however, the attenuated use of Latin in the last of a number of phases in the language's historical development. Until the Renaissance, Latin was the language of Western European philosophy, law and culture. From its early stages, it has been the language of the Catholic Church. Before that, it was the language of the Roman Empire and, before that even, it was the language of Republican Rome. Parts of modern English law, which have their origins in the Medieval common law (for example, habeas

---

29   Mortimer, J, 'Rumpole and the younger generation', in *The Best of Rumpole*, 1993, London: Viking, p 27. See the answer to Question 55 for the mode of address used here.

corpus, certiorari and so on) the law of ancient Rome or canon law, the law of the Catholic Church, tend still to require its use today.

37   Should I use Latin in my moot presentation?

There is no doubt that Latin is associated very closely in the public mind with a particular kind of lawyer. Equally, the use of Latin is associated in the minds of *lawyers* with a particular kind of lawyer, Mr Justice Everglade, for example (see the answer to Question 36). However, following the implementation of the proposals contained in Lord Woolf's report, *Access to Justice*, these associations may gradually evaporate. The Woolf Report, as mentioned elsewhere in this book, provided the background to the Civil Procedure Rules 1998. Not only do these rules remove Latin tags from certain types of civil proceedings (for example, an *ex parte* application becomes an application made without notice), but their introduction has begun a strong debate about whether Latin phrases, as well as archaisms of the English language, should have any place in substantive law.[30] At the time of writing, there is some indication that the use of Latin and English archaisms is meeting increasing judicial hostility (see, for example, *Fryer v Pearson and Another* (2000) *The Times*, 4 April, *per* May LJ). In addition, there is a belief that one result of Lord Justice Auld's review of the criminal process will be the suppression of such language.

Unless you can justify the use of Latin in your moot presentation for a particular reason (see below), our advice is that you use equally precise English instead. This is in line with the spirit of Woolf and much modern thinking on the issue. One justification for the continued use of Latin is the preciseness of expression which it encourages. Precise expression should be possible in English too.

The use of Latin is justified where it is used to describe something by lawyers that is virtually universal. Obvious examples of this are *mens rea* and *actus reus* in criminal law, and the expressions *ex turpi causa non oritur actio*, *volenti non fit injuria* and *res ipsa loquitur* in tort. These expressions are so universally used that, for you, as a mooter, not to use them would seem eccentric. It remains to be seen what the fate of such words and phrases will be.

The use of Latin may also be justified if used with discretion, simply for effect. Knowledge of the meaning of the Latin words and expressions in Appendix 8 may provide you with just the right phrase at just the right time. We suspect that the neatness and felicity of the Latin 'tags' still in common use is the reason why they have survived. For instance, the ideas expressed in *volenti non fit injuria* and *ex turpi causa non oritur actio* can only be expressed quite clumsily in English.

---

30   See, eg, Rufford, N, 'Court jargon to suffer GBH' (1999) *The Sunday Times*, 5 December.

Generally, however, there is no doubt that the use of Latin in the legal context sounds pompous and unnecessary. It is also something of a confidence trick. Very few lawyers today are classical scholars, so very few speak Latin as though it were 'a second language'. For example, could any lawyer today equal Sir Thomas More (c 1477–1535), Lord Chancellor from 1529–32, who could both speak and write in Latin? (His published Latin works included the philosophical work *Utopia*, epigrams, religious tracts and four dialogues of the Roman writer Lucian.)

What should be avoided at all costs is entirely gratuitous and inappropriate use of Latin. You will know when the use is entirely gratuitous and inappropriate, because you will be met with a Rumpolian rebuff (see the answer to Question 36). In similar vein, Keith Evans recounts the story told of an encounter in the Court of Appeal, between Serjeant Sullivan, the great Irish advocate, and a hapless Lord Justice of Appeal: 'Serjeant Sullivan, hasn't your client ever heard of *in pari delicto potior est conditio defendentis*?' – 'My Lord, in the hills and dales of Killarney where my client plies his trade as a shepherd, they talk of little else!'[31]

The leading article in *The Guardian* of 1 February 1999 should perhaps have the last word in this answer. '*Ab initio* it should be said that there is a good *prima facie* case for the decision of Lord Irvine, the Lord High Chancellor, to simplify the language used in court as part of the civil law reforms which bear the imprimatur of the Master of the Rolls, Lord Woolf. From 26 April, Lord Irvine wants lawyers, *pro bono publico*, to be much more straightforward in the way they speak *pendent lite*.'

38 Can I learn anything from great advocates of the past?

This is one of those questions which, even if you have never asked, then you *ought* to ask! On one very elementary level, the answer is an obvious 'no'. Why should I need to know about great advocates of the past, in order to make a good moot presentation? On another level, however, the answer is an emphatic 'yes'. That is the level at which, as one author has said, you aspire to the true art to which advocacy can rise.[32]

Thus, the same author, a barrister, says that you should:[33]

Familiarise yourself with the 'greats' of the past. There are excellent biographies and memoirs of those advocates, and although styles change you can learn a lot from

---

31 Evans, K, *The Golden Rules of Advocacy*, 1993, London: Blackstone, p 16. For Serjeant Sullivan, see the footnotes to the answer to Question 53.

32 Evans, K, *Advocacy at the Bar – A Beginner's Guide*, 1983, London: Financial Training, p 27.

33 *Ibid*, p 6.

their careers. There really ought to be no single Bar student looking for a pupillage who cannot say at once who it was [who] asked, 'What is the coefficient of expansion of brass?', or who it was [who] began a lethal cross-examination with the stark little question: 'Did you like her?' It is, of course, possible to become a good advocate without much knowledge of the past but an awareness of it can do nothing but good.

Admittedly, this advice is directed at aspiring barristers and, whilst you may aspire to be a good mooter, perhaps you do not aspire to be a barrister. Equally, the advice comes from a book about the art of the advocate in the setting mainly of a trial or mock trial (see the answer to Question 2). Mooters, to put it blandly, are almost exclusively concerned with appeal hearings – simulated ones at that. Nonetheless, the same advice holds true for a mooter, in the authors' contention. Knowledge of the feats of the great advocates of the past will help to build up your confidence as a mooter. The author who wrote the above extract recommends Richard Du Cann's *The Art of the Advocate*;[34] we would do the same. As it happens, the authors are at liberty to divulge the first of the great advocates mentioned in the quotation above. However, it is up to you, should you wish to do so, to find the other!

The great advocate who asked the question, 'What is the coefficient of expansion of brass?' was Norman Birkett, later Lord Birkett, and he did so, well over half a century ago now, in 1931. He used it to begin one of the most devastating cross-examinations on record (see the answer to Question 2). You can read the full story in H Montgomery Hyde's biography of Lord Birkett.[35] Briefly, Norman Birkett, as he then was, was prosecuting in a case which involved, so it was alleged, the murder of a man, followed by the burning of the car in which the dead body had been left by the defendant. Crucial to the prosecution's case was showing that the defendant had loosened a nut on a brass petrol pipe, in order to douse the car with petrol, before igniting it. The defendant's case was that the nut would have become loose in the blazing vehicle in any event. The defendant's legal advisers produced an expert witness to that effect and, following the examination-in-chief (see the answer to Question 2), Birkett cross-examined the witness, beginning with the notorious question: 'What is the coefficient of expansion of brass?' One after another, the questions came. But the expert witness's answers were all wrong, right from his initial '... the what?', through to, 'I'm a practical engineer, not a theoretical one', with which the cross-examination ended.

The consequence of the collapse of the evidence of the defendants' expert witness was that the defendant was executed. Even though the defendant's confession was published in a national newspaper the day after the execution,[36]

---

34 Du Cann, R, *The Art of the Advocate*, 3rd edn, 1982, London: Penguin.

35 Montgomery Hyde, H, *Norman Birkett – The Life of Lord Birkett of Ulverston*, 1965, London: The Reprint Society, pp 297–310. The relevant passage is extracted in Gilbert, M (ed), *The Oxford Book of Legal Anecdotes*, 1986, Oxford: OUP, pp 30–32.

36 *Ibid*, Montgomery Hyde, p 310.

it gives the story a somewhat macabre air. This, as much as anything else, is why you can learn a lot from the careers of the great advocates. You learn something about the adversarial system in which they worked and the matters of life and death which have been their daily fare. More than that, many of the skills used in the course of trials by a great advocate such as Norman Birkett were exercised also by him on the hearing of appeals. So we too would recommend that you read and know something about the great advocates of the past. Richard Du Cann's *The Art of The Advocate* is an excellent introduction, although there are also biographies of Sir Edward Marshall Hall (1858–1929), Rufus Isaacs, Lord Reading (1860–1935) and Sir Patrick Hastings (1880–1952). These are well worth reading because each of these great advocates, in different ways, led eccentric and very testing lives and their experiences are valuable even today.

Look at any of these books and you will notice that all are by and about men. There were very few women barristers, or solicitors, for that matter, more than 25 years ago. Not only that, but none of the authors of these books are from an ethnic minority. Although this situation is slowly changing, you will probably look in vain for books of reminiscences by women or by advocates from ethnic minorities. If you would like to read the insights of an eminent woman barrister of today, you should look out for the book by Helena Kennedy QC, now Lady Kennedy, *Eve Was Framed – Women and British Justice*, as well as a very interesting book of reminiscences by a junior barrister, Charlotte Buckhaven, called *Barrister-By-and-Large* .

These are two very different types of book. *Eve Was Framed* is, in the words of its author, 'a polemic about the law, not an academic exercise', which looks at 'the treatment of women in British justice as a paradigm of the faults and blindnesses of the legal system as a whole'. *Barrister-By-and-Large* was described, in the words of John Mortimer QC, which are reproduced on its cover, as: 'A funny and truthful account of the uphill task of becoming a Portia in the 1980s.' Vastly different in scope and spirit though these two books may be, they offer insights into the legal career of an advocate, in particular, that of a barrister, which the books mentioned above cannot offer.

Particularly relevant, if you can find them, are reminiscences of great advocates which tell you something about the way in which they spoke when they argued cases. We therefore end the answer to this question by reaching back in time, to the description given of the art of Sir Samuel Romilly (see the answer to Question 4). As you read this passage, try to ignore the archaisms of style and attitude and focus on the qualities which are being emphasised by the writer:[37]

> As an advocate I think Sir Samuel Romilly approached in his own line as near perfection as it is possible for man to attain ... When any great occasion arose,

---

37 Quoted in Holdsworth, W (Sir), *A History of English Law 1903–72*, in Goodhart, AL and Hanbury, HG (eds), 1952, London: Methuen/Sweet & Maxwell, Vol 13, p 218.

especially when he came to reply at the close of a long and important case, in which the feelings were at all engaged, nothing could be finer. Usually restating his case ... not always exactly as he had opened it, but as, after the discussion which it had undergone, it could be presented with the best prospect of success; not using all the arguments which had been used against him, and which admitted of an answer; ... clear, powerful, and logical when he was right; discreet and adroit when he was wrong; never introducing an unnecessary sentence, seldom using a word that could be altered for the better; always energetic, often earnest and impassioned, never degenerating into violence, either of language or tone; with a noble countenance, a stately figure ... and a voice distinct, deep, and mellow, always, as it seemed to be modulated with singular skill, the exhibition was one which it was impossible to witness without admiration and delight. Probably those who have heard ... Sir Samuel Romilly have heard the most exquisite specimens of eloquence ever addressed from the bar to the bench ...

These qualities in Sir Samuel as an advocate are extremely close to ones which we would extol today, qualities of a good mooter ('never introducing an unnecessary sentence, seldom using a word that could be altered for the better'), no less than any other good advocate. If you turn back to the answer to Question 4, you will see that Sir Samuel Romilly had been one of the few barristers of his generation to have been a mooter as a student. We do not suggest, of course, that if you moot as a student you will, like Sir Samuel, be honoured for your efforts!

39 How can I obtain old cases?

By old cases, we mean those cases dating from before 1865, when the semi-official law reports began to be produced. Before that date, law reports were produced by private individuals, and published under their own names. For this reason, these reports are often referred to as the *nominate reports*.

Just occasionally, you may need to rely on a case reported in the nominate reports. Locating such a case gives rise to two main problems. The first of these is the way in which the name of the reporter or reporter is abbreviated. A few examples will give you an idea of the nature of the problem. Esp is the abbreviation for *Espinasse's Reports*; De GF & J By is the abbreviation for *De Gex, Fisher and Jones's Bankruptcy Reports*; Tur & Rus is the abbreviation for *Turner and Russell's Reports*; E & B is the abbreviation for *Ellis and Blackburn's Reports* and so on. These series of nominate reports cover short periods of years over a vast period of time, roughly from the time of Henry VIII (see the answer to Question 26) to 1865. Help is at hand, however, since there are a number of published tables giving the meanings of the abbreviations mentioned above and many more. First, there is a chart which is to be found in many law libraries, which gives the full names for the abbreviations. Second, there is a volume published with the *English Reports* (abbreviation ER, as to which see below), which again gives the full names for the abbreviations, and is to be found in law libraries which hold the *English Reports*. Finally, there is *Osborne's Concise Law Dictionary*, again to be found in many law libraries, which also contains a table showing the full names for the abbreviations.

Having identified the series of reports in which the case you are looking for is located, the second problem is how to locate that volume itself. Most law libraries do not have the originals, some of which (like the reports of the great Elizabethan lawyer, Edmund Plowden (1518–85)) are extremely rare and very valuable.[38] What they have instead is a massive series of very large volumes called the *English Reports*. These contain, in very closely printed text, reprints of the nominate reports. Because of the comparative ease of availability of the *English Reports*, all citations by you of cases in the nominate reports should be by reference to the *English Reports*. Indeed, in some competitive moots and assessments, this is compulsory.

There is also the *All England Reports Reprint* (abbreviated to 'All ER Rep'). The latter contains only the most famous of cases decided before the *All England* series began, in the 1930s (see the answer to Questions 39 and 40). It is therefore not very likely to contain the case you are looking for, unless it is a particularly famous one, such as *Spencer's Case* [1558–1774] All ER Rep 68.

40   What report do I use of an old authority?

Because the nominate reports were produced by private individuals, and published under their own names, there was no co-ordination of the reports that were produced. Lord Lindley, writing in the first ever edition of the *Law Quarterly Review*, said:[39]

> A multiplicity of law reports is a great evil. The evil was once intolerable; it may become so again; whether it will or will not depends on the profession and the Council [that is, the Incorporated Council of Law Reporting]. Let us hope it never will. If it does, a great effort will have failed, and its failure will prove the necessity for legislative interference and for a monopoly of law reporting.

Very often, therefore, if a case is reported in one set of nominate reports, it will also be reported in another. In this situation, it will be up to you to decide which reference to cite.

The general rule of common sense is that you should choose the fullest report. There are, however, a number of glosses on this general rule. Some of the series of nominate reports are of worse quality than others. Espinasse, who produced reports of cases at *nisi prius* between 1793 and 1807, is notoriously bad. If you have any choice in the matter, therefore, avoid that series. Similarly,

---

38   Edmund Plowden was greatly admired by Sir Edward Coke and was said to be the origin of the (sometimes heard) saying among lawyers: 'The case is alter'd, quoth Plowden.'

39   Lindley, N, 'The history of law reports' (1885) 1 LQR 137, p 149.

Barnardiston's Reports, of which there are two volumes, reprinted at volume 94 of the *English Reports*, and which report cases in the Court of King's Bench between 1726 and 1734, were bad. So bad, in fact, that Lord Lyndhurst is reported to have exclaimed to counsel:[40]

> Barnardiston, Mr Preston! I fear that is a book of no great authority; I recollect, in my younger days, it was said of Barnardiston that he was accustomed to slumber over his notebook, and wags in the rear took the opportunity of scribbling nonsense in it!

Other series, without being totally bad, may omit some vital piece of information which may make the report incomprehensible. In a famous essay,[41] Professor Goodhart mentioned the well known old contract case of *Williams v Carwardine*. The report of the case usually cited is (1833) 4 Barnewall and Adolphus 621. However, that report omits to mention a material fact which is, however, referred to in the report of the case at (1833) 5 Carrington and Payne 566, p 574. In the Barnewall and Adolphus report of the case, the facts merely show that the defendant offered a reward and the claimant offered information for reasons not connected with the reward. It is not mentioned that the claimant knew of the offer. This makes nonsense of the report. However, in the Carrington and Payne report of the case, p 574, Lord Denman CJ is reported as saying to counsel: 'Was any doubt suggested as to whether the plaintiff knew of the handbill at the time of her making the disclosure?' To which counsel for the defendant, Mr Curwood replies: 'She must have known of it, as it was placarded all over Hereford, the place at which she lived.'

41   Is an authority ever too old to use?

In principle, the common law subscribes to a declaratory theory of law, namely, that judges do not create law but merely declare what the law has always been. (It is a theory which has some resonance with natural law jurisprudence.) It follows from a strict adherence to this theory that a case will be valid, no matter how old it is; and judicial obedience to the doctrine of *stare decisis* (see the answer to Question 85) goes some way to enshrining this philosophy as a practical reality. The law reports are full of cases where counsel have dusted off very old authorities with the intention of binding or persuading modern courts.

---

40   Wallace, JW, *The Reporters Arranged and Characterised with Incidental Remarks*, 1882, Boston: Soule and Bugbee, p 424; quoted in Williams, G, *Learning The Law*, 11th edn, 1982, London: Stevens, p 35. Glanville Williams does not record counsel's reply to Lord Lyndhurst's admonition: '... I trust I shall show your Lordship that it may be said of Barnardiston, "*non omnibus dormio*" [*Qu Anglice*; "I've got one eye open"]' (Wallace, p 425).

41   *Op cit*, Goodhart, 1931, fn 3, pp 11, 12; and (1959).

An example is the recent case of *Cambridge Water Co v Eastern Counties Leather plc* [1994] 2 AC 264, in which an authority which had lain dormant since 1884 and had been practically forgotten, namely *Ballard v Tomlinson* (1884) 26 Ch D 194, was brought to the attention of the Court of Appeal. Their Lordships, feeling unable to distinguish *Ballard* from the facts of the case before them ([1994] 2 AC 264, p 275D), followed it, despite the dramatic consequences which flowed from their judgment, that is, that polluters of water sources could be made liable for nuisance, even when harm was not a foreseeable result of their action. (The judgment of the Court of Appeal was in the event later reversed by the House of Lords: see [1994] 2 AC 264 also.)

This example, and there are many others like it, shows that as a general rule common law judicial authorities do not die of old age. In fact, when it suits a judge to do so, he or she will often accord particular respect to older authorities, precisely because they have not been overruled nor otherwise disturbed for a long period of time. Nor do authorities cease to have value merely because they have not been referred to for tens or hundreds of years. There is no principle of desuetude applicable to judicial authorities. Authorities do not have a 'use-by date'.

Having said all that, it is possible to argue that a case has become, in effect, out of date, or should not be afforded the status it once had. The explanatory note which accompanied the House of Lords' *Practice Statement* of 1966 on the doctrine of *stare decisis* (see Question 87 and Appendix 4) acknowledged as much: 'An example of a case in which the House might think it right to depart from a precedent is where they consider that the earlier decision was influenced by the existence of conditions which no longer prevail, and that in modern conditions the law ought to be different.'

However, this technique for avoiding precedent is apparently not limited to the House of Lords. After the coming into force of the Variation of Trusts Act 1958, courts of *first* instance were at first willing to use their new statutory jurisdiction to extend the investment powers granted to trustees by their trust instruments. Then, in 1961, Parliament enacted the Trustee Investments Act. In cases heard in the years immediately following the 1961 Act the courts were far more reluctant to extend trustees' investment powers, taking the view that to do so would be inconsistent with the statutory scheme of investment powers recently laid down by Parliament: see *Re Cooper's Settlement* [1962] Ch 826; *Re Kolb's Will Trusts* [1962] Ch 531. By the early 1980s, this approach had become somewhat out of date and inconvenient, with the result that courts were more willing to extend the investment powers granted by the 1961 Act. An examination of two such cases reveals an intriguing divergence of judicial technique for avoiding the inconvenient precedents set in 1962. In *Mason v Farbrother* [1983] 2 All ER 1078, Blackett-Ord VC (see the answer to Question 58) noted that the rule in the 1962 cases was not an absolute one, and that courts were still free to enlarge trustees' investment powers in 'special circumstances'.

The Vice Chancellor of the County Palatine of Lancaster (again, see the answer to Question 58) concluded that inflation since 1961 was a special circumstance and, on that basis, proceeded to grant the trustees the extension they sought. In the slightly later case of *Trustees of the British Museum v Attorney General* [1984] 1 All ER 337, Sir Robert Megarry VC, when considering a similar application by trustees, politely disapproved of the reasoning in *Mason*, noting that inflation was a 'general', not a 'special' circumstance.[42] Sir Robert Megarry VC concluded instead that the principle laid down in the 1962 cases should no longer be followed: 'Though authoritative, those cases were authorities only *rebus sic stantibus*; and in 1983 they bind no longer.'[43] Note that if the judges in the 1962 authorities had not based their decisions on the temporally specific fact that Parliament had recently enacted the Trustee Investments Act, it is doubtful that their judgments could have been distinguished by Sir Robert as having been decided *rebus sic stantibus* (see Appendix 8).

A similar, but subtly different, technique for avoiding judicial authority, on the basis that it has been 'overtaken by events', is to argue that legislation enacted *since* the judicial authority was laid down has provided a basis upon which to distinguish the judicial authority, so that it need not be followed in modern times. So, for example, the strongly persuasive *obiter dicta* of the judges of the Court of Appeal in *Pharmaceutical Society of Great Britain v Boots Cash Chemists (Southern) Ltd* [1953] 1 QB 401, to the effect that customers in supermarkets are contractually bound to purchase goods even if they discover that they have forgotten their money after the goods have been rung through the cash register, might be avoided on the basis that the Sale of Goods Act 1979 is more recent evidence of a general parliamentary intention to provide greater consumer protection.

If it is not a realistic possibility to argue that a case was decided *rebus sic stantibus*, or that it has been weakened by supervening statute, it may still be possible to argue on other grounds that an old authority should no longer be accorded the status generally attributed to it. A good example of this is provided by the recent decision of the Judicial Committee of the Privy Council in *Royal Brunei Airlines Sdn Bhd v Tan* [1995] 2 AC 378 (see Appendix 1). In that case, Lord Nicholls, delivering the advice of the Judicial Committee, observed that the long standing and much followed authority of Lord Selborne LC's *dictum* in *Barnes v Addy* (1874) 9 Ch App 244 had for many years wrongly been accorded the status of statute, an approach which Lord Nicholls described as being 'inimical to analysis of the underlying concept'.[44] This tendency to recite leading judgments as if they were passages of statutes drafted with all the circumspection of the

---

42 [1984] 1 All ER 337, p 343e.

43 *Ibid*, p 342f.

44 [1995] 2 AC 378, p 386B–C. Even Lord Atkin's famous *dictum* in *Donaghue v Stevenson* [1932] AC 562, p 580 has been cautioned against on this ground (see, eg, Lord Reid in *Home Office v Dorset Yacht Co Ltd* [1970] AC 1004, p 1027.

parliamentary draftsman and enshrining the full intent and purpose of Parliament is all too common. Look out for it when you moot. Frequently, the strongest judicial authority cited against you will be susceptible to this fundamental criticism.

In conclusion, the question whether an old case is as good as a newer case is itself a somewhat mootable one. On the one hand, the declaratory theory of law and the doctrine of precedent mean that judges will usually accord great respect to old cases. On the other hand, cases may have been specific to their time and may have been superseded by supervening conditions or expressions of parliamentary intention. Furthermore, even the most respected of old statements of law, if afforded too much judicial deference, may potentially be avoided if a modern court concludes that it has habitually been given an interpretation or attributed a status which the original author of the statement probably never intended it to have.

42 How do I prepare the law for my moot presentation?

The answer to the question of how you prepare for a moot presentation has a number of aspects including, among other things, the purely practical ones of *learning* the substance of what you finally decide to argue, and how you should dress for the moot. The answers to those questions are dealt with elsewhere in this Guide. In this answer, we focus on the methodology for assembling the substance of the legal argument itself, including the question of how you choose your authorities.

We have divided the process into a number of steps, taking a ground of appeal in an imaginary, and fairly simple, land law moot as an example. This imaginary moot and the relevant ground of appeal are discussed below. If you wish to see the points illustrated further, however, we suggest that you turn to Appendix 1 and that you select, on a random basis, one or other of the grounds of appeal in the moot problem, and one or other side to that ground to argue. You can then adopt the methodology set out below and see whether your argument corresponds to its counterpart in the Appendix 1 moot. Bear in mind, however, that the arguments in the Appendix 1 moot are designed to be *illustrative only*.

Imagine that you have to tackle a land law moot, the assessment of which forms part of your course, and that you have been told that you are the Junior Appellant (see the answer to Question 14). The facts of that second ground of appeal are as follows. In February 1992, Mr Leonard Lombard signed a document letting his holiday home, Yokel Cottage, to Miss Thomasina Trent for a period of 12 years. Title to Yokel Cottage was unregistered. Although the time period of the agreement was certain, the document did not comply with the formalities for a deed contained in the Law of Property (Miscellaneous Provisions) Act 1989. One of the terms of the agreement was that Miss Trent would keep the property in good and tenantable repair throughout the term of the agreement. In March 1995, Miss Trent assigned the agreement to Mr Tony Allen. By April 1997, Yokel Cottage had fallen into serious disrepair, and Mr Allen had refused to carry out any repair work on the property. Mr Lombard brought proceedings in the High Court of Justice, Chancery Division, to enforce the promise to repair contained in the agreement.

Wiseman J gave judgment for the claimant, holding that the agreement ranked as an equitable lease and that the promise was therefore enforceable by Mr Lombard against Mr Allen. Mr Allen, the defendant, appealed to the Court of Appeal, contending that the promise to repair was not enforceable against him, since the agreement did not constitute a legal lease.

You have received the problem and you know you act for the Appellant on this ground of appeal. This is the crucial question, since the answer to it will shape the substance of everything you have to say on the ground of appeal. You know that your argument will be that the promise is *not enforceable* against your client, Mr Allen.

Secondly, you need to check what the ground of appeal from the decision of Wiseman J is. It is that the promise to repair is not enforceable against Mr Allen, since the agreement does not constitute a legal lease. You note that Mr Allen is the assignee of the original tenant. You can guess from these points that there is some judicial debate, or even conflict of authority, on the question of whether a promise in an agreement for the letting of land which is not a deed, can be enforced by the original 'landlord' against an assignee of the original 'tenant'. At this stage, however, you do not know where that debate is to be found.

The third stage, although it does not apply here, is to check whether any cases are referred to in the moot problem. If there were, the next stage would be to check whether those cases are referred to in your lecture or tutorial or seminar notes. If they were referred to in this way, then the next question would be what the notes actually said about those cases. In other words, do your notes generally support or undermine Mr Allen's ground of appeal?

Whether or not the moot problem refers to cases, and whether or not it has been possible to form some view of the strength of your client's case from your notes, the fourth question is whether the *alleged principle involved* in the ground of appeal is referred to in your notes.

Assuming that it is not so referred to, although even if it is, the fifth question is whether your land law tutor is willing to discuss the alleged principle involved in the ground of appeal (see the answer to Question 24). This is worth thinking about for a moment. In the situation discussed here, the moot has been given to you as an assessment. You cannot, therefore, ask your tutor what his or her comments on the moot problem itself are. What you could perhaps do, however, if you were a little artful, would be to ask the tutor what he or she thought of the general principle that a promise in an agreement for the letting of land which did not constitute a deed was not enforceable by the landlord against an assignee of the agreement (but see, again, the answer to Question 24).

Whether your tutor has been willing to discuss this principle or not, the sixth question is whether the principle is referred to in the textbook or textbooks which you use for studying land law. Thus, for example, you might turn to the index of MacKenzie and Phillips's *A Practical Approach to Land Law*,[45] where you would see the heading 'Lease' and, within that heading, 'creation' of a lease, pages 101–07. If you then read those pages, you would see, pages 104–06, that there is a section headed 'Is an equitable lease as good as a legal lease?'. You are getting warmer. Then, just less than half way down page 106, a very helpful passage indeed:

> ... if the tenant agrees in an equitable lease to decorate the interior of the property the burden of this agreement cannot be transferred to a person purchasing the lease from the tenant. The original tenant will remain contractually liable for any breach of the agreement but the landlord will not be able to take action against the new tenant [*Purchase v Lichfield Brewery Co* [1915] 1 KB 184; but see also *Boyer v Warbey* [1953] 1 QB 234].

Hmm, you think. What does a bigger textbook say? So you turn to, say, *Gray's Elements of Land Law*.[46] The task is easier now, since you have the *Purchase* case as a peg to hang your explanations on. You look up *Purchase v Lichfield Brewery Co* in *Gray*. Sure enough, there it is, pages 870, 871 and 872. Looking at page 871, your enthusiasm wanes: 'It is widely accepted that the result generally attributed to *Purchase v Lichfield Brewery Co* is anomalous ...' You read on and, there, referred to slightly lower down, is *Boyer v Warbey*. That case contains an attack on *Purchase v Lichfield Brewery Co* by Denning LJ, no less. Your spirits revive as you form the distinct impression that Denning LJ's comments were either strictly *obiter*; or that *Boyer v Warbey* can be distinguished from the present case and, what is more, seems to overstate the case: see the answers to Questions 88 and 89.[47] Thus are the battle lines drawn up. The issue has become one of demonstrating why *Purchase v Lichfield Brewery Co* is correctly decided and why the comments of Denning LJ in *Boyer v Warbey* are wrong.

The seventh stage is to remind yourself what you are arguing for. You are arguing for the principle that the promise is not enforceable against your client, Mr Allen, since the lease is not a legal one. In other words, that *Purchase v Lichfield Brewery Co* is correctly decided.

---

45 MacKenzie, J-A and Phillips, M, *A Practical Approach to Land Law*, 6th edn, 1996, London: Blackstone.

46 Gray, K, *Elements of Land Law*, 2nd edn, 1993, London: Butterworths.

47 *Ibid*, p 872.

The eighth stage is to look at the academic writing on the two cases. You already have a fair idea from Gray what this writing may say. You can, however, pick up any land law/landlord and tenant law textbook and find an opinion on the issue. If you wish to check whether there has been any recent writing on the subject, check the *Legal Journals Index*, which is published regularly.

Finally, check whether there have been any case law or statutory developments since the materials you have looked at so far were produced. You might consult in this context, for example, *Current Law*, especially the *Current Law Yearbooks*, as well as the most recent editions of *Halsbury's Statutes* and *Current Law Statute* – you never know whether the common law position has been interfered with by legislation. Sure enough, you find the Landlord and Tenant (Covenants) Act 1995, which came into force on 1 January 1996, has been enacted, although you conclude that it has no effect on this situation, the running of covenants in an equitable lease granted prior to 1996.

Armed with the arguments on each side, you begin the process of assembling and writing your argument against *Boyer v Warbey*. You will need to know at least all the materials discussed above, if not more. You will also need to have formed a critical judgment as to why *Purchase v Lichfield Brewery Co* should be upheld. As you formulate each proposition of your argument in your mind, you will need to consider it critically, in order to decide whether you fully understand it and how it could possibly be questioned by the moot judge.

To summarise, these are the nine minimum stages you will need to go through in preparing to argue the law:

(1) Check whether you are Appellants or Respondents.

(2) Check what the ground of appeal from the decision of the first instance judge is.

(3) Check whether any cases are referred to in the moot problem.

(4) Ascertain whether your subject tutor is willing to discuss the case or alleged principle involved in the ground of appeal (to be used sparingly, see the answer to Question 24, especially where your moot presentation is being assessed as part of your course):

    (a) if so, look the case or principle up in a textbook, to see how it is discussed; or

    (b) if not, check whether the *alleged principle involved* in the ground of appeal is referred to in your lecture or seminar/tutorial notes.

(5) Ascertain whether the principle or case is referred to in the textbook or textbooks which you use for studying the relevant subject.

(6) Remind yourself what you are arguing for.

(7) Check whether there is any academic writing on what you are arguing for.

(8) Check whether there have been any case law or statutory developments since the materials you have looked at so far were published.

(9) Finally, write and learn your argument, testing each statement made.

43   How do I practise my moot presentation?

We have included detailed suggestions on how you should practise your moot presentation in the answer to Question 46. This is because practising your moot presentation thoroughly is the key to conquering nerves before a moot presentation. Even if you do not suffer from nerves, it is still important to practise your presentation. In that situation, you may simply be telling yourself that you are not nervous when the reality is that you are lulling yourself into a false sense of security.

Thus, on a very basic level, you can at least try to get an impression of yourself from speaking in front of a mirror. Unless you stand stock still, however, you will not be able to watch yourself. If you want to see what you will actually look like in full flow, so to speak, you will need to obtain video recording facilities. As a partially sighted mooter, you would not of course obtain any benefit from this, but there is still the potential for hearing your performance on audio tape. Even for the fully sighted mooter, audio taping your moot presentation – obviously without the moot judges' questions – will nonetheless give you a good impression of what you will sound like, and will enable you to correct any idiosyncrasies of expression with which you are not entirely satisfied.

Finally, it may be possible to enlist friends at least to hear your presentation. Obviously, they must be trusted friends – otherwise you run the risk of your confidence being undermined rather than increased by their reaction. You may even be able to get friends who are lawyers to simulate the functions of the moot judge by questioning you on your submissions.

44   How can I develop a professional courtroom manner?

In attempting to develop a professional courtroom manner, you should take account of the following general points:

- Dress smartly (see the answer to Question 50). It is remarkable how neatness and sharpness of attire can sharpen and neaten the mind.

- Whilst you are on your feet, imagine that you have a real client to represent and a real case to argue, without ever losing sight of the fact that the moot exercise is a hypothetical one. It may help, for instance, occasionally to refer to 'the Appellants' or 'the Respondents' by their names, for example, 'Mr Smith' or 'Mrs Jones'.

- Be positive. You may be only too well aware of the weak aspects of your case. But do realise that the onus of persuasion lies on you and you must do everything you can to persuade the moot judge that your argument is a sound one, not being afraid to acknowledge, for example, the lack of authority for, or novelty, of the argument (see the answer to Question 60).

- Use formal and disciplined language. Take great care in the selection of words to communicate your submissions to the moot judge. Sloppy, flippant, vague or overfamiliar expressions will only endanger your case.

45 May I talk to my colleague during the moot?

In short, no. If it is absolutely necessary to communicate, it should be perfectly acceptable to bring your colleague's attention to a note in as discreet a manner as possible. You should, of course, confer with your colleague if the moot judge so requests, and you may even ask for the judge's leave so to confer. However, you should only confer with your colleague as an absolute last resort, if, for example, you are unable to answer the judge's question and believe that your colleague may be able to do so.

You will naturally be tempted to speak with your colleague during the other side's presentation of its case. At that time, new thoughts may occur to you, together with new strategies to defeat the other side. Nevertheless, do not whisper your ideas. Scribble them down quietly, discreetly and without fuss. Your colleague will ideally be seated in a position from which he or she will be able to read what you have written.

What you must *on no account do* is to register any reaction at all when it looks as though your opponent is performing badly or suffers any rebuke from the judge. The judge will find nothing to be more offensive than smug whispers between mooters who, in self-congratulatory mood, see fit to pass disparaging comments on the efforts of their opponents. Nothing, that is, apart from disparaging comments about the judge!

46 How do I conquer nerves?

Imagine it. The moot judge has just asked you a question. You have uttered the introductory words to your answer, words such as: 'In my submission, my Lord ...' Suddenly, your eyes dart around the moot court. You have an adrenaline rush. You see the moot judge, impassive. You see the mooters on either side of you. Your hands feel damp with sweat. Try as you might, you can't fix your mind on the question. You feel your throat tighten into a knot. You feel your face muscles subside into blankness. The rest is silence ...

This is the nightmare feared by every mooter, feared by everyone who has to speak in public. You think you have done the research. You tell yourself you know the law. You have read not only your own cases, but your opponent's too. Somehow, however, you have simply imagined that controlling your nerves when speaking in public will come naturally to you. Like the law itself, however, this needs preparation. In the answer to this question, we look at some of the points you need to assess about your personal response to speaking and arguing in public, and how nervous energy can be channelled positively, to convey enthusiasm and confidence in dealing with your material, rather than fear of it. We then briefly consider what you should do if, despite your best laid plans, you find yourself succumbing to nerves after all, in other words, what you should do if your mind goes blank.

As a newcomer to mooting, one of the reasons you will feel nervous about the task ahead is the very idea that any speaking in public is something to be endured rather than enjoyed, perhaps even feared. It is the simple idea of speaking in public that instils fear in you, fear of failure in it.[48] You would not be alone in this. Surveys suggest that some people are more frightened of speaking in public than they are of dying. There is little doubt that, in any straw poll of students, only a small percentage of them will say that they actually enjoy the task of speaking in public, least of all, speaking in public in a moot. For the rest, it will be a matter of tolerance or even dread. You must aim to be one of those who actually *enjoys* it. See the moot as a game, as a dialogue between you and the moot judge, and enjoy it. As we have stressed, this enjoyment of mooting is a skill which can actually be cultivated by you. Consider some of the points you need to assess about your personal response to speaking and arguing in public.

First, consider the way you stand. Stand up straight, with your arms relaxed at your sides, or behind your back. If you use a lectern for your notes, hold it by all means, but do not lean on it. Experts believe[49] that most people tend to stand by locking one hip and relaxing the other when speaking in public, and that this tendency is especially prevalent when they stand behind a lectern. The effect of this is to trap nervous energy and the effect of this, in turn, is to tend to make

---

48 See the interesting discussion in Higgs, N, 'Failure is a positive force' (1995) 31 Training Officer 1, p 21.

49 See Telford, A, 'Controlling nervousness in presentations' (1995) 31 Training Officer 1, p 16. The authors would like to acknowledge the assistance obtained by them from this most interesting article.

you want to pace up and down or gesticulate to emphasise points, neither of which are permitted by the etiquette of a moot court.

Secondly, do not be afraid to pause at appropriate moments when you are speaking. The pause can serve the dual purpose of giving emphasis to a point which you are making and also of giving you time to think.

Thirdly, spend some time practising slow, deep breaths, before going into the moot court, or while you are awaiting your moment to speak. One writer on controlling nerves advises her readers to do this as follows:

> Close your eyes so that you can concentrate solely on your breathing and try to shut out everything else. Listen to the sound of your outward breath and, as you do so, feel your shoulders and the rest of your body becoming more relaxed.
>
> Alternatively, try gradually tensing up all or part of your body. Tense your muscles as hard as you can and then release them on an outward breath. You should feel all your body's tension slip away. Repeat this a few times until you begin to feel completely relaxed.[50]

Fourthly, organise your written material so that you can refer to it easily. If you do this, you will reduce the chances of stumbling or making mistakes, and thus reduce the scope for nervous reactions. Many mooters do this by producing cards on which are set out the various points of their argument. If this works for you, then fine. If not, you might want to try what has been called the Columnary Speech Process,[51] a technique which has been used once at least, to the present writers' knowledge, by a Chancellor of the Exchequer in delivering a Budget speech! This involves dividing each sentence of what you are going to say into small groups of words or short phrases which are, for some people at least, easier to read than a continuous script or list of points. Setting the text out in this way on numbered sheets avoids the dangers associated with shuffled cards. You can keep your thumb by the place you have reached in your presentation.

We can illustrate this technique by taking a segment of speech from the example moot in Appendix 1, para 8.21:

> ... it is clear from this passage that *Lumley v Gye* has already been extended to cover the procurement of the breach of fiduciary obligations of a purely equitable nature. Therefore, I submit that there can be no good reason to deny its application to cases where a person has procured the breach of equitable rights existing under a trust.

You may find that this becomes easier to handle by dividing it up using the Columnar Speech Process, as follows:

---

50 Rawlins, K, *Presentation and Communication Skills – A Handbook for Practitioners*, 1993, London: Macmillan Magazines, p 69. We are indebted to this author for a number of the useful insights here.

51 *Op cit*, Telford, fn 49, p 17.

it is clear from this passage
that *Lumley v Gye* has already been extended
to cover the procurement
of the breach of fiduciary obligations
of a purely equitable nature.

Therefore, I submit that
there can be no good reason
to deny its application to cases
where a person has
procured the breach of equitable rights
existing under a trust.

There is no special magic to this, except that the end of each short line must fall where there would be a slight pause in your (normal!) speech. An elaboration of the process would involve indenting each new sentence, and you may find that this makes your material still easier to use. Once you have formatted the text in this way, you can either run it down one side of each sheet of paper, or set it out on two columns on each sheet of paper, depending on which you find easier.

Fifthly, maintain eye contact with the judge. We have referred to this elsewhere as being of general importance. Believe it or not, it will also assist you in dealing with the question the judge has put, since it operates as an aid to concentration.

Sixthly, you may like to try a technique used by sports people, which involves visualising success in the task ahead. It is commonly known as 'psyching up'. You imagine yourself dealing calmly and clearly with all the questions asked by the judge and being warmly congratulated on an excellent performance by your friends and by the judge. That this may require a leap of faith on your part should not deter you – you don't have to tell anyone you are doing this!

Seventhly, imagine the judge as an individual like you, rather than as some sort of malevolent creature seeking your destruction. Particularly if you are mooting before a member of your law school faculty, the judge will actually want you to succeed and will tend not to be interested in making you look foolish.

Eighthly, practise what you are going to say. Then practise it again and again. Use a full length mirror if you can. Alternatively, ask someone whom you trust to give a constructive opinion on what you are proposing to say in your moot. Don't do this, however, until you are almost ready to give your moot presentation and make sure the person in whom you confide can be trusted not to undermine your confidence with negative comments/suggestions. Again, if you try this out too early, you may find you feel discouraged by your performance and/or by the comments of the friend you have confided in.

If the worst happens, and you find yourself losing your thread in the way we saw at the beginning of this answer, stay calm. Count to five, in your head, whilst looking at an empty space on the desk. Silences are never as long as they feel when you are speaking in public!

Finally, remember that a certain amount of nervousness is actually essential to success in addressing the moot court. As Glanville Williams, robustly says in his *Learning the Law*: [52]

> If you are nervous, console yourself with the thought that the initially nervous speaker often performs far better than the stolid [person] with no nerves ...

We would argue that a little nervousness is no bad thing. It shows that you actually care about doing a good job and that, as one of the writers quoted above has said, 'Nerves can have a positive effect by releasing adrenalin into your bloodstream, which will provide you with additional energy and vigour'.[53]

47 How can I improve my pronunciation of English words generally?

If you turn to Question 48, you will see that it is obviously related to this one. The answer to that question, however, is concerned with a more specific issue than this, since it is concerned specifically with the pronunciation of *personal* and *place names*. As mentioned there, the considerations which apply to personal and place names are in many ways quite different from those which apply here. Here, we shall be considering briefly how you might improve your pronunciation of English words generally. Before doing that, however, we shall be considering whether indeed you ought even to *bother* to do so! In other words, we would like to comment briefly on the merits of so called *received pronunciation*. We shall then move on to look briefly at Latin and law-French pronunciation in the context of mooting.

Received pronunciation is also known as 'BBC English'. It is taken to refer to the pronunciation of English by those educated at public schools in England and Wales.[54] It is interesting that the Preface to the *BBC Pronouncing Dictionary of British Names* describes BBC English as a 'myth' which has died hard. Be that

---

52 *Op cit*, Williams, fn 4, p 169. 'Fearnley-Whittingstall [see the answer to Question 50] ... was tall and thin, and incredibly and continually nervous ...' (*Op cit*, Du Cann, fn 34, p 48.) Elsewhere, William Arthur Fearnley-Whittingstall KC was described as 'a fighter' (see Pugh, J, *Goodbye For Ever – The Victim of a System*, 1981, London: Barry Rose, p 27).

53 *Op cit*, Rawlins, fn 50, p 67.

54 Pointon, GE (ed), *BBC Pronouncing Dictionary of British Names*, 1983, Oxford: OUP.

as it may, the learned editor says that this myth continues to have an important place in broadcasting:[55]

> The good announcer remains, as far as the BBC is concerned, the pleasant, unobtrusive speaker who does not distract attention from his subject matter by causing embarrassment, unwitting amusement, or resentment among intelligent listeners.

Obviously, mooting is not the same as broadcasting. Moreover, to the authors' knowledge, received pronunciation has never been favoured at the English bar above any other. However, the aims of avoiding unintentional amusement, embarrassment or resentment are no doubt useful ones to bear in mind when mooting. Any of these things will detract from the success of the moot presentation made by you.

Notice, however, that we are not commenting on the merits – or otherwise – of *regional accents* here. The above quotation says nothing about accents and, no doubt, what may have been perceived as unobtrusive 50 years ago could easily seem amusing today. The comedian Harry Enfield's 'Mr Cholmeley-Warner' character (see the answer to Question 48!), after all, trades on this dilemma. If you are worried about your accent, therefore, our first reaction would be to tell you not to be worried. All that is necessary in order to make a good moot presentation is that you can be heard clearly and distinctly by the moot judge. There is no need to aim for a form of received pronunciation by seeking to eliminate all trace of a regional accent from your speaking voice.

However, having said this, although it is in this sense a matter of personal choice as to whether you seek to develop a neutral accent – so called received pronunciation – we recognise that there may be other factors at work, beyond mere personal choice. You may be happy with your accent but you may feel that it puts you at an unnecessary disadvantage with others in relation to the way in which they speak. No doubt, the reasons for this are quite wrong, but it is a fact of life, even so. Therefore, if you wish to develop a more neutral accent, a form of received pronunciation – and this is largely a matter of personal choice – you cannot do much better than making a practice of, say, listening to BBC Radio 4. You may actually find it enjoyable. Again, however, as his hearers will testify, the question of accent was not a point which troubled that one-time rural-Hampshire speaker, the former Master of the Rolls.

We now need to look briefly at Latin, law-French and English pronunciation. This is not a matter of received pronunciation. It is instead a reflection of the common language – the common custom – of the Bar. There is an old convention of the English Bar that non-English words are to be pronounced in

---

55 *Op cit*, Pointon, fn 54, p v.

an English manner.[56] This has nothing to do with received pronunciation, as we have said. It is a throw-back to the days when the language of the common law was law-French. The convention certainly encompasses Latin and law-French words and expressions. Although recent developments, particularly the growing amount of EC case law which has to be referred to by advocates, means that this convention no longer applies with quite the same rigour as it once did, it is as well to bear in mind that there is still such a convention and that there are therefore no prizes for an idiomatic pronunciation of Spanish, say. (This should come as a great consolation to all non-linguists!) However, it remains essential for you to be able to tease every syllable out of the word that you are pronouncing.

Of course, it follows from the comments made above that, if you are using a word which is traditional law-French (see Appendix 8 for some common examples of this), you will pronounce it in as English a way as you can. Even this is sometimes misleading, however. The classic example is that of the expression *cestui que trust* (plural *cestuis que trust*), which means 'beneficiary/beneficiaries', and pronounced by the tradition of the Bar as 'settee kee trust' (plural 'settees kee trust').[57] Our advice would be to avoid the problem of pronunciation here if you can and refer simply to the *beneficiary* or *beneficiaries* of a trust![58]

We are not concerned here with the pronunciation of EC law case names, for example, which contain non-English words. We save that for the answer to Question 79, in which we offer some quite specific suggestions about pronouncing words which, as an English-speaking lawyer, may be foreign to you.

48 How can I improve my pronunciation of English (and Welsh!) names?

As mentioned in the answer to Question 47, the considerations which apply to personal and place names are in many ways quite different from those which apply to the pronunciation of other English words. So much, at least, is laid down in the preface to the *BBC Pronouncing Dictionary of British Names*.[59]

The *BBC Pronouncing Dictionary of British Names* professes to set out the pronunciation of personal and place names which as closely as possible 'represents the usage of the inhabitants of the place or of the family bearing the

---

56 *Op cit*, Williams, fn 4, p 62.

57 *Op cit*, Williams, fn 4, p 10.

58 If you find you have no choice, you might refer to Williams, *op cit*, fn 3, pp 61–66, for guidance as to the pronunciation of certain commonly encountered law-French and Latin expressions (see, also, Appendix 8).

59 *Op cit*, Pointon, fn 54.

name listed'.[60] As to the latter, one of the authors was pleased to find his own name rendered there (that is, as 'Wott'), although the other was not so lucky as to find a pronunciation for his own name! Be that as it may, this dictionary is very useful when you are mooting, and maybe even if you aren't. Did you realise, for example, that what is pronounced *chumli* may be written as *Cholmondeley* or *Chomley* or even *Chulmleigh*; or that *Featherstonehaugh* may be, and often is, pronounced *fán-shaw*?

Say, for example, you wished to refer in your moot presentation to the names of any or all the following judges:

Lord Simon of *Glaisdale*; Lord Bridge of *Harwich*; Lord Goff of *Chieveley*; Lord Justice *Farquharson*; Lord Justice *Staughton*;

the dictionary will give the pronunciations of the italicised words as being as follows:

gláyzdayl; *hárritch*; *che'evli*; *fa'arkwarsson*; and *stáwton*.

And, as is said, there are many more where those come from!

Assistance is also given by the dictionary in relation to *Welsh* place names and personal names. In the author's experience, the following present difficulties of pronunciation:

Mr Justice *Ungoed-Thomas*.

Using the dictionary, we find that his Lordship's name is pronounced:

Mr Justice *íng-goyd-tómass*.

An abiding mystery, however, is 'Vinelott' – how *is* Mr Justice Vinelott's name pronounced?! Otherwise, using the dictionary, you should not have any difficulty with old favourites, such as Sir Edward *Coke* (pronounced 'kook') and Lord *Thankerton*, pronounced – please forgive this(!) – 'thánkerton'.

49 Should I write out my speech and may I read it or should I learn it by heart?

It is not advisable to read a speech to a moot judge. Indeed, in the English-Speaking Union Moot, judges are specifically instructed that 'rigidly scripted speeches, in particular, should be penalised'.[61] To read a good speech may display your skills as a researcher, and show off your literacy and elocution, but it will do little to display your skills as a mooter.

---

60 *Op cit*, Pointon, fn 54, p vii.

61 See Appendix 5 under the heading 'Guidance for judges'.

The foremost of the mooting skills is to respond to the judge's questioning flexibly and with good legal arguments. Similar to it is the ability to respond flexibly to the Appellants and the ability to reply *ex tempore* to the Respondents. Sound preparation will assist here, but a rigid speech will usually serve only to hinder you. This is not to say that you should avoid writing out your submissions in full, in order to practise before you moot. To do so will elucidate the logical structure of your argument and show up any gaps in the step by step sequence of your reasoning (see the answer to Question 31). Having written out your submissions read them out loud to test their duration and grammatical construction. If you can, read them to a friend. If you have no willing friend, you might record your submissions, into a tape recorder and play them back. To learn your submissions off by heart for use within the moot is, of course, preferable to reading from a script during the moot, but may still dispose you to inflexibility.

One approach which we can recommend is that you should distil each of your submissions from its crude beginnings until it emerges as a single refined phrase. This phrase should be used to outline your submission to the moot judge at the beginning of your 'speech' (see below) and should be written at the top of a handy sized piece of card. Underneath this title phrase on the card, you should write a number of bullet points which expand upon your submission. The exact phraseology used should be invented during the moot itself if you have sufficient confidence. The merit of this approach is that the order of your submissions can be altered if the moot judge so requests or desires, and the individual points which you wish to make in support of your main submissions can be omitted or adopted at will during the moot. The Columnar Speech Process described in the answer to Question 46 could be adapted to suit this approach. In the example moot in Appendix 1, the mooters display precisely these skills.

Despite the foregoing call to flexibility, there are certain parts of every moot that you will do well to commit to memory. In particular, you should memorise your opening and your conclusion. Some suggested formulae can be found in the Appendix 1 (see also the answers to Questions 83 and 84). Not only does this formal language make your moot presentation more polished, it has the added advantage of relaxing you at the beginning of your moot (see the answer to Question 46). A good conclusion, furthermore, gives you the confidence of knowing that, no matter what confusion may unfortunately have gone before, the last thing the judge will hear from you will sound professional and eloquent.

50 How should I dress for a moot?

Mr Justice Croom-Johnson: 'I cannot see you, Mr Fearnley-Whittingstall.'

Mr Fearnley-Whittingstall: 'My Lord, I am before you wigged and gowned.'

Mr Justice Croom-Johnson:	'I still cannot see you, Mr Fearnley-Whittingstall.'
Mr Fearnley-Whittingstall:	'My Lord, is it my yellow waistcoat that you cannot see?'
Mr Justice Croom-Johnson:	'Yes, it is.'
Mr Fearnley-Whittingstall:	'Well, my Lord, you can see me.'
Mr Justice Croom-Johnson:	'Oh, very well, let's get on with the case.'[62]

As we have said elsewhere (see the answer to Question 68), this exchange says quite a lot about the nature of legalistic wit. More importantly for present purposes, it emphasises the traditional importance attached to correct dress at the Bar.

We would suggest that this approach should in principle extend to the moot court. We would certainly not recommend the wearing of barristers' wigs in the moot court. It is certainly not necessary to wear gowns, either. Having said this, however, you may find that the wearing of a gown will do quite a lot for your self-confidence, as it will give you a kind of anonymity, of the type the existence of which is often given as a justification for the wearing of robes in court.

We would, however, recommend that in other respects the dress code of the Bar, for barristers appearing in court, is observed by you. Thus, men must wear suits – preferably dark – and women should wear either a dark suit or a dark skirt and a white blouse. The relevant guidance laid down by the General Council of the Bar, which is obviously a useful guide for the mooter, states that:[63]

> In court a barrister's personal appearance should be decorous, and his dress, when robes are worn, should be compatible with them.

This guidance used to be laid down in a series of annual statements, and used to be highly prescriptive. For example, for women barristers, it used to say:[64]

---

62 Pugh, J, *Goodbye for Ever – The Victim of a System*, 1981, London: Barry Rose, pp 27–28, reproduced in Gilbert, M (ed), *The Oxford Book of Legal Anecdotes*, 1986, Oxford: OUP, p 119.

63 General Council of the Bar, *Written Standards for the Conduct of Professional Work*, 1998, amendment 5, Annex F, para 5.12. The authors are most grateful to Ms Helen Wagner of the General Council of the Bar for her assistance on this point. It should be noted that this guidance is not referring to the barrister's obligation to wear wig, gown and bands in the Supreme Court (including the Crown Court) and in county courts: see, eg, *Practice Direction (Court Dress) (No 3) (1998)* (unreported), available at: http://www.courtservice.gov.uk

64 Boulton, W (Sir), *Conduct and Etiquette at the Bar*, 1975, London: Butterworths, pp 85–86 (superseded) (and supplement). Lord MacKay of Clashfern LC re-affirmed the rules on dress for advocates in court in *Practice Direction (Court Dress) (No 2)* [1995] 1 WLR 648, following consultation with the professions on the wearing of wigs by solicitor-advocates. The rules are set out in full in *Practice Direction (Court Dress)* [1994] 1 WLR 1056. For an extensive survey of *Court Dress*, see the consultation paper of that title, issued on behalf of the Lord Chancellor and the Lord Chief Justice, August 1992. See, also, Rozenberg, J, *The Search for Justice*, 1994, London: Hodder & Stoughton, pp 165–69.

... blouses should be long-sleeved and high to the neck ... [H]air ... should be drawn back from the face and forehead and if long enough should be put up. No conspicuous jewellery or ornaments should be worn.

Although this guidance is today superseded (see footnote 53), you may find it useful if you wish to cultivate quite a conservative appearance.

51   In addition to reading the report of a judgment of a case, should I also read counsels' arguments?

You will be expected to have read the full report of the judgment in every case which you or your opponents have cited and you may be required to answer questions on any part of the judgment. In addition, it is helpful in preparing your moot presentation to read how counsel argued before the court which decided the relevant cases in the law reports (see the answer to Question 20). For example, did counsel fall into error by making a bad concession,[65] or by failing to plead a particular matter?[66]

It is more likely, of course, that counsel's arguments will provide you with a helpful example of how the relevant submissions should be distilled and presented. As well as providing positive guidance on the main issues in the moot problem, counsel may perhaps offer some clue as to how best to phrase your submissions. It is often most impressive to witness the economy and lucidity with which leading counsel are able to communicate complex points, although do not be overawed – counsel's submissions as set out in the law reports are, of course, summarised by the reporter. You should, however, never repeat verbatim counsel's form of words as it appears in the law reports, not least because your moot judge or opponents in the moot will probably be alert to your tactic and will be quite willing to expose it.

52   Where can I obtain a transcript of a recent unreported case?

If you are unable to visit the library of the Royal Courts of Justice in the Strand, where copies are kept of all transcripts, copies may be obtained by post from the following sources (details correct at the time of going to press):

---

65   See *Baden v Société Générale de Commerce SA* [1983] BCLC 325, where counsel conceded that constructive (and not merely 'actual') forms of knowledge are relevant in fixing liability as a constructive trustee on a stranger who has dealings with a trust. Doubt was later cast upon the wisdom of that concession by Vinelott J in *Eagle Trust plc v SBC Securities Ltd* [1992] 4 All ER 488, p 499.

66   See the answer to Question 17.

House of Lords

> The Judicial Office of the House of Lords
> House of Lords
> London SW1A OPW
> Tel: 020 7219 3111

(A small charge (currently £5) may be made for copies. Transcripts may also be accessed on the internet http://www.parliament.uk.)

Court of Appeal (Criminal Division until 31 March 1993)

> Criminal Appeal Office
> Room C223
> Royal Courts of Justice
> London WC2A 2LL
> Tel: 020 7936 7344

(There is a small charge for each page (£1 for each of the first five pages, 25 p for each additional page) of the transcript copied.)

Court of Appeal (Both Divisions for the period 1 April 1993–31 March 1996)

> John Larking Verbatim Reporters
> Temple Chambers
> 3–7 Temple Avenue
> London EC47 0DT
> Tel: 020 7404 7464

(The price is £29 per transcript, plus VAT and postage.)

Court of Appeal (Both Divisions from 1 April 1996)

> Smith Bernal Reporting Ltd
> 180 Fleet Street
> London EC4A 2HG
> Tel: 020 7404 1400

(The first copy transcript costs £40 plus VAT and postage (next working day).)

High Court of Justice

> Mechanical Recording Department
> Room WB11
> Royal Courts of Justice
> London WC2A 2LL
> Tel: 020 7936 6154

(Price will vary according to the length of the transcript. Decisions are available only for the six years prior to the month of the inquiry.)

Remember to check the rules of the assessed or competitive moot, to determine whether you will be allowed to rely on transcripts during your moot presentation (see, also, the answer to Question 34).

It should be noted that it will generally be far more financially viable to obtain transcripts of unreported cases from an electronic source (see the answer to Question 34).

53 How should I manage my time?

A very excellent and learned friend of mine, not, however, famed for his brevity, had been for some considerable time enforcing his arguments before a Kentish jury. Mr Justice Wightman, interposing, said, 'Mr – you have stated that before', and then, pausing for a moment, added, 'but you may have forgotten it, it was a very long time ago'.[67]

One of the most crucial things to remember before you rise to address the moot court is your watch. If you forget it, you will disadvantage yourself unnecessarily, because you will have no idea of the passage of time when you are delivering your moot presentation.

Timing your presentation should be an important feature of your preparation, whatever the moot. In many moots, you will be penalised if you overrun, although, obviously, the judge's questions should not eat into the timing of your presentation.

The clerk of the moot court will assist you to keep within the time limits by bringing your attention to cards which indicate the time remaining for your presentation (see the answer to Question 11).

Time management is, of course, a bigger task than merely staying within the minutes allotted to your submissions in the moot presentation. The really big tasks of time management arise the very moment you receive the moot problem and are informed on which side you will be advocate. The tasks are as follows: research; drafting; meetings with colleagues; photocopying; putting together your bundle of notes and authorities; practising your presentation (see the answer to Question 43). To these sometimes mundane tasks should be added

---

67 Ballantine, R (Serjeant Ballantine), *Some Experiences of a Barrister's Life*, 7th edn, 1883, London: Richard Bentley, p 155. Before 1846, Serjeants were a select guild or order of pleaders in the Court of Common Pleas. In 1846, the Common Pleas was opened to the whole Bar. Serjeant Sullivan (see the answer to Question 37), often called 'the last Serjeant', was not a serjeant in the English sense of being a member of this English guild of Serjeants at Law. He was the last surviving King's Serjeant in Ireland (see Baker, JH, *An Introduction to English Legal History*, 3rd edn, 1990, London: Butterworths, p 182, note 11). (See, generally, also, Baker, JH, *The Order of Serjeants at Law: A Chronicle of Creations, With Related Texts and an Historical Introduction*, 1984, London: Selden Society.)

that most vital of ingredients, that is, intellectual reflection, the 'think' before you speak.[68]

To manage your time properly, you should be fully aware of the size of each task and allocate a proportional amount of time to each one. You will only know how much total time you have to divide between the tasks if you know when the moot is due to take place. You will also need to calculate how much time your other studies will demand between the moment you receive the moot problem and the day on which the moot takes place.

The calculation of the time to be allotted to each task is the easy part. The hard part is being disciplined enough to adhere to your timetable.

54 Where can I find out more about mooting?

There is almost no substitute for actually watching a moot, as a way of finding out more about mooting. Most law schools hold moots which are open for all students to watch, although moots forming part of a course of legal study will often be held in private.[69] Mooting as a rather bizarre spectator sport is encouraged by competitive moots. You may find the idea of hiring a coach and travelling to another law school miles away, to watch an 'away' moot fixture, a rather surreal one.

If you are unable to see a live moot performance, it may be possible to view a video recording of a past moot. The organisers of the various moot competitions may be able to provide copies for sale or on loan (see answer to Question 96). The library at your law school may even stock copies.

Discussions of mooting in printed texts is more scarce than you might imagine. There is a good general discussion in Glanville Williams's famous book *Learning the Law*. In addition, we would recommend KN Llewellyn's *The Bramble Bush – On Our Law and Its Study* and Professor Twining's *Blackstone's Tower: The English Law School*. Full details of these volumes are given in the bibliography at the back of this Guide.

We say there is *almost* no substitute for watching a real moot. The reason for this is that a visit to a sitting of the Court of Appeal will give you a rich insight into the contrast between the reality and the moot court (see the answer to Question 3).

---

68 See Savage, N and Watt, G, 'A house of intellect for the profession', in Birks, P (ed), *What are Law Schools For?*, 1996, Oxford: OUP.

69 See CPR, r 39.2.

3   Performance

55   How do I address the moot judge?

The correct answer to this question depends on the court in which the moot is imagined to be taking place. For mooters who are students of law schools in England and Wales, the moot will usually be set in the Court of Appeal or in the House of Lords. The reason for using these settings is that moots are concerned with questions of *law* and, although both the Crown Court and the High Court of Justice are part of the Supreme Court of England and Wales (see s 1(1) of the Supreme Court Act 1981), these courts are generally concerned with establishing questions of *fact*, as well as questions of *law*.[1]

The mode of address in court for individual judges of both the Court of Appeal and the House of Lords is 'my Lord' or 'my Lady', as appropriate. Advocates observe this convention as a matter of tradition and it is odd that, although you will find the mode of address stated in a leading dictionary[2] and in Debrett, *Civil Procedure*[3] does not tell you how judges should generally be addressed. The nearest there seems to be to an authority on the mode of address of a Court of Appeal or House of Lords judge seems to be a Practice Direction[4] which, by implying that a High Court judge is to be addressed as 'my Lord' or 'my Lady', as appropriate, suggests that Court of Appeal and House of Lords judges are to be so addressed also.

The mode of address of more than one judge of both the Court of Appeal and the House of Lords is 'my Lords'. This is apparently the case even where one of the judges is female (for example, where Butler-Sloss LJ is sitting with another, or two other, Lords Justices of Appeal).[5] In the context of a moot, it is fairly unusual for there to be more than one moot judge, even in the settings of the Court of Appeal or the House of Lords. Where the Court of Appeal or the

1   For historical reasons, the House of Lords is not part of the Supreme Court. See Bailey, SH and Gunn, MJ, *The Modern English Legal System*, 3rd edn, 1996, London: Sweet & Maxwell, pp 99–100.

2   *The Oxford English Dictionary*, 2nd edn, 1989, Oxford: Clarendon, Vol 9, p 27.

3   *Civil Procedure*, 2000, London: Sweet & Maxwell.

4   *Practice Direction (Judges: Modes of Address)* [1982] 1 WLR 101.

5   The authors are indebted to Mr Peter Laight, clerk to Butler-Sloss LJ, for clarifying this point of practice.

House of Lords is represented by a single moot judge, it is unnecessary to address that judge in the plural, even though he or she is representing the whole court.

There are no exceptions to these rules, whether you are mooting in the imagined setting of the Court of Appeal or that of the House of Lords. It is, therefore, irrelevant whether you are addressing a Lord of Appeal in Ordinary in the House of Lords; a Lord Justice of Appeal in the Court of Appeal; or a judge of the High Court. Irrelevant, also, is the fact that a Lord of Appeal in Ordinary may be a life peer (for example, Baron Denning of Whitchurch); that male judges of the High Court and Court of Appeal are Knights (so, for instance, Harman J is Sir Jeremiah LeRoy Harman and Russell LJ is Sir Thomas Patrick Russell); or that female judges of the High Court and Court of Appeal are Dame Commanders of the British Empire (Arden J, for example, is Dame Mary Howarth Arden, DBE, whilst Butler-Sloss LJ is Dame Ann Elizabeth Oldfield Butler-Sloss, DBE).[6] These simple rules should not present the mooter with any problems. The key to using them easily is to try to forget that you, the mooter, are addressing a postgraduate student, a member of staff of your law school or a member of the local bar, as the case may be, and to imagine that you are addressing a real judge. Even if you are addressing a real judge, he or she must be addressed in his or her capacity as a moot judge of the court in which the case is imagined to be taking place. If a Court of Appeal or House of Lords judge is male, he is addressed as 'my Lord'; if such a judge is female, she is addressed as 'my Lady'. Having said all this, however, you will need to be able to steer clear of certain common mistakes, which we shall discuss below.

We also need to emphasise that the Court of Appeal and the House of Lords are not the only courts in which a moot could be set, even in an English or Welsh university. A moot, especially a competitive one, could very easily be set in the International Court of Justice, in the European Court of Human Rights or in the Court of Justice of the European Communities (that is, 'the European Court'). Where the court is one of these three, or any other court except the Court of Appeal or the House of Lords, you may have to address a judge in ways other than 'my Lord' or 'my Lady'. Indeed, if you are mooting in a competition, there may be a specific direction in the competition rules regarding how you must address the judge or judges. In the European Court of Human Rights, an English barrister will address the president as 'Mr President', possibly using 'my Lords' in the same way as he or she would do at home.[7]

Again, in the European Court, although there are no strict rules regarding the mode of address for its judges in court, national rules of legal etiquette apply,

---

6   This list is illustrative only; for example, Harman J is now retired, whilst Butler-Sloss LJ was appointed President of the Family Division on 1 October 1999.

7   The authors are grateful to Mr Paul Mahoney, Deputy Registrar of the European Court of Human Rights, for this information.

with appropriate adaptations. This means that English barristers appearing before the European Court will address the President of the Court as 'my Lord President' and any other judge of the Court as 'my Lord'. In the same way that the president of the Court is addressed as 'my Lord President', the Advocate General is therefore addressed as 'my Lord Advocate General'. To date, there have been no female judges of the European Court, so the question of the correct mode of address of a female judge of the European Court has not arisen. By parity of reasoning with the above, however, the modes of address of 'my Lady President' and 'my Lady' would presumably be used. Interestingly, there has been a female Advocate General (Mrs Simone Rozes of France, Advocate General from 1981–84), who later became the First President of the French *Cour de Cassation*.[8] A female Advocate General is addressed as 'my Lady Advocate General'.

Reverting to moots in the setting of the Court of Appeal or the House of Lords, you can see an example of the proper mode of address of a judge of the Court of Appeal in Appendix 1, para 7.3. There, Miss Felicity Fowler, who appears as leading counsel for the Appellant, addresses Scales LJ with the words: 'My Lord, in the instant case there are two grounds of appeal ...' Although the point is not suggested in Appendix 1, the words 'my Lord' might be pronounced by her in a mannered or hurried way and, of course, you will see this represented in novels, and so on, as 'my Lud' or 'm'Lud'.[9] By the same token, if the moot in Appendix 1 were imagined to be taking place in the House of Lords, the mode of address of the judges would be exactly the same as this. The rule being so simple, you might ask, how could you get it wrong?

First, you might confuse the correct use of 'my Lord' or 'my Lady' with the use of 'your Lordship' or 'your Ladyship'. Notice that, earlier on in Appendix 1, para 7.1, Miss Fowler begins her submissions by saying, 'May it please your Lordship ...'. Unfortunately, explaining when counsel uses 'my Lord' rather than 'your Lordship', and vice versa, involves us discussing some fairly arcane points of grammar. 'My Lord', as used by an advocate, is the vocative case of the noun 'my Lord' or 'milord',[10] and its equivalents in everyday speech are the various ways in which each of us might address another individual: 'Hello, Simon,' 'Goodbye, madam,' or 'What's the problem, dad?', for example. Having used

---

8   See Weatherill, S and Beaumont, P, *EC Law*, 2nd edn, 1996, London: Penguin, p 160, note 31.

9   Or even 'mlud', as in Dickens, C, *Bleak House*, 1985, London: Penguin, p 53. This representation of the pronunciation seems to be found less frequently in more modern fiction. Sir John Mortimer QC's Rumpole of the Bailey studiously addresses the appropriate judge as 'my Lord', for example (see the answer to Question 36).

10   In modern English usage, 'my Lord' does not usually appear, except in the *vocative* case, when addressing a High Court judge for instance. You can affect an archaic nominative use of it, however, as shown below in the text and thus: 'Does my Lord wish to refer to Bundle A?' See also *Bleak House*, where Dickens talks about 'my Lady Dedlock', *ibid*, p 56.

'Simon', 'madam', 'dad' or 'my Lord' vocatively in this way, however, it will be necessary for you to refer to the person you are addressing *in the course of what you are saying,* either by using a pronoun (for example, a possessive pronoun) or possessive adjective.[11] Examples of the former in everyday speech would be, for instance, 'How are you?' or 'I am very grateful to you'. Examples of the latter would be: 'That book is yours' or 'This is your book'. Applying these to the situation where you have used 'my Lord' or 'my Lady' as a mode of addressing a judge, you would say: 'How is your Lordship/Ladyship?' or 'I am very grateful to your Lordship'; and 'That book is your Lordship's' or 'This is your Lordship's book'. As you can see, what is happening here is that the words 'your Lordship' or 'your Ladyship' are being politely substituted for the pronoun 'you', the possessive pronoun 'yours' or the possessive adjective 'your'.[12]

You can see these points illustrated further in the following exchange reported at the end of an income tax case called *Brumby (Inspector of Taxes) v Milner* 51 TC 583, pp 609H–10A, in the Court of Appeal:

Davenport [*Counsel for the Crown*]:	My Lord, I ask for the appeals to be dismissed with costs.
Russell LJ:	We seem a bit thin on the ground.
Davenport:	We have telephoned. Mr Turner, who was Mr Nourse's Junior, comes from Liverpool, and whether something has gone wrong in communications or in the train, I do not know. If your Lordships would prefer this application to be made later, we would have no objection if the application were considered by two of your Lordships, if my Lord Russell LJ were unable to be here.

Here, of course, you can see the proper mode of address of Russell LJ; 'your Lordships' in place of the personal pronoun 'you' (plural) and an archaic nominative use of 'my Lord Russell LJ'.

A second way of getting the mode of address wrong might be to address the judge in a moot set in the Court of Appeal or House of Lords as 'your Honour', 'your Worship' or even 'Sir/Madam'. All of these are quite wrong in the context of such a moot, since 'your Honour' is the mode of address of a circuit judge[13] and 'your Worship' (or simply 'Sir/Madam') is the mode of address of a justice of the peace, that is, a magistrate (although, apparently, barristers do not address magistrates as 'your Worship'). Circuit judges may or may not have a title (his Honour Sir David Hughes-Morgan, Bt, CB, CBE, for example, does, although his Honour Judge Blennerhassett QC does not) but they are never

---

11 See Williams, G, *Learning The Law,* 11th edn, 1982, London: Stevens, pp 143–44.

12 Thus, 'begging your pardon' becomes 'Begludship's pardon' in *Bleak House, op cit,* fn 9, p 54.

13 Circuit judges are judges of the Crown Court (see *op cit,* Bailey and Gunn, fn 1, p 218).

addressed as 'my Lord' unless they are sitting at the Central Criminal Court (that is, 'the Old Bailey'); or as deputy High Court judges (see s 9(1) of the Supreme Court Act 1981); or where they hold the office of honorary Recorder of Liverpool, honorary Recorder of Manchester or honorary Recorder of Cardiff.[14] 'Sir' is the mode of address for Masters and district judges. You will not have to address any of these judicial officers in a moot, although you may accidentally use these modes of address, especially if you are suffering from nerves (see the answer to Question 46). It is also worth noting that lawyers will sometimes encourage a non-lawyer witness in a trial, for instance, to address the judge as 'Sir' or 'Madam' rather than 'my Lord/Lady' or 'your Honour', on the basis that these modes of address sit more easily in the mouth of a lay man or woman than 'my Lord' or 'my Lady'.

Having learnt the general rule and avoided the common mistakes, you should regard all of this information as a tool to be used to your advantage. As you will know if you have an unreliable memory for people's names, it is extremely difficult to address someone politely if you have forgotten that person's name. Legal procedure helps you to avoid such difficulties of politeness, by requiring you to address judges in a way which honours their office as judges, rather than requiring you to remember their names! Naturally, you are not entitled to subvert these practices by using the polite forms we have discussed above to say what is actually very rude. The tale is told[15] of how Richard Bethell, a famous Victorian barrister, once replied to a judge who had told Bethell that he would turn a point over in his mind and reserve it, with the words: 'May it please your Lordship to turn it over in what your Lordship is pleased to call your Lordship's mind?' However, this approach is not recommended with a moot judge!

56 How should I relate to the moot judge during my presentation?

In relating to the moot judge, you should take account of the following general points:

---

14 See *op cit, Civil Procedure*, fn 3, Vol 2, p 297, reproducing [1982] 1 WLR 101. See, also, *Practice Direction (Modes of Address)* [1999] 2 All ER 352.

15 *Op cit*, Williams, fn 11, p 162, note 3, where Bethell is also reported once to have said to a judge: 'Your Lordship is quite right, and I am quite wrong – as your Lordship usually is.' Richard Bethell (1800–73) became Lord Chancellor as Lord Westbury (see Simpson, AWB, *Biographical Dictionary of the Common Law*, 1984, London: Butterworths, p 49). As Lord Westbury, he refused one George Jessel promotion to QC in 1861 (see O'Keeffe, D, 'Sir George Jessel and the union of judicature' (1982) 26 *American Journal of Legal History* 227, p 229.

- As a fully-sighted person, maintain eye contact with the judge in order to reassure him or her that you are not merely going through the motions of a speech. By maintaining eye contact, you will also pick up on subtle visual hints from the judge that he or she is impatient with, bored with or simply unconvinced by your submissions. You should respond to any such hints appropriately, even if this requires you to expand or curtail your explanation. You may even feel it wise to abandon a submission entirely, if the judge has made it clear that he or she is displeased or unimpressed with the submission. Listen to what the judge says to you and to the other mooters. Gauge how he or she will react to your arguments and modify your submissions accordingly.

- Pause if the judge clearly wishes to make a note. The judge cannot fully listen to your argument if he or she is writing down a previous point, so you lose nothing by waiting until the judge nods to indicate that he or she is ready for you to proceed with your submission. It is a good discipline to keep an eye on the judge's pen and not to speak until he or she has stopped writing.

- Be polite, calm, respectful and courteous but also courageous and firm. You have an imaginary client to represent and you must be as firm as possible, but not in any way irritable, impatient or aggressive. Instead, divert your intellectual energy to trying to win the case by persuading the judge that your argument is sound. Stand your ground, whilst being willing to respond to points being raised by the moot judge.

- You need to project your voice so that the moot judge has no difficulty in hearing your arguments, although do not speak too loudly. Use the tone of your voice to be persuasive and to convey the conviction in your argument. A crisp, business-like, forceful voice will be an asset. Remember to stress important or key quotes from cited cases.

- You need to keep alert. Even when you are not on your feet addressing the moot court, you should remain alert because the moot judge may at any time call upon you to assist the court in dealing with a difficulty which has arisen. Do not forget to stand up when giving such assistance to the court.

- Occasionally, a judge will be rude to you and you must learn how to respond appropriately (see the answer to Question 62). It will rarely, if ever, be appropriate to be rude back, as the Latin maxim tells us: *injuria non excusat injuriam* (two wrongs don't make a right)!

- If used sparingly, good humoured witticisms will assist you in relating to the moot judge and may endear the judge to your case (see the answer to Question 68).

- As an unsighted, or partially-sighted mooter, you may be able to gauge the same points from the tone of the judge's voice.

57 Should I take account of the identity, character and standing of the moot judge?

The answer to this question depends on the moot in which you are about to take part. The authors' advice would be to obtain all reliable information you can about the approach that your moot judge is likely to take.

In the context of a moot forming part of your course, it will be relatively easy for you to ascertain the approach taken by the member of staff who is assessing you. Beware of exaggerated stories from colleagues, however.

Equally, if you are appearing in a competitive moot and the moot judge will be a real judge, it may be possible to form something of a picture – however sketchy – of him or her, from his or her entry in *Who's Who*.

58 How do I refer to judges?

The correct answer to this question is dictated by the court to which the judge you are referring belonged, when he or she delivered the judgment or speech, as the case may be, in the relevant case. If you are mooting in a law school in England and Wales, the authorities on which you will mainly rely will be decisions of the superior courts in that jurisdiction, namely the High Court, the Court of Appeal or the House of Lords. This being so, you will need to know how to refer to the judges of those courts properly.[16] However, you may also need to refer to the first instance decision from which the appeal in the moot problem has been made and, if so, you will obviously need to refer correctly, in speech, to the name of the first instance judge also.

For example, if you look at the specimen moot in Appendix 1, you will see that the first instance judge was Risky J who, as we shall see, is referred to in speech as 'Mr Justice Risky'. The proper way of referring to a judge of the Court of Appeal is as 'Lord Justice X', where the Lord Justice of Appeal is male, and 'Lady Justice Y', where the judge is female. It may become necessary, therefore, for you to ascertain whether the relevant judge is male or female. (One way of addressing this problem is discussed briefly below.) Thus, if you had to refer to either of them as a judge in a case you were citing, you would have to refer, for example, to 'Lord Justice Nourse' and 'Lady Justice Butler-Sloss'.[17] On paper,

---

16 This is because the general rule in that jurisdiction is that the moot court need only follow a decision of another court at the same, or higher level, in the hierarchy of courts (see the answer to Question 85).

17 Obvious as this may seem, it was not always the case. Between 1988 and 1994, Butler-Sloss LJ was referred to as 'Lord Justice Butler-Sloss', since there had never previously been a female Lord Justice of Appeal and this was the designation provided for by the Supreme Court Act 1981, s 2(3). In 1994, a Practice Note was issued designating her as 'Lady Justice Butler-Sloss' (see *Practice Note (Mode of Address: Dame Elizabeth Butler-Sloss)* [1994] 1 FLR 866, now *Practice Direction for the Court of Appeal, Civil Division* [1999] 2 All ER 490).

their names would appear as 'Nourse LJ' and 'Butler-Sloss LJ', respectively. The situation in relation to judges of the House of Lords is much simpler. A House of Lords judge is, generally speaking, referred to simply as 'Lord X'.[18] The reason why the situation is much simpler than in relation to the Court of Appeal is that, in the case of a judge of the House of Lords, his or her designation would appear in full in print in the report to which you were referring. Thus, Lord Roskill would appear as 'Lord Roskill' in the report, so there would be no need to remember the meaning of any abbreviation. The obvious exception is the Lord Chancellor, when he or she is sitting in his or her judicial capacity. All of these points require some qualification and we shall consider the judges under the headings below. We shall end with a discussion of judges who will appear in old cases in now outmoded jurisdictions, such as the Court of Common Pleas or Court of Exchequer.

House of Lords' judges

House of Lords' judges have the official designation of 'Lords of Appeal in Ordinary'[19] and are known, unofficially and almost universally, as 'Law Lords'. Nowadays, they are life peers, a fact which is reflected in the fact that it is sometimes necessary to refer to them by referring to the style that they have taken on being dignified in that way. Thus, for instance, if in your argument, you were referring to passages from the Law Lords' speeches in *R v Brown*,[20] you would refer to two of the judges by their full style ('Lord Jauncey of Tullichettle' and 'Lord Slynn of Hadley') and to the other three simply as Lord Templeman, Lord Lowry and Lord Mustill. The latter three also have styles (for instance, Lord Templeman's is 'Lord Templeman of White Lackington in the County of Somerset'), although they are not referred to as such in the law reports. As we have already said, the Lord Chancellor sits with the Law Lords in some cases and, if you have to refer to him, you do so by saying, for example, 'Lord Hailsham of St Marylebone, the Lord Chancellor', even though the abbreviation given in the law reports will be 'Lord Hailsham of St Marylebone LC'.[21] The current Lord Chancellor, Lord Irvine of Lairg, was appointed on 7 May 1997.

---

18 There have, as yet, been no female House of Lords judges. Possibly, Butler-Sloss LJ will be the first one. Sometimes a House of Lords judge will be referred to by another title, such as 'Viscount' or 'Earl', eg, 'Viscount Dilhorne'.

19 For an explanation of this term, see Denning (Lord), *The Family Story*, 1981, London: Butterworths, p 184.

20 [1994] 1 AC 212.

21 Lord Hailsham of St Marylebone LC was Lord Chancellor from 1970–74 and from 1979–87, as a cabinet minister in the Conservative governments of Edward Heath and Margaret Thatcher.

Court of Appeal judges

As mentioned above, a full time Court of Appeal judge is referred to as 'Lord/Lady Justice X'. This is because he or she has the official designation of a Lord or Lady Justice of Appeal. However, they are not the only judges who may sit in the Court of Appeal and you will encounter judges with special, or at least different designations, sitting as Court of Appeal judges. The most obvious of these are the Lord Chief Justice of England and the Master of the Rolls. The Lord Chief Justice is the president of the Criminal Division of the Court of Appeal. The Master of the Rolls is the president of the Civil Division of the Court of Appeal.[22] In the law reports, the Lord Chief Justice's name and title will be abbreviated to 'Lord X CJ' and that of the Master of the Rolls to 'Sir X/Lord Y MR'. Needless to say, in argument, you must not use the initial letters of their specific judicial offices. Instead, if, for example, you were referring to the judgment of Lord Widgery CJ in *R v Cato*,[23] you would refer to him as 'Lord Widgery, the Lord Chief Justice'. By the same token, if you were referring, for example, to the judgment of Sir George Jessel MR in *Bennett v Bennett*,[24] you would say 'Sir George Jessel, the Master of the Rolls'. In fact, two further points can be made in relation to this. First, if the holder of the office of Lord Chief Justice or Master of the Rolls is not a life peer (as, originally, in the case of Sir Thomas Bingham MR, who became Lord Chief Justice in June 1996), you will have to refer to his or her forename. If this is not given in the report of the case you are looking at, you will need to check it from the full list of judges at the front of the *Law Reports*, from which your citation of the case itself should ideally be made (see the answer to Question 21). Secondly, you can make the reference even more elegant, when you are referring to a Lord Chief Justice or Master of the Rolls from days gone by, by adding the word 'then' before the judge's name, for example, 'Sir George Jessel, the then Master of the Rolls'. The insertion of the word 'then' is easy where you are referring to a 19th century judge such as Sir George Jessel. However, you may have to make a careful check where a judge has only recently ceased to hold the relevant office (for example, as in the case of the late Lord Taylor of Gosforth, who retired as Lord Chief Justice in June 1996). One way of making this check is to refer to the lists of judges at the front of the *Law Reports* which helpfully show when a judge was appointed and when he or she retired.

Finally, occasionally, just occasionally, you may have to contend with the fact that judges other than Lords Justices of Appeal may sit in the Court of Appeal. To take just a few examples. Law Lords may sometimes sit in the Court of

---

22 Supreme Court Act 1981, s 3(2). By the Access to Justice Act 1999, s 69(1), the Lord Chancellor may appoint a Court of Appeal judge to be Vice President of the Queen's Bench Division.

23 [1976] 1 WLR 110, p 121n.

24 (1879) 10 Ch D 474.

Appeal;[25] High Court judges may sit in the Court of Appeal, especially in criminal law cases;[26] High Court heads of division (see below),[27] circuit judges[28] and former judges of the High Court/Court of Appeal may also sit in the Court of Appeal.[29] It will be relatively easy for you to deal with these, in view of the points made above and below.

High Court judges

As indicated above, there are a number of contexts in which you might have to refer to a High Court judge correctly. The most obvious one is that of a reference to a decision of a High Court judge in the course of your argument. The other is that you may need to refer to a decision of the hypothetical first instance judge given in a moot problem.

There are three divisions of the High Court: the Queen's Bench Division, the Chancery Division and the Family Division.[30] All High Court judges are attached to one of these three Divisions. If he or she consents, a High Court judge attached to one division may be transferred to one of the others and may act as an additional judge of one of them at the request of the Lord Chancellor.[31] It is worth checking to see *where* a case decided by a High Court judge was decided – they may sit at both the Royal Courts of Justice in the Strand, London and at 26 centres outside London. You will be able to see from the report if a case was decided in Manchester or Birmingham, for example. With the exceptions mentioned below, all High Court judges are referred to simply as 'Mr Justice X' or 'Mrs Justice Y', as in 'Mr Justice Blackburne' and 'Mrs Justice Arden', for example. In addition, a circuit judge sitting as a deputy High Court judge under s 9(1) of the Supreme Court Act 1981, is referred to as, for example, 'his Honour Judge John Finlay QC, sitting as a Judge of the High Court'.[32] One mistake which you must not make is to assume that the initial 'J' refers to a circuit judge; this is the abbreviation for 'Mr / Mrs Justice X'.

---

25 *Barnes v Addy* (1874) 9 Ch App 244, actually a decision of the Court of Appeal in Chancery (see text), where the presiding judge was Lord Selborne LC.

26 *R v Wilson* [1996] 3 WLR 125 (Bracewell J, ie, 'Mrs Justice Bracewell').

27 Eg, *Grant v Edwards* [1986] Ch 638 (Sir Nicolas Browne-Wilkinson VC).

28 Eg, *R v Wilson*, above, his Honour Judge Capstick QC.

29 Eg, *Midland Bank Trust Co v Green* [1980] 1 Ch 590, where Sir Stanley Rees, who had retired from the Family Division of the High Court at the end of 1977, sat with Lord Denning MR and Eveleigh LJ. (See the answer to Question 20.)

30 Supreme Court Act 1981, s 5(1).

31 Supreme Court Act 1981, s 5(2) and (3).

32 See *Practice Direction (Judges: Modes of Address)* [1982] 1 WLR 101 and *Kingsnorth Finance Co v Tizard* [1986] 1 WLR 783 (note the wording of the marginal note to the headnote).

Each of the three divisions of the High Court of Justice has a head, to whom you might have to refer. The head of the Queen's Bench Division is, as we have said, the Lord Chief Justice. The head of the Family Division is referred to as the President of the Family Division. You will see the President of the Family Division referred to as 'Sir X P'. Of course, you pronounce this as, for example, Sir Stephen Brown, the President of the Family Division. The head of the Chancery Division is the Vice Chancellor, whose title is abbreviated to VC in the *Law Reports*. Again, you will see the Vice Chancellor referred to as 'Sir X VC'. You pronounce this, for example, 'Sir Donald Nicholls, the Vice Chancellor'.

Note that, for historical reasons, there is also a Vice Chancellor of the County Palatine of Lancaster. This was a post held by a circuit judge, the last of whom was his Honour Judge Blackett-Ord VC. The post has since been held by a justice of the High Court.

Crown Court judges

These may be justices of the High Court (see above), circuit judges or recorders. There are also deputy circuit judges[33] and deputy recorders. In the context of a moot, you are only likely to encounter them as having decided a case, especially a criminal case, at first instance. You will need to refer to them correctly in making your submissions. Circuit judges are referred to as 'his or her Honour Judge X'.[34] Thus, if you are referring to a circuit judge, you might say, for example 'his Honour Judge Burford' or 'her Honour Judge Linda Davies'. If you are referring to a deputy circuit judge, you would say, for example, '*his Honour* Malcolm Weisman, sitting as a deputy circuit judge'. Recorders are referred to as 'Mr (or Mrs) Recorder X', although not 'Miss Recorder', it would appear, although this seems to be an oversight, given our next point.[35] Assistant recorders are referred to as 'Mr or Mrs or Miss X, sitting as an assistant recorder'.[36]

Outmoded jurisdictions

Finally, you may have to refer to a judge in an old case from a jurisdiction which is now defunct or which has been assimilated to a modern one (for example, the Court of Common Pleas, the Court of Exchequer or the Court of Exchequer Chamber). Broadly speaking, the judges who sat in these courts over the centuries were referred to as 'Justice X' or, in the 19th century, as 'Mr Justice X'. They were denoted with the abbreviation 'J'. Which of the two applied in

---

33 See, eg, *R v Lawrence* [1982] AC 510, p 512A, where the trial judge was his Honour Malcolm Weisman, sitting as a deputy circuit judge.

34 *Practice Direction (Judges: Modes of Address)* [1982] 1 WLR 101.

35 *Op cit*, Bailey and Gunn, fn 1, p 218, note 15. It may be a tasteful oversight (imagine 'Miss Justice', ie, 'misjustice')!

36 *Practice Direction (Judges: Modes of Address)* [1982] 1 WLR 101.

speech in their own day is something we can now only glean from external sources, such as novels, newspaper reports, contemporary accounts, and so on. Today, it is best to use the latter, as though you were referring to a High Court judge. You will encounter exceptions, however. First, note that between 1851 and the Judicature Acts 1873–75, there was a court called the Court of Appeal in Chancery, whose judges were the Lord Chancellor and a number of Lords Justices (the same etiquette applies in referring to these as to modern Lords/Lady Justices and Lord Chancellor).[37] Secondly, note also that the abbreviation 'B', as in, for example, 'Huddleston B', denoted judges referred to as 'Exchequer Barons'. Again, this abbreviation seems to have been rendered as 'Baron' or 'Mr Baron' and, again, the latter would seem to be the better choice in a moot court. Odd as 'Mr Baron' may sound, it does indeed seem to have been the formal usage, as the following advertisement from an 1854 edition of *The Times* shows:

> TEN POUNDS REWARD – LOST OR STOLEN from Westminster, on or about the night of 21 February, a FULL BOTTOMED WIG, the property of MR BARON ALDERSON ...[38]

The outmoded jurisdictions had Chief Justices or Chief Barons, abbreviated in the reports to 'CJ ' and 'CB'. The practice seems to have been to refer to these simply as 'Chief Justice X' or 'Chief Baron Y'. Thirdly, note that before October 1966, criminal appeals were heard not by the Court of Appeal (Criminal Division), as they have been since, but by the so called Court of Criminal Appeal.[39]

Everything we have said should now enable you to refer to judges correctly. Only a couple of final points need to be made by us. This is, by a process of reasoning, parallel to that used in the answer to Question 55. Where you do not refer in full to a judge's name, in other words, you need to use a pronoun, it is always good to use 'his Lordship or her Ladyship', rather than 'him or her'. By the same token, in referring to a circuit judge, 'his or her Honour', rather than 'him' or 'her' is appropriate. When referring to the trial judge, it is good to say 'the learned trial judge' or 'the learned judge at first instance' or simply 'the learned judge'.

Our final point is a warning. Where two or more judges share a surname – however odd you may think it is – do not assume which one of them is being

---

37 The Court of Appeal in Chancery became the model for the Court of Appeal, not surprisingly. Famous decisions of the Court of Appeal in Chancery include *Pilcher v Rawlins* (1872) 7 Ch App 259 (classic statement of the *bona fide* purchaser doctrine in jurisdictional terms by James LJ).

38 Quoted in Lewis, JR, *The Victorian Bar*, 1984, London: Robert Hale, p 46.

39 Originally set up by the Criminal Appeal Act 1907. See, eg, *R v Gibbins and Proctor* (1918) 13 Cr App Rep 134.

referred to in a report. One of the authors saw the dangers of this demonstrated vividly in a moot judged by Robert Goff LJ (as his Lordship then was). One mooter simply assumed that the Goff J in the case he was referring to was the same judge. In fact it was Sir Reginald Goff. Robert Goff J dealt with the matter with the utmost tact but, of course, this type of mistake hardly boosts the self-confidence of the advocate who makes it!

59   What should I do if I feel ill during the moot?

If you feel ill while making your submissions, the answer is obvious. Ask the moot judge if you may be seated or if you may be excused from the moot court for a few moments – but do not let the mask of the mooter slip. If at all possible, follow all the conventions of etiquette you have used in the rest of your presentation. If you feel well enough to resume your moot presentation, the fact that you conducted yourself with decorum, far from having damaged your presentation, may even have endeared you to the judge.

If, at the moment you ask to be excused, you are not actually speaking, then this will be one of the rare occasions when it will be proper to interrupt the mooter who is speaking. However, if possible, it will be a good idea to stand, in order to ask to be excused.

If the fact that you feel ill means that you really cannot continue, you should be prepared to entrust your presentation to the other member of your team. One of the authors has witnessed this happen, in the context of a competition moot. There, a mooter was too ill to continue and, because his colleague had been wise enough to familiarise himself with the other's presentation, he was able to continue in his stead.

The mooter, appearing as Junior Respondent, who fell ill on that occasion, felt faint during his presentation and knew that he would be unable to stay on his feet for very much longer. Very politely, he requested permission to be seated and to hand over the remainder of his submissions to the Lead Respondent. The Lead Respondent took up where his junior had left off, and did so with aplomb. The Respondents won the moot. Thus, the unfortunate illness proved to be the perfect opportunity for both Respondents to show off the depth of their teamwork and their ability to moot with flexibility and flair.

60   What do I do if it looks as if I cannot win on the law?

If you ever practise as a barrister do not be surprised if, one day, you receive a brief from your instructing solicitor at close of business on a weekday evening with the instruction to appear on the matter in an obscure provincial court the following morning. It will be too late to change the pleadings, you must simply turn up and persuade the court that someone else's argument is correct.

This is what advocacy is all about. The word 'ad-vocate' means, literally, to 'speak on behalf of'. It may be that someone has made a pig's ear of the case before it falls into your hands. Nevertheless, it is down to you to make a silk purse out of that sow's ear. Similarly, a mooter cannot attempt to alter or avoid the ground of appeal which has fallen to them to argue (except in the case of a manifest error in the wording of the appeal, and with the agreement of both sides to make the necessary alteration). If it looks, at first sight, as if your ground of appeal is unarguable, think again. Are you sure that you have considered all possible lines of legal argument? Could it be argued, for example, that the binding authorities against you are in fact outdated (see the answer to Question 41)? Even if you have considered all the legal authorities, could there yet be strong arguments of legal principle or public policy which might persuade the court to favour your interpretation, albeit an imaginative interpretation, of the authorities (see the answer to Question 74)? Or again, could it be that a case cited against you has no true *ratio*. Consider the following extract from a note by Sir John Smith QC, in relation to *R v Steele* [1993] Crim LR 298, p 300:

> There are occasions when decisions of the House of Lords are so obscure that it is impossible to extract a *ratio decidendi* and they come to be regarded as 'confined to their own special facts' and cease to be authority for anything else. An example of this rare species in the civil law is *Elder Dempster & Co Ltd v Paterson, Zochonis & Co Ltd* [1924] AC 522. *Director of Public Prosecutions v Warner* [*sic* (1969) 52 Cr App R 373] seems, in practice, to be in this class. The court in *McNamara* [1988] Crim LR 440, having respectfully discussed the speeches in *Warner*, in effect abandoned the search for the impossible and went back to the opinion of the *Warner* Court of Appeal and Lord Guest who dissented in the Lords. The snag is that *Warner* will continue to plague the courts unless and until someone in authority is bold enough to declare it dead.

You should, therefore, never be downhearted in the face of an apparently unbeatable legal argument. Rather, see it as the best opportunity to display all your skills as an advocate. We have already seen that it is quite possible to win a competitive moot despite failing to win on a point of law. There are a number of techniques which can be employed to turn bad odds in your favour.

First, stealing your opponent's thunder. If you appear on behalf of the Appellant on a comparatively weak legal argument you have probably come to the conclusion that your argument is weak because you know that there are certain strong authorities on the Respondent's side. There are a number of ways of turning this to your advantage. The safest is to alert the judge to the fact that you are fully aware of the apparent weakness in your case. You will generally come a cropper if you try to disguise that fact. One could say, for example, 'my Lord, it is possible that learned counsel for the Respondents will argue X, Y and Z and will rely upon the well known authorities A, B and C. Accordingly, I am bound to argue the opposite'. This, or some similar phraseology, serves to make the Respondent's submissions sound somewhat hollow and repetitive when they are heard for the second time! Describing the Respondent's authorities as 'well known' suggests that your opponent has displayed no great skill in discovering them. Emphasising the fact that you are 'bound' to argue the opposite suggests to the judge that, given the opportunity, you would perhaps have drafted your ground of appeal differently. If your arguments which follow are good they will be all the more impressive for your having suggested to the judge (whether it be strictly true or not) that you had the harder case to argue.

It is said that a barrister once pursued a somewhat riskier variation on this theme in a case where he was appearing on behalf of an Appellant. He actually put the Respondent's arguments to the judge as if they were his own, and in such a way that the judge rejected them out of hand. After her Ladyship had launched her criticism at the Respondent's arguments in the inelegant form in which the Appellant's counsel had put them, counsel for the Appellant simply added, 'Of course, my Lady, it is not I, but the Respondent who relies upon these arguments. I merely raise them to show their weaknesses. For my part, I am entirely in agreement with your Ladyship's criticisms'.

Secondly, be audacious. Moot judges usually admire the courage of a mooter who proposes an audacious solution, unless their audacity is interpreted as disguising a lack of ability to see the more straightforward argument. Therefore, if you are going to attempt the audacious, let the judge know that you are fully aware that your argument is unorthodox. Arguments of this sort should, ideally, be kept up one's sleeve and used only in addition to more orthodox arguments, and only then if you are convinced that the judge is an interested listener and willing to 'play the game'.

We shall attempt to illustrate what we mean by an audacious submission, by taking as our example what may be the most unorthodox submission of them all:

My Lord, I am well aware that the weight of authorities is against me, but it is my submission that in your Lordship's House all authority has only a persuasive quality and thus my Lord is free to dispose of this case according to broader issues of principle and policy. My Lord, there are a number of sound reasons to support the view that today the doctrine of precedent should have no application in the House of Lords. First, their Lordships by their Practice Statement of 1966 [see Appendix 4] stated that the House would thereafter depart from its previous decisions whenever it appeared 'right to do so' and would be reluctant so to depart in only a limited number of circumstances – none of which is relevant here [see Appendix 4]. Second, there has been an important development in the hierarchy of our courts since 1966. In 1972, the United Kingdom accepted as its ultimate court of law on issues of European law, the Court of Justice of the European Communities, a court which does not consider itself to be bound by its own decisions. It seems to be a distinction unwarranted in principle for our superior domestic tribunal to be more constrained in matters of our domestic law than the European Court is in matters of European law, the import of both types of law being equally great in the lives of our citizens. Finally, the doctrine of precedent has as its aim the attainment of certainty in the law. Certainty, however, is not the principle aim of the law. The principal aim of the law is justice and to achieve justice, certainty and flexibility must be kept in some sort of balance. The balance I urge your Lordship to achieve today is to expressly limit the doctrine of precedent to those courts below your Lordship's House, and to free your Lordship's House entirely from its shackles in the interests of the chief end of law, justice, and so as to achieve the only just outcome in the instant case.

We are sure that you will agree that the above line of argument is somewhat unorthodox. A real Law Lord may or may not give it short shrift. A moot judge will be more likely to give you credit for your inventiveness and sheer audacity.

61 What do I do if the moot judge has misunderstood my point?

I'll never throw dust in a juryman's eyes

(Said I to myself – said I),

Or hoodwink a judge who is not overwise

(Said I to myself – said I) ...[40]

The image of a judge, perhaps an elderly one, who is slow on the uptake, is a feature of legal iconography. Whatever the reality, however, you are unlikely to encounter such a judge in a moot. As a student, it is usually safe to presume that lack of judicial understanding of your arguments is a symptom, not of the judge's inability to understand, but of your inability to make yourself understood.

The answer to this question is, therefore, a fairly commonsense one. It is that you should be prepared to re-phrase, explain and expand upon the point until the judge does understand it. The greatest danger you face in this situation is that you will become impatient – after all, you will have practised your presentation a thousand times! If you do become impatient, however, you will most certainly antagonise the judge. It is the type of thing which could cost you the moot, however good your submissions are.

Occasionally, and most regrettably, the presumption in favour of the moot judge's ability is rebutted by obvious signs that the judge has not made the effort to become acquainted with the moot problem in advance of the moot. In such a situation, it is unfortunately the case that, the greater the sophistication of your submission, the less likely the moot judge is to be persuaded by it. A good mooter will react to the judge's lack of understanding constructively,

---

40   Gilbert, WS, *Iolanthe*, Act 1, lines 481–84, in Bradley, I (ed), *The Complete Annotated Gilbert and Sullivan*, 1996, Oxford: OUP, p 295.

perhaps prefacing their submission with the gambit, 'My Lord, my point is in fact a simple and straightforward one. It is ... ', or words to that effect. The judge may, for fear of looking foolish (knowing full well that he or she is under-prepared), be reluctant to quiz you any further on that submission if prefaced in this way. A bad mooter, as we suggest above, will simply become irritated by the judge's obvious lack of preparation, and will foolishly allow this irritation to show.

62   How do I respond to a moot judge's rudeness?

The Judge: Stuff and nonsense!

Sir Humphrey: I beg your Lordship's pardon?

The Judge: I said 'Stuff and nonsense!' Sir Humphrey, and I say it again, with a satisfaction that I am unable to conceal. This case wearies me –

Sir Humphrey: May it please your Lordship –

The Judge: It does *not* please my Lordship ...[41]

This question highlights what is, or at least what ought to be, an important difference between the game of mooting and the harsh reality of advocacy in court. You are extremely unlikely to encounter deliberate rudeness on the part of a moot judge, since moot judges should strive to be courteous and friendly under all circumstances (see the answer to Question 100).[42]

Should you be so unlucky, however, one type of riposte is to take the line which FE Smith took in the extract set out below. Unless the moot judge is willing to take a fairly light-hearted view of him or herself, however – by taking such a riposte in good part – you risk alienating them by adopting this approach:[43]

When, rising to address the jury in a case before Mr Justice Ridley, the latter had unjudiciously observed: 'Well, Mr Smith, I have read the pleadings and I do not think much of your case.' Stung by this remark, he answered: 'Indeed, My Lord, I'm sorry to hear that, but your Lordship will find that the more you hear of it the more it will grow on you.'

Rather more reliable than such a riposte is, we would suggest, to be extremely patient. This is much more difficult than it may sound. Not least of the reasons for this difficulty is the fact that, if the moot judge is rude, your initial reaction will be one of shock. We cannot over-emphasise the fact that rudeness from a moot judge is quite unacceptable. Quite beyond the pale is for a mooter to be

41   Herbert, AP, *Uncommon Law*, 4th edn, 1942, London: Methuen, p 279.

42   For some real life examples of judicial rudeness, taken from the US, see Pannick, D, 'American judges behaving badly in the courtroom' (1999) *The Times*, 16 November.

43   Birkenhead (Second Earl), *The Life of FE Smith, First Earl of Birkenhead, By His Son*, 1960, London: Eyre & Spottiswoode, p 98 (quoted in Gilbert, M (ed), *The Oxford Book Of Legal Anecdotes*, 1986, Oxford: OUP, p 279).

rude to the moot judge, although on one occasion one of the authors witnessed a moot *won* through just that! The setting was the quarter-finals round of *The Observer* National Mooting Competition some years ago. The approach of the judge on that occasion was, to say the least, forthright – perhaps even domineering. Indignant at the judge's latest vexatious interruption, one mooter snapped: 'If your Lordship would only let me get a word in edge-ways ... ' The judge smiled, fell silent at last and ultimately awarded the moot to the team of which this mooter was a member. His expressed reason for so awarding the moot was his pleasure in the mooter having dealt so firmly with the judge's irritating manner.

What lesson can be drawn from this story? It is, arguably, that, despite the rule that one should never be rude to a moot judge, it may, on the very rare occasion, be prudent to breach the rules if the judge, him or herself, demonstrates little respect for them. It must be said, however, that the mooter who succeeded on that occasion impressed everybody with other aspects of his mooting, and might well have won even if he had not stood up to the judge in such dramatic fashion. Less able mooters should advance with caution!

63 May I interrupt or correct the moot judge and my opponents?

The next time you are in a bar with a group of friends, listen to the animated conversation. How rare it is that the speaker manages to finish the story which he or she is relating before, in a very good-natured and quite natural way, someone else interrupts. Indeed, a number of people often seem to be speaking at the same time! Certainly, if somebody starts to ask a question and you precisely anticipate the question that they are going to ask, you are tempted to answer immediately, aren't you?

How different is the dialogue of a moot court. Here, your natural instinct to interrupt must be curbed. Here, interruptions are regarded as very bad etiquette indeed. You must never interrupt the moot judge and, if you do so by mistake, you must apologise. Whether you wish to agree or disagree with a judicial comment, you must wait until the judge has finished making his or her point before making yours.

As for interrupting an opponent, in *LA Law* and *Murder One*, the American courtroom dramas, the advocates frequently jump to their feet and interject with the shout of 'Objection, your Honour!'. It would be such fun to do the same in your moot, but is it permissible? The first point to be made is that objections of any sort are usually much more appropriate to a trial, usually a criminal trial, rather than the appellate hearings simulated in the moot court. So the bulk of the 'objections' that you hear on television will relate to matters which might unfairly influence the jury, such as the presentation of evidence which it is claimed is inadmissible or asking leading questions of a witness in examination-in-chief (see the answer to Question 2). They find an echo in an English criminal trial, albeit in a less dramatic form, as in 'I must object to my learned friend's question, my Lord/your Honour, for the following reasons ...'. However, in a moot court, the facts are not in dispute and, thus, raising objections of this sort will rarely, if ever, be appropriate.

So when is it ever permissible to interrupt? Surely, you might ask, it must be permissible to point out that an opponent is breaching the rules of the moot competition or assessment? This happened in the 1993 Final of the United Kingdom round of the Philip C Jessup International Law Moot Court Competition, between the Universities of Strathclyde and Nottingham Trent. One of the mooters rose to his feet and objected to the fact that his opponent was dealing with points in his sur-rebuttal which had not been raised in rebuttal. To deal with points in the sur-rebuttal which had not been raised in rebuttal was a clear breach of the rules of the competition.[44] Nevertheless, the mooter who objected to this breach received a mild rebuke when one of the moot judges thanked him for pointing out that the moot court was failing to apply its own rules of procedure. The clear message was that the breach had already been recognised and that the opponent would have been penalised by the judges without any prompting from the mooter. The authors' conclusion is that interruptions should ordinarily be avoided at all costs (for an exception, see the answer to Question 59).

If interrupting the moot judge is fraught with risks, how much more so is any attempt to correct the judge. It may be the case, for example, that a judge has referred to a case incorrectly, perhaps the case of *McPhail v Doulton* [1971] AC 424 when he or she meant to refer to *Re Baden's Deed Trusts (No 2)* [1973] Ch 9. In such a situation, it would be perfectly acceptable for you to seek clarification of the case to which the judge meant to refer. However, even to correct a judge in such a situation as this should be avoided unless absolutely necessary. What you should avoid at all costs is to correct what you perceive to be the moot judge's error of law or understanding. It is prudent to assume that the error is yours and, even if you are convinced of the contrary, the safest course is to assume that the judge will not appreciate being corrected in this way, particularly when there is an audience present.

64 What general points should I bear in mind when answering the moot judge's questions?

You should certainly take account of the following general points:

---

44 Following the CPR 1998, these terms seem no longer to exist: permission is needed to go past a reply.

- Listen to the question carefully. This is the cardinal rule. Indeed, as a Cardinal once said: 'Reflect, Gentlemen, how many disputes you must have listened to, which were interminable, because neither party understood either his opponent or himself. Consider the fortunes of an argument in a debating society, and the need there so frequently is, not simply of some clear thinker to disentangle the perplexities of thought, but of capacity in the combatants to do justice to the clearest explanations which are set before them ...'[45]

- Do not be frightened of silence. It is never as long as you think.

- Do not look down and rifle through your papers.

- It is never a bad idea to acknowledge the thrust of the moot judge's question, thus showing that you have actually understood it, for example: 'Thank you, My Lord/Lady, yes I can appreciate that at first sight it might appear that my second submission contradicts my first submission. They are, however, with respect, perfectly consistent for the following reasons ...'

- If you actually do have an authority that is going to help you answer the judge's question, then by all means say: 'Would your Lordship/Ladyship give me a moment to find the authority that might assist?' This is a particularly good technique if you actually intended the case to be part of your original argument!

- If you have understood the question/comment, pause to think whether the interruption is friendly or hostile. Pause anyway even if you have predicted the question and know the answer. It looks better to appear to have considered a point and to have answered it on your feet.

- The judge may just be seeking clarification of what you have been saying or he or she may be trying to assist you with a new line of thought or assist you with an improved manner of expressing the point you have been trying to make. If the judge assists you in this way then you might say, 'I am much obliged, my Lord/Lady', before expressing your agreement with the judge's comment. Similarly, if the judge makes an assertion with which you agree say, 'My Lord/Lady, your Lordship/Ladyship is quite correct. I'm grateful'.

- Maintain eye contact with the judge so that you can assess how your argument is being received and whether you need to extend your answer in order to satisfy the judge.

- Always begin your answer with something like 'My Lord/Lady' or 'Indeed, my Lord/Lady' or 'I am much obliged, my Lord/Lady' or 'No [or Yes] my

---

45 Henry, J (Cardinal Newman), *The Idea of a University*, 1959, New York: Image, p 448.

Lord/Lady, I submit ...' or 'No, my Lord/Lady, with respect I would submit ...' or 'My Lord/Lady I hesitate to disagree but in my respectful submission that is not the case. I submit that the correct position is ...'. Never say 'I quite agree' or 'That is a good point'.

- It is easy for a lack of confidence to cause you to lower the volume of your speech. Try to maintain your audibility, but don't shout. You are attempting a dialogue, not a lecture.

- Try hard to sound firm and positive, even if you feel as though you are treading on thin ice.

- Even if the question is complex, try to be as concise as possible in your answer, but at the same time, if the judge is clearly not satisfied with your answer, 'bounce back' with further explanation to try to persuade him or her that your view is sound.

- Remember that the onus to persuade is on you. Emphasise words in order to make your arguments sound more persuasive.

- If you feel that the exchange between yourself and the judge is taking you away from your argument, and you are confident that the point raised by the judge is not more material than the points you had planned to make, do your best to give a reasonable reply to the judge, pause slightly and, without showing irritation, try to return to your argument. If you have completed your arguments on a particular submission you can simply say 'With your Lordship's/Ladyship's permission, I shall proceed to my second submission'. If it is quite clear that the judge would like further argument on a point that he or she has raised but there really is nothing that you can usefully add to your previous response, you could say 'My Lord/Lady, I do not think that I can assist the court any further in the development of this particular point but I do stand by my previous submission'.

65 What do I do if I cannot understand the moot judge's question?

If, having really thought about what the moot judge has said, you quite simply do not understand the question, then in those circumstances, and only in those circumstances, you might say: 'My Lord/Lady, I should be obliged if your Lordship/Ladyship could clarify the question.' Or 'I am afraid I do not understand your Lordship's/Ladyship's point' or 'I'm afraid I do not grasp your Lordship's/Ladyships meaning'. Responses such as these will *usually*, unless you are most unlucky, solicit a helping hand from the judge, if nothing else they will at least maintain the communication between yourself and the judge and thus avoid an awkward silence.

On no account must you use this as a device for gaining more time in a situation where you have understood the question. In that situation, it is far better simply to take your time in thinking of and formulating an appropriate response.

For some mooters, when presented with a question which they do not immediately understand, their first instinct is to muddle together some sort of answer – *any* sort of answer. This approach must be resisted by you. Think about it: what good can this do you? The answer is very little. On the contrary, it can do the following harm. First, if the judge was seeking a specific answer to his or her question, your woolly reply is unlikely to contain it. In fact, your vague response is likely merely to highlight your *lack* of understanding. Secondly, if the judge had no particular answer in mind, the judge will not be too disappointed if you admit frankly that no particular answer has leapt to your mind. It can only do harm to give an immediate and imprecise answer, for it merely encourages the judge to ask you to expand upon it. Before you know it, you will be taken away from your main argument by a side discussion on an answer that you wish you had not given in the first place.

To conclude, if you really do not understand the judge's question, the best thing to do is to admit it. If you are lucky, the judge may merely have been speculating. There may in fact be no sensible answer to the question!

66 How can I turn judicial questions to my advantage?

> Rejoice when the court asks questions ... If the question does nothing more it gives you assurance that the court is not comatose ... Moreover, a question affords you your only chance to penetrate the mind of the court, unless you are an expert in face reading ...[46]

When you moot you will perceive questions from the moot judge to be of two crucially different types. On the one hand, there are questions to which you will immediately have a good answer, on the other hand, there are questions to which you will have no ready response. Each type of question presents you with an opportunity to impress, so how can you make the most of each opportunity?

Let us consider first your response to an 'easy' question. When the judge asks you a question which you may have been expecting, and to which you have a ready rejoinder, you should straightaway make it utterly apparent to the judge that you grasp the issue that he or she has raised. One way to do this is

---

46 Davies, JW, 'The argument of an appeal', address to the Association of the Bar of the City of New York AQ Ar.

immediately to rephrase the judge's question. You might say, 'I understand the issue your Lordship raises, my Lord wonders whether if X, then Y necessarily follows'. However, having shown with impressive alacrity that you understand the question, you should not so readily blurt out a solution. If you appear too expeditious in solving the issue the judge may assume that you have researched and prepared well, but is unlikely to credit you with that most impressive of intellectual skills – thinking on your feet. Far better for you to begin to answer, 'It would be my submission ...', then to pause ever so slightly, so that the judge can imagine the cogs in your brain whirring, then to give your impressive response. It is most important to make the most of your 'easy' questions in this way, or some similar way, because if you fail to answer a hard question later on in your moot the judge cannot immediately conclude, as he or she might otherwise have done, that you are unable to extemporise.

Now let us consider your response to what you perceive to be hard questions. The hardest question of them all to respond to is the one where you simply do not comprehend the judge's meaning (as to which, see the answer to the previous question), for other hard questions the important thing is to remain calm and composed as you formulate your response.

Of course, the very best response to a hard question is a good *ex tempore* display of your legal knowledge, common sense and wit. Unfortunately for you, it is beyond the scope of this book, and presumably any book, to furnish you with these skills. They can, however, be fostered by good preparation and thorough familiarity with your authorities and those of your opponent. Norman Birkett QC (by then Lord Birkett (see the answer to Question 38)) wrote about this when he said:[47]

> ... Whatever the case and whatever the court, the first and vital thing is that the advocate shall know the case he desires to make with complete thoroughness. He must have a complete mastery of the facts and he must have the power to present them in the most attractive way. He must have a quick mind and an understanding heart. He must acquire in some way an insight into human nature and a natural and unforced sympathy with all sorts and conditions of men. Above all, he must have what I can only call an intuitive recognition of what the circumstances of the case require as it slowly unfolds itself before the court.

Finally, never forget that there are a number of different reasons why a judge might choose to ask a question. Rarely will it be because he or she does not know the answer. It is more likely that the judge is wanting to test your advocacy skills and/or your substantive legal knowledge. Do not assume, however, that the judge is trying to catch you out. It is at least as likely that the judge is merely seeking clarification of your arguments. It may even be that the

---

47   Birkett, N, 'The art of advocacy', in *Six Great Advocates*, 1961, London: Penguin, p 108.

judge can see that you are struggling and has chosen to throw you a lifeline in the form of a question, 'Mr Smith, are trying to say A, B, C?'. If a judge throws you such a lifeline, try to recognise it as such, and do not instinctively respond, 'My Lord, no!'. Too many mooters presume that judicial interventions must by their very nature be hostile. Indeed, the authors have witnessed nervous mooters inadvertently argue against their own submissions when judges have put the mooter's own arguments to them. Gratefully accept judicial questioning and, as we have said earlier, rigorous questioning is often a sign that you are doing well – it may well indicate that the judge has had to go to great lengths to find the bounds of your ability.

67 May I tell the moot judge that I will deal with his or her question later in my presentation?

One thing you should never do when faced with a hard question is attempt to brush it under the carpet. The moot judge is unlikely to accept the brush-off!

Mooters are often tempted to tell the judge that they will deal with the question later, especially if they know that they had actually intended to deal with the judge's particular question during the course of their submissions in any event. This is unacceptable and unwise mooting practice. It is unacceptable for a number of reasons. First, it is somewhat discourteous to keep the judge waiting for an answer. Secondly, it suggests to the judge that you are rigidly adhering to a pre-prepared moot speech and, thirdly, having asked the judge to wait for your response you might deliberately or inadvertently commit the cardinal sin of concluding your submissions without having dealt with the judge's question – in which event you will almost certainly lose the moot. However, if you are utterly confident that you will not forget to answer the question, it is acceptable to respond to the judge's question thus: 'My Lord, I had intended to deal with precisely that point at a later stage of my submissions, however if your Lordship prefers I will deal with that issue now.' This response is both courteous and displays flexibility.

It is unwise mooting practice because a judicial question is an opportunity to shine and a postponed answer takes the shine off your performance. If you do know an answer to the judge's question, and had intended to give it at a later stage in your presentation, why wait until then? The surest way to impress the judge is to deal with his or her questions as and when they arise.

68 May I be witty in my presentation?

'Mr Smith, have you ever heard of a saying by Bacon – the great Bacon – that youth and discretion are ill-wed companions?'

'Indeed I have, your Honour; and has your Honour ever heard of a saying by Bacon – the great Bacon – that a much talking judge is like an ill-tuned cymbal?'

The judge replied furiously: 'You are extremely offensive, young man', and FE added to his previous lapses by saying: 'As a matter of fact, we both are; the only difference between us is that I'm trying to be, and you can't help it. I have been listened to with respect by the highest tribunal in the land and I have not come down here to be brow-beaten.'[48]

This is mere anecdotage concerning the advocacy style of FE Smith, politician and barrister, who was ultimately to become Lord Chancellor as Lord Birkenhead.

We use it to illustrate the fact that, although it may be extremely helpful to the persuasiveness of your manner to be witty, your barbs should never be directed at the moot judge. If they are, it will defeat the object of your presentation, which is – in some part – to persuade the moot judge of the correctness of your submissions.

It is worth bearing in mind, also, that legal wit has certain characteristics. It tends to mock, often quite subtly, the rules and conventions under which lawyers operate, and the subtleties of language which are traditionally meat and drink to them. You can see quite a good example of this in relation to court dress, in the answer to Question 50.

69 May I gesticulate to emphasise the points I am making in my presentation?

For my early cross-examinations I would take off my battered Timex watch, lug out my bundle of keys held together with a piece of frayed string and pace up and down, firing off what I hoped were appropriate questions backwards. I continued with this technique until an unsympathetic judge said, 'Do try and keep still, Mr Mortimer. It's like watching ping-pong'.[49]

This, as John Mortimer QC tells us, was the rather grotesque result of his attempts to emulate, early in his career, the considerable panache of another great advocate. It does, however, illustrate another important feature of style in

---

48 *Op cit*, Birkenhead, fn 43.

49 Mortimer, J, *Clinging to the Wreckage – A Part of Life*, 1982, London: Weidenfeld & Nicolson, pp 96–97.

moot presentations, which may be at odds with your conception of things, especially if you have not mooted before.

The convention of the English Bar always seems to have been to keep gesticulations to a minimum. Truly great advocates, such as Sir Edward Marshall Hall (see the answer to Question 38) were always able to flout the convention, with success, especially when seeking to persuade a jury, rather than a judge. To say that you should keep your gesticulations to an absolute minimum, when making your moot presentation, cannot be bad advice, however.[50] The authors have heard this expressed in the somewhat dark and obscure motto, 'handcuffs and shackles'. Translated, however, it seems to mean that a barrister and, by parity of reasoning, a mooter, should make his or her presentation as though incapable of moving any part of their body but their face muscles. Doubtless, this is an extreme motto and, doubtless, there are valid departures from it. Work done by the National Institute for Trial Advocacy at Nottingham Law School indicates that an advocate on so called interim hearings in real courts, where most advocacy is conducted sitting down, must develop the skill of using effective and persuasive body language in presenting the case to the judge. For example, if the judge is sitting back in his or her chair to hear the advocate's submissions, then the advocate should do so too. Obviously, it may not be possible to combine this, as a mooter, with not moving any part of your body but your face muscles. Nonetheless, skillful use of body language, involving some assessment of that of the judge, may make your submissions more persuasive to the judge, even when you are standing still.

Part of the reason for the convention, we suspect, is that it is extremely difficult for a judge to concentrate on assimilating highly detailed information if the advocate or mooter behaves any differently from the way dictated by the motto. Conversely, as an advocate or mooter, you do not want to create unnecessary barriers to the acceptance of your submissions by the judge.

---

50 Defending one Marie Hermann at the Old Bailey on a charge of murder using an iron bar, Marshall Hall '... made a dramatic reconstruction of the crime before the jury, and acted the part of Marie Hermann with the iron bar, showing that what he suggested had actually taken place' (see Birkett, N, 'Sir Edward Marshall Hall KC', in Six Great Advocates, 1961, London: Penguin, p 15).

70 Should my style of presentation be aggressive or thoughtful?

> ... I greatly admired the smooth and elegant advocacy of [Cyril] Salmon, who seemed to me to win his cases with all the noise and bluster of a perfectly tuned Rolls-Royce coasting down hill.[51]

So writes Sir John Mortimer QC, in his autobiography, *Clinging to the Wreckage*. He goes on to say that his admiration for the advocacy of Lord Salmon, as Cyril Salmon was later to become, led him unsuccessfully to emulate his style (see the answer to Question 69).

The moral of this story as, doubtless, many others, is that you must be your own man or woman, as is said. There is no point in adopting an aggressive style of delivery if self-awareness tells you that you are not an aggressive individual in everyday life. You will probably be unmasked, as the moot judge's questions become increasingly searching!

Not only this but, as Norman Birkett (see the answer to Question 38), once wrote, dipping his pen in acid, contrasting trial before judge with trial by jury:[52]

> To attempt eloquence before a judge alone is slightly ridiculous ...

71 Do I need to outline the facts of the moot problem to the moot judge?

If you are the Lead Appellant, you are obliged to outline the facts of the case to the moot court or, at the very least, to ask permission from the moot judge to be excused from doing so. Try not to waste the very limited time at your disposal by reading *verbatim* the full statement of facts set out in the moot problem. Instead, simply give a brief outline of the facts. An appropriate form of words would be: 'My Lord/My Lady, I don't know whether your Lordship/Ladyship would find a brief summary of the facts of this case helpful?' If the judge says 'yes', you should then proceed to outline only the salient facts of the moot problem and pause from time to time, to emphasise those facts which are especially important. Do not, however, selectively highlight only those facts which support your submissions. Part of the role of the Lead Appellant is to assist the moot judge in familiarising him or herself with the facts of the moot problem.

An example of how to stress the most important facts is found in the example moot in Appendix 1.

---

51   *Op cit*, Mortimer, fn 49, p 96.

52   See Birkett, N, 'Sir Patrick Hastings, KC', in *Six Great Advocates*, 1961, London: Penguin, p 25.

72 Is it ever possible to put an interpretation on the facts in order to favour my hypothetical client?

There should be very little scope for doing this in the context of a moot. This is because, as mentioned in the answer to Question 99, in a good moot problem, the facts are crystal clear. It is only the law relating to those facts which should be in doubt.

There should, therefore, be no opportunity for you to put an interpretation on the facts designed to favour your hypothetical client. This, subject to what is mentioned below, contrasts with the situation in a mock trial (see the answer to Question 2), where the object of the exercise is to establish the facts of the case.

Even were you to be appearing for the parties in a mock trial, your freedom to put a favourable interpretation on the facts would be restricted by the duty which, as an advocate, you would be taken to owe to the court. The duty of real barristers generally in this regard is expressed in the Bar Council's *Written Standards for the Conduct of Professional Work*, as follows:[53]

> A barrister must assist the court in the administration of justice and, as part of this obligation and the obligation to use only proper and lawful means to promote and protect the interests of his client, must not deceive or knowingly or recklessly mislead the court.

That said, as is mentioned in the same document:[54]

> A barrister must at all times promote and protect fearlessly and by all proper and lawful means his lay client's best interests.

It follows from these points that, in the rare situation where it might be possible to favour your client by putting a particular interpretation on the facts, you should not do so. This would be against both the spirit of the game, so to speak, but would also defeat one of the objects of the mooting exercise – to follow as closely as possible the conventions of argument used in a real court.

73 Do I need expressly to apply the law to the facts of the moot problem?

Having referred to a *dictum* in the report of a judgment in a case, you must explain the relevance of it to the submission with which you are then dealing. It

---

53 See General Council of the Bar, *Written Standards for the Conduct of Professional Work*, 1998, Annex F, para 5.2.

54 *Ibid*, para 5.1. See, also, Access to Justice Act 1999, s 42, and The Law Society, *The Guide to the Professional Conduct of Solicitors*, 1999, London: The Law Society, paras 21.01–21.02.

is an absolutely vital part of your submissions to apply the proposition of law to the facts of the moot problem, in the light of the authority you have cited. Do not leave it to the moot judge to perform this exercise for you. You cannot assume that he or she will oblige. Spell out the connection between the law and the facts clearly. It is poor mooting practice simply to draw out a string of statutory sections and judicial *dicta* and to forget to tie the string to the particular facts of the moot problem.

In the example moot in Appendix 1, the Lead Appellant shows how the law should be applied to the fact of the moot problem (see para 7.57) and the Lead Respondent provides an even better example later on (see para 9.5). The Junior Respondent (see para 10.6) shows how an opponent's authorities can be efficiently distinguished from the facts of the moot problem, and thus de-fused. Nevertheless, all the mooters in the example moot missed opportunities expressly to apply the law to the facts of the moot problem. A useful exercise for you to embark upon would be to read through the example moot and to add in pencil further statements which could have been made in order to tie-in the law more closely to the facts.

74   When and how do I use policy arguments?

Policy arguments must be used with great care. This is for two reasons. The first is that you will only be free to use them in very specific situations. This reason underpins the answer to the question: when? The second is that you must be careful to ensure *what* exactly a policy argument *is*, as well as how it should be articulated by you. This reason underpins the answer to the question: how?

Although it is possibly foolhardy for us to do so, we would suggest that the situations in which policy arguments can be used are as follows:

- Virtually always when you are making a submission on a ground of appeal in a moot which is set in the House of Lords. You may obviously do this where any other House of Lords cases cited are distinguishable from the facts of the moot problem (see the answers to Questions 88 and 89). However, even if they are not so distinguishable, you may still advance policy arguments, although you must ensure that your submission can be brought within the terms of the 1966 Practice Statement (that is, *Practice Statement (Judicial Precedent)* [1966] 1 WLR 1234). If you turn to Appendix 4, you will see that the 1966 Practice Statement shows that the House of Lords may depart from its previous binding decisions 'when it appears right to do so'. However, if you also read the Explanatory Note for the Press, again set out in Appendix 4, you will see that even the discretion conferred by the 1966 Practice Statement is not as wide as it may at first appear.

- Sometimes when making a submission on a ground of appeal in a moot set in the Court of Appeal. You may obviously do this where any other Court of Appeal cases cited are distinguishable from the facts of the moot problem (see the answers to Questions 88 and 89). However, even if they are not so distinguishable, you may still advance policy arguments, although in that case you must ensure that your submission can be brought within the terms of the exceptions in *Young v Bristol Aeroplane Co Ltd* [1944] 1 KB 718, if the moot problem concerns civil law or, if the moot problem concerns criminal law, within Lord Goddard CJ's *dictum* in *R v Taylor* [1950] 2 KB 368 (see the answer to Question 87).

If you turn to the answer to Question 87, you will see that, although the Court of Appeal may depart from its previous binding decisions in certain situations, these situations are very restricted indeed, for civil cases, although somewhat less so for criminal ones.

It follows that, whichever of these points fits the moot problem, it is always desirable, and sometimes *essential*, to check that there is no binding authority on the moot court *before* using policy arguments. Were you to fail to do this, a rigorous moot judge might ensure that your submissions fell at the first fence, as it were, by challenging your use of policy arguments in the first place.

The second reason for exercising great care in your use of policy arguments, as mentioned above, is that you must be careful to ensure that you are clear as to what *exactly* a policy argument is, as well as how it should be articulated by you in relation to the submission you are making. This enables you to know *how* policy arguments should be used. The nature of policy arguments was rigorously explored by Professor John Bell in his book *Policy Arguments in Judicial Decisions*.[55] Texts other than Professor Bell's deal with related areas of judicial activity but, as will be apparent in a moment, his book identifies some crucially useful issues for mooters, which relate to the *nature* of policy arguments, and therefore provide good guidance as to how those arguments might be framed.

Professor Bell invites us to be clear as to what *exactly* is encompassed by the term 'policy arguments'. The definition which he gives is that of ' ... substantive justifications to which judges appeal when the standards and rules of the legal system do not provide a clear resolution of a dispute'.[56] He therefore contrasts policy arguments with purely legal arguments. The latter are arguments which rely on ' ... *authority* reasons, where reliance is placed simply on the clear rules and principles' (emphasis added).[57] Policy arguments are therefore, in honesty,

---

55   Bell, J, *Policy Arguments in Judicial Decisions*, 1st edn, 1983, Oxford: Clarendon. The authors would like to thank John Hodgson Esq, Solicitor, Principal Lecturer, Nottingham Law School, for his comments on an earlier draft of the answer to this question.

56   *Ibid*, pp 22–23.

57   *Ibid*, p 23.

political arguments. If a policy argument is adopted by a judge, then his or her decision is a political act, that is to say, it is the exercise of some power by a judge which gives direction to society.[58] Thus, provided that you are free, as a mooter, to advance policy arguments (as to which, see above in the answer to this Question), your arguments must be directed at providing *substantive reasons* for the outcome which is sought by you.

Professor Bell contends that substantive justifications can be either *ethical* or *non-ethical*. If they are ethical, your submissions will be to the general effect that the outcome for which you contend is *fair*, that is, that it meets some articulated standard of justice. If they are non-ethical, by contrast, then they are *goal-orientated*. In that case, your submissions will be to the general effect that the outcome for which you contend will *provide a greater benefit to the community* than the one which is being contended for by your opponents. He illustrates his argument by, *inter alia*, considering the development of the duty of care in tort,[59] an area characterised by policy arguments. However, his classification of the policy arguments used in these cases into five types should hold good in other areas of law, too. Some of these types of policy argument may be more prevalent in one area of the law than in another.

He finds five types of policy argument in the cases on the area. All except the fourth, *fairness* itself, are goal-orientated policy arguments. The first type of policy argument is that which draws on *social factors*. Thus, Lord Pearce remarks in *Hedley Byrne v Heller* [1964] AC 465, p 536, that 'How wide the sphere of the duty of care in negligence is to be laid depends ultimately upon the courts' assessment of the demands of society for protection from the carelessness of others'. Thus, if you argue the importance of social factors, you will be arguing about what society demands that the outcome of the case should be.

Secondly, there are *administrative factors*. Relying on administrative factors, you will be arguing *either* that a particular outcome will be workable in the future *or* that it *will not* be workable. Workable, here, may be used in the narrow sense, that is, that it is actually practicable, or in a broader sense, that it will produce the wrong result. The so called 'floodgates' argument relies on workability in the latter sense. It is sometimes expressed in the *dictum* of Cardozo J in *Ultramares Corporation v Touche* 255 NY 170 (1931), p 444: liability '... in an indeterminate amount for an indefinite time to an indeterminate class'. Unfortunately, the 'floodgates' argument has a listless existence on the lips of the weaker mooter struggling with policy arguments. This was the argument put by the defendant in *McLoughlin v O'Brian* [1982] 2 WLR 982, a case which is discussed by Professor Bell. Whilst accepting that the plaintiff in *O'Brian* ought

---

58 *Op cit*, Bell, fn 55, p 6.

59 It should be noted that his discussion pre-dates important recent developments in this area, including *Caparo Industries plc v Dickman* [1990] 2 AC 605 and *Murphy v Brentwood District Council* [1991] 1 AC 398.

to be able to recover damages for psychiatric injury, Lord Wilberforce, with whom Lord Edmund-Davies agreed, had to accept that there was some force in the 'floodgates' argument. Accordingly, he imposed *policy* limits on the existence of a duty of care, in addition to the reasonable foreseeability of psychiatric injury.[60] Lord Wilberforce's policy limits were applied by the House of Lords in *Alcock v Chief Constable of South Yorkshire* [1991] 3 WLR 1057.

Again, if you rely on the third of Professor Bell's type of policy arguments, *constitutional limitations*, you will be arguing that a particular outcome is a matter for Parliament rather than the courts. This issue is considered fully in the answer to Question 93. In this connection, however, note also the speech of Lord Scarman in *O'Brian*, arguing against the application of this form of policy argument.

The fourth of Professor Bell's types of policy argument is fairness. About fairness, he says this:[61]

> It involves the propositions that people should be treated according to what they deserve in terms of the scale of values applied and that people in similar positions should receive similar treatment.[62]

Fairness is not a simple stand-alone policy argument, however. The first part this quotation can be found in one aspect at least of the 'floodgates' argument, which might be seen as a *goal-orientated* policy argument, since the 'floodgates' argument carries the strong implication that a defendant should not have to bear an undue burden of expense. Finally, the fifth of Professor Bell's types of policy argument is that based on the *economic analysis approach*. This type of policy argument relies on the proposition that, given that resources are scarce, judges *cannot but* pay attention to whether the loss caused by the defendant was a result of the wasteful use of those resources.[63] It should be said that he found that this did not often explicitly commend itself to judges, with the exception of Lord Denning MR.

It is worth the mooter noting, however, that Professor Bell detects an *absence* of policy arguments which might have been expected to have been present in these cases. The fact that the defendant was insured, for instance, was generally ignored by the judges, with the exception of Lord Denning MR, who referred to this factor in both *Spartan Steel & Alloys Ltd v Martin & Co (Contractors) Ltd* [1973] 1 QB 27 and, in the Court of Appeal, in *Morgans v Launchbury* [1973] AC 127 (HL); [1971] 2 QB 245 (CA) (a case on the limits of policy arguments).

The point for the mooter, in Professor Bell's analysis of these five types of policy argument is that, if you are free to use a policy argument in a submission

---

60 See [1982] 2 WLR 982, pp 989E–G and 990B–D.

61 *Op cit*, Bell, fn 55, p 73.

62 *Op cit*, Bell, fn 55, p 75, referring to Posner, R, *Economic Analysis of Law*, 3rd edn, 1977, New York: Little, Brown.

63 See *Spartan Steel & Alloys Ltd v Martin & Co (Contractors) Ltd* [1973] 1 QB 27.

on your ground of appeal, then it will be a good idea to test which of the five categories it falls within. Do not content yourself with bland assertions about, for example, the 'floodgates' argument. Rather, focus on the outcome which you are seeking to achieve. Ask yourself *what* the *substantive reasons* are for urging a moot judge to exercise his or her 'political discretion', or not, as the case may be in your favour.

Finally, bear in mind that, even if you are not advancing a policy argument, a moot judge could still ask you whether the purely legal solution you are arguing for should be the policy of the law. In this situation, it is useful to be able to base your answer on one or more of the five types of policy argument referred to above.

75 Will a moot judge make a ruling on my arguments before the conclusion of the moot?

No, the judge will not usually make a ruling on legal points raised by the moot problem until he or she gives judgment after the mooters have concluded their presentations. On no account must you ask the judge to do so, by for example, asking 'Does your Lordship/Ladyship accept that point?'. Even worse is to ask the judge whether he or she has understood your argument!

There may, however, be strong indications that the moot judge accepts a point you are making, in which case refrain from arguing that point further. Alternatively, he or she might well say, 'If I reject that argument do you have any alternative arguments?' and again you must discontinue that argument and move on to any alternative arguments that you might have. Similarly, if there are indications that the judge is very unlikely to accept one of your submissions, it is prudent not to pursue it, provided that you are satisfied that you have said everything possible to persuade the court to change its mind. Instead, you should proceed to your next submission or to the close of your argument.

76 How and when should I address and refer to my colleagues and my opponents?

You should refer to your colleague as 'My learned junior (or senior), Mr/Mrs/Miss ...'. You should refer to your opponent as 'My learned friend, Mr/Mrs/Miss ...' or as 'Learned counsel for the Appellant' or 'Learned counsel for the Respondent'.

Introductions are made by the Lead Appellant. He or she should allow the moot judge time to organise any papers that he or she has. When the judge indicates that he or she is ready, the Lead Appellant should rise and introduce all the mooters by name, stating who is appearing for which party.

Incorporating the characters from the example moot in Appendix 1, the usual opening formula would be: 'May it please your Lordship, my name is Miss Felicity Fowler, I appear in this case with my learned friend Mr Neil Wright for the Appellant, and my learned friends Mr Amir Khan and Miss Sally James appear for the Respondent.'

In fact, in the example moot, Mr Dearing and Mr Holmes, the Respondents, represent different imaginary clients. Consequently, the introduction actually takes the following form: 'May it please your Lordship, my name is Miss Felicity Fowler, I appear in this case with my learned friend Mr Neil Wright for the Appellant, my learned friend Mr Amir Khan appears for the Respondent, Mr Dearing and my learned friend Miss Sally James appears for the Respondent, Mr Holmes.'[64]

You should say who is dealing with the separate grounds of appeal. The example moot takes the following form: 'My Lord, in the instant case, there are two grounds of appeal. First, the issue whether the Respondent trustee, Mr Dearing, is liable to make good losses caused to the trust fund through the defaults of his agent, Mr Holmes; and, secondly, the issue whether Mr Holmes can himself be said to have committed the tort of procurement of a breach of trust in advising Mr Dearing to make unauthorised investments. My Lord, I shall be dealing with the first ground of appeal and my learned junior will be dealing with the second ground of appeal.'[65]

Advocates appearing before the International Court of Justice do not introduce the advocates on all sides but merely introduce the advocates on their own legal team. Consequently, Notes for Guidance in the Telders International Law Moot Court Competition recommend the following formula: 'If it pleases the honourable court my name is ... and I together with my co-agent ... appear in the case for the government of ... .' It is, then, usually the case that the advocate, that is, the agent, will go on to state which agent will cover which aspect of the questions presented to the court for determination.

77   How can I win the moot judge over?

The very best way to win a moot is to win the moot judge's mind. To win the judge's mind, you must capture the judge's imagination. One method of achieving this, which we have seen used to great effect by our students, is to shoot an arrow phrase, and to shoot repeatedly, until you are satisfied that your point has finally struck home.

An example of such an arrow phrase appears in the example moot in Appendix 1. There, the arrow phrase was in fact provided by the judge but the

---

64   Appendix 1, para 7.1.

65   Appendix 1, para 7.3.

mooter very shrewdly shot it back at him. The particular phrase was 'the law should not protect honest fools'. It is neither a legal rule, nor an established principle of law. It is merely a pithy statement, the internal logic and the linguistic appeal of which the mooter hopes the judge will find irresistible and, equally as important, highly memorable. Read a judgment or speech closely, particularly one by a judge noted for an imaginative turn of phrase, and you will see that the judgment or speech is full of potential arrow phrases.

Consider how an arrow phrase might be used to make a complex point in succinct and memorable terms. Imagine you are trying to convince the moot judge that, even though your client had knowingly accepted a lift from a cab driver whose vehicle smelt of beer, your client should still be able to sue the driver for injuries suffered by your client by reason of the driver's negligent driving. An arrow phrase you might wish to use is to be found in somewhat extended form in a *dictum* of Asquith J in *Dann v Hamilton* [1939] 1 KB 509, p 518, where the judge considers the issue of *volenti non fit injuria* in the following terms:

> There may be cases in which the drunkenness of the driver at the material time is so extreme and so glaring that to accept a lift from him is like engaging in an intrinsically and obviously dangerous occupation, intermeddling with an unexploded bomb or walking on the edge of an unfenced cliff.

Having quoted the *dictum*, the key image might be put in slightly altered form, as an arrow phrase. Something like this: 'A cab smelling of beer presents no obvious risk; it is not an unexploded bomb.' By use of a phrase such as this, you will hopefully capture the judge's imagination. If the arrow phrase is lodged firmly enough in the judge's mind, such that it cannot be shaken free, you might win over the judge and win the moot on the strength of it.

78   I can't act: is that a problem?

The answer to this question is a definite no!

It is a common mistake to imagine that mooting is the law degree equivalent of drama lessons at school. In fact, mooting is an exercise in the clear communication of ideas and the art of persuading another, the moot judge, to accept those ideas. You will generally perform better in a moot by simply being yourself. Far from drawing an impressive mask over your anxiety or lack of confidence in your own argument, acting can often result in nothing but a transparent veil. Be real, in other words, do not try to convince the judge you are right, unless you have first of all convinced yourself.

If you are an aspiring actor, however, do not fear that your talents may go entirely unused, for, even if ill suited to mooting, they may yet find a home in the practice of law. As Sir John Mortimer QC observes:[66]

An English criminal trial is a very theatrical occasion – the barristers and judges wear wigs and gowns, some of the judges are in scarlet and ermine and, on State occasions, carry bunches of flowers (once necessary to protect their noses from prison stench). I often left court to go to a rehearsal of a play I had written and felt I had left the world of fantasy and make-believe at the Old Bailey for the harsh reality of the world of art.

79   How do I pronounce foreign case names in a moot?

The short answer to this question is that you should not attempt to adopt a foreign pronunciation. As mentioned elsewhere, the tradition of the English Bar is to use anglicised pronunciations, as in relation to Latin and law-French. A similar convention seems to apply to foreign case names.

That said, however, it is important to pronounce every syllable of the name, so that it can clearly be heard. Some notes on how you might ensure that you do this are included in the answer to Question 47.

First, when you realise that you will have to pronounce a non-English word, for example, in the EC law context, the name of a case, write it down. If necessary, split it up into its component syllables. For instance, say you were seeking to rely on a point from the EC law case of *Klaus Biehl v Administration des contributions du grand duche de Luxembourg*, Case C-175/88 [1990] 3 CMLR 143. If you are even an elementary linguist, you will immediately recognise the language of one of the parties as being German and the other as being French. Unusually, perhaps, the German name does not involve so many syllables. You might find it helpful to split the French party's name up, however, thus:

Ad/mini/stra/tion des/ contri/bu/tions/ du/ grand/ duche/ de/ Lux/em/bourg.

There is no science in this. All you are doing is dividing the words into their component parts, making it easier to pronounce them. The next stage is to find a good French dictionary and to see from there how these words should be pronounced. You will need to do the same with the German words. Having said this, you may not immediately recognise the language of the case name. In that situation, it will be necessary for you to look at the case itself, to see from which Member State(s) of the EC the parties originate, and to check the relevant

---

66   Mortimer, J, 'Introduction', in *The Best of Rumpole*, 1993, London: Viking, p 1. Scintillating though John Mortimer's point is, however, a salutary view is put by Helena Kennedy QC: 'The criminal trial is a terrifying process. Those who are most affected by it, the victims and defendants, are those who are most neglected and alienated by the ambience and the procedures' (Kennedy, H, *Eve Was Framed – Women and British Justice*, 1993, London: Vintage, p 13).

dictionary accordingly, for example, *Frans-Nederlandse Maatschappig voor Biologische Producten*, Case 272/80 [1981] ECR 3277.

Now, you may think that all of this sounds a little bit excessive in relation to every single case. Well, true. We are only suggesting that you go through the process set out above in relation to those cases which you eventually need to cite in your moot presentation. The correct pronunciation should be one of the final points you check before going into the moot court or, having produced your submissions, when you are practising them orally for the first time.

In this situation, it might even be sensible to translate the names of the parties into English.

80   Do I need to recite law and facts from the cases upon which I am relying?

Law

When you cite an authority, you will be expected to cite a passage from the judgments or speeches, as the case may be, in that authority. If you do not intend to do so, then inform the judge immediately that you do not intend to refer to any particular passage from the judgment or speech. Be warned, very rarely will you be justified in referring to a case or other authority for such and such, without actually quoting support from the judgments or speeches, as the case may be.

It must be stressed that any reference you make should ordinarily be to the judgment or speech itself and not to the headnote or other part of the law report. It is usually far better to refer to what a judge actually said, rather than what the law reporter has interpreted the judge as having said. The law reporter, remember, writes the headnote, although in the semi-official law reports, it is approved by the judges. If you wish to make unorthodox use of a law report (see, for example, the approach of Miss Felicity Fowler in the example moot in Appendix 1, with the case of *Re Brier*), be honest and open with the moot judge. In other words, let the judge know that you are fully aware that what you are doing is unorthodox but that you have good reason for taking the unorthodox course.

Facts

Having referred to a case by name and citation (see the answer to Question 81), you should always deal with the facts before taking the judge to any passage of law. To deal with the facts, it is never necessary for you to read them out in full. You should always have brief summaries of the facts of each case ready to assist the judge. The best approach is to ask the judge 'Is your Lordship familiar with the facts of this case?' or 'Would your Lordship wish to be reminded of the facts?' or 'Would a brief summary of the facts be helpful, my Lord?', and so on. The risk inherent in this approach is, of course, that the judge may say 'No, thank you'. If you are very keen to refer to the facts, you should therefore avoid this risk by saying at the start 'The facts of the case are as follows ...' or 'The facts of the case are most relevant. They were ...' or, simply, 'The case involved ...'. When summarising the facts of a case, you must do so honestly. Any attempt to omit facts which are unhelpful to your hypothetical client will be severely disapproved of by the judge.

Finally, what if you cite a case but do not wish to refer to it at all during your presentation? Can you simply ignore it? The straightforward answer is yes. However, the judge and your opponent will be aware of the existence of the authority (from your list of authorities: see the answer to Questions 19–21). If the reason you have chosen to ignore the case is that it actually hinders your submissions, you can be sure that either the judge or your opponent will mention it, as they will be perfectly entitled to do. Therefore, do not throw away your notes on the case, even if you do not intend to rely upon it. In fact, if you do not wish to rely upon a case appearing in your list of authorities, it is best to put the omission in a positive light. Inform the judge that you cited the case merely to reinforce your main point, and that you are confident that your submissions are strong enough without it.

81 What is the correct way to refer to a case?

When you are referring to cases in the course of your moot presentation, avoid using abbreviations for the printed or written references.

An appropriate way of referring to an authority would therefore be:

In support of this submission, I would refer your Ladyship to the case of *Carlill and The Carbolic Smoke Ball Company*, reported in the first volume of the *Law Reports*, Queen's Bench Division, for 1893, p 256.

Similar wording would be used, the necessary changes being made, by the mooters in the example moot in Appendix 1.

Notice that the 'v' in the name of the case is pronounced 'and', not 'versus' or 'vee', and that the details of the volume are spelt out in full. Alternatively, you may use the word 'against' to express the 'v' orally. In the interests of euphony, this may be used where there is more than one defendant, for example, *R v Gibbins and Proctor* ('The Crown against Gibbins and Proctor' arguably sounds more elegant than 'the Crown and Gibbins and Proctor').

As an illustration of how seriously the courts have taken these decencies in the past is the story told by Glanville Williams, involving an exchange in the course of argument, between Lord Esher, the Victorian Master of the Rolls, and a junior barrister. It involved the kind of play on words that the Victorians, especially Victorian lawyers, seemed to like so much. Briefly, the barrister in question had referred to '2 QB'. 'That is not the way you should address us', said Lord Esher. When counsel protested that he merely intended to use a brief and ordinary form of words, Lord Esher replied: 'I might as well say to you, "U B D".' Translated, this means of course 'You be damned'. The authors shouldn't be surprised if, Pooter-like, Lord Esher awoke in the night, laughing at his own joke. It illustrates the general point, however.

In addition, remember that the 'R', in the name of a criminal case, is pronounced 'The Crown' and in Privy Council cases as 'The Queen' or 'The King', depending on who the sovereign is, or was, at the time the case was decided (see the answer to Question 26).

A more general point to remember, when referring to an authority, is to pause while the moot judge finds the appropriate volume and page reference. Give a brief summary of the facts of the case you are referring to, unless the facts are not relevant to your submissions, in which case, make that point, and ask the judge's permission to ignore them. For example, if the purpose of referring to a passage from a case is to use it as illustrative of a general rule of law, it is appropriate to say something like: 'The facts of this case are not material and, with your Lordship's permission, I would refer, in support of the rule of law which I have stated, to the passage in the judgment of ...'

82   May I give my personal view of the relevant law?

It is the role of mooters, just as for counsel in the setting of a real court, to make submissions as to what the correct interpretation of the law should be. Accordingly, if you examine the example moot in Appendix 1, you will observe that the mooters frequently introduce an argument with the phrase, 'I submit that ...' or 'It is my submission that ... ' or 'In my respectful submission ... '. This is a commendable approach. It may also be appropriate, although somewhat less formal, to say 'I would argue that ... ' or 'It is my contention ... '.

This approach should be contrasted with the following, more personalised approach, which some mooters erroneously take. Frequently, we hear mooters commence a submission with the phrase 'I feel that ... ' or 'I believe that ... '. Such an approach is quite inappropriate for two reasons. First, because it is in nature judicial as opposed to advocatory. It suggests that the mooter has reached a personal conclusion as to the proper outcome in the case. This is the province of the judge. Secondly, it lacks objectivity. An advocate is never neutral, of course, but an advocate must always be objective.

83 How do I introduce myself and my submissions?

You should begin your moot presentation with one of a number of rather stylised forms of introduction. As we shall see in a moment, there are illustrations of some of these forms in the example moot in Appendix 1. However, as long as you adopt a substantially similar form of wording, observing the correct etiquette in addressing the judge, for example (see the answer to Question 55), you will be observing the general conventions of mooting.

Even before using one of the forms of introduction set out below, you may wish to begin with the time-honoured formula, now slightly archaic perhaps, but nonetheless very appealing 'May it please you, my Lord' or 'May it please your Lordship' (for the difference between these two, see the answer to Question 55). The advantage of adopting either of these formulae is that they give you yet another opportunity to find your voice before beginning the substance of your presentation.

The rather stylised forms of introduction used in the example moot in Appendix 1, embodying the time-honoured formulae mentioned above, are as follows. They are slightly different for each mooter, bearing in mind the need for the Lead Appellant to introduce all the mooters in turn:

Lead Appellant:

[*Standing up to lead in the case*] May it please your Lordship, my name is Mr/Miss/Mrs A, and I appear in this case with my learned friend Mr/Miss/Mrs B for the Appellant. My learned friend Mr/Miss/Mrs C appears for the Respondent, X, and my learned friend Mr/Miss/Mrs D appears for the Respondent, Y.

Junior Appellant:

[*Standing up*] May it please your Lordship, as has already been indicated, my name is Mr/Miss/Mrs B and I appear for the Appellant on the second ground of appeal.

Lead Respondent:

If it pleases your Lordship, may name is Mr/Miss/Mrs C and I represent the Respondent together with my learned junior, Mr/Miss/Mrs D.

Junior Respondent:

[*Standing up*] May it please your Lordship, as has already been indicated by my learned friend, Mr/Miss/Mrs C, my name is Mr/Miss/Mrs D and I appear for the Respondent on the second ground of appeal.

Having used substantially the relevant introduction set out above, the Lead Appellant should pause in order to give the moot judge the opportunity to write down the name of each mooter. There is obviously no need for the other mooters to pause in this way.

Please refer to the answer to Question 27 for other points relating to the form which your submissions should take.

84 How do I conclude my submissions?

As you reach the end of your moot presentation, you will possibly be holding on quietly – but very firmly – to the thread of your submissions.

The moot judge, no less than yourself, will want to be clear as to the essential points in those submissions. This will be the case particularly if you have been questioned closely on your submissions. Therefore, if you get the opportunity to do so, you should conclude your submissions by summarising their essential points. The opportunity to do this should obviously be taken account of by you in timing your moot presentation.

In addition, ask the moot judge to dismiss or allow the appeal as appropriate. Having concluded your submissions, you should always offer the moot judge a final opportunity to ask you concluding questions. Alternative formulae which may be used before finally sitting down are: 'Unless I can assist the court further, that concludes my submissions on this ground of appeal' or 'Unless your Lordship has any further questions, that concludes my submissions' or even the old favourite 'Unless I can assist the court further, I rest my case'.

4 Principles and Practice

85 When is an authority binding on a moot court?

As we have already observed, most moots on English points of law are set in the Court of Appeal or the House of Lords. Only occasionally will a moot be set in the High Court (the High Court is, however, often chosen as the forum for mooting issues of judicial review). It follows that one of the most important issues you must grasp is to know which legal authorities are binding upon the Court of Appeal and upon the House of Lords.

Some basic rules can be stated:

- All judicial tribunals in England and Wales, even the Court of Appeal and the House of Lords, are bound to follow effective EC law directly.[1] This is notwithstanding any inconsistent provision appearing in a statute enacted by the UK Parliament. It is generally thought that until such time as the UK Parliament decides to repeal the European Communities Act 1972, the UK Parliament and the UK courts will remain subject to the law of the European Community. It is not, however, clear how the English courts would treat a UK statute which purported to disapply EC law.[2]

- Judgments of the Court of Justice of the European Communities made in relation to questions of EC law are binding upon the Court of Appeal and House of Lords (Arts 10 and 234, EC Treaty, as renumbered by the Treaty of Amsterdam).

- Authorities arising out of overseas domestic jurisdictions, even when heard on appeal by the Judicial Committee of the Privy Council, are not binding, and are, therefore, of *merely persuasive* authority in English courts. However, some overseas authorities are more persuasive than others. As was acknowledged in the explanatory note for the press appended to *Practice Statement (Judicial Precedent)* [1966] 1 WLR 1234 (see Appendix 4): 'The relaxation of the rule of judicial precedent will enable the House of Lords to pay greater attention to

---

1   See Weatherill, S and Beaumont, P, *EC Law*, 2nd edn, 1996, London: Penguin; Groves, PJ, *Lecture Notes on European Community Law*, 1995, London: Cavendish Publishing, for a detailed consideration of those circumstances.

2   See, generally, the *dictum* of Lord Denning MR in *McCarthy's Ltd v Smith* [1981] 1 QB 180, p 200E–F.

judicial decisions reached in the superior courts of the Commonwealth, where they differ from earlier decisions of the House of Lords.' (For more detail of the way in which the Practice Statement relaxed the rule of judicial precedent, see the answer to Question 86.) Although a judgment (correctly referred to as an 'advice') of the Judicial Committee of the Privy Council, is of only persuasive authority, an English court will rarely depart from it. This is because the Judicial Committee often comprises five Lords of Appeal in Ordinary and is, thus, similar in its constitution to the House of Lords sitting in its judicial capacity. There is often an overlap of personnel between the two appellate bodies. Indeed sometimes a Privy Council case actually contains a clarification of the law as previously laid down in a domestic forum by the judge delivering the opinion. For example, Lord Roskill in the House of Lords in *R v Seymour* [1983] 2 AC 493, when comparing motor manslaughter to the then statutory offence of causing death by reckless driving contrary to s 1 of the Road Traffic Act 1972 held that there are degrees of turpitude which will vary according to the gravity of the risk created by the manner of the defendant's driving and that manslaughter should only be charged if 'the risk of death from a defendant's driving was very high ...'.[3] This led commentators to speculate that the two offences had different *mens rea* elements. Clarification that this was not the case occurred two years later when the same Law Lord said, in the Privy Council in *Re Kong Cheuk Kwan* (1986) 82 Cr App Rep 18, that: 'The model direction suggested in *Lawrence* [1982] AC 510 and held in *Seymour* [see above] equally applicable to cases of motor manslaughter, requires ... proof that the vehicle was in fact being driven in such a manner as to create an obvious and serious risk of causing physical injury to another ...'.[4] After such a clarification, it would be fruitless for a mooter to claim in a manslaughter case that the *mens rea* for manslaughter is recklessness in respect of a high risk of death. You can, after all, hardly submit that that is what Lord Roskill had meant in *R v Seymour* when he has subsequently said that he did not.

- Whatever law the Queen enacts in Parliament is binding upon both the Court of Appeal and upon the House of Lords sitting in its judicial capacity. Such primary legislation is enacted in the form of a statute (that is, an Act of Parliament). Subordinate legislation, which is legislation created by bodies other than the Queen in Parliament, under law making powers delegated, either directly or indirectly, by Parliament, is similarly so binding, assuming it has been validly created. You are most likely to encounter subordinate legislation in the form of statutory instruments.[5]

---

3   [1983] 2 AC 493, p 508D.

4   *Ibid*, p 525.

5   Where a body purports to create subordinate legislation outside the powers delegated to it by Parliament, such legislation may be declared void by a court of law as being *ultra vires* (see Appendix 8). Subordinate legislation can also by challenged in the courts, if it is formally defective.

- According to the doctrine of *stare decisis* (which literally translates as 'to stand by things decided' and is commonly known as the *doctrine of precedent*) any court (let us take, for example, the High Court) is bound to follow certain statements of law made by any court superior to the High Court in the judicial hierarchy (the Court of Appeal and the House of Lords).[6] However, for the purposes of the doctrine of *stare decisis*, not every judicial pronouncement will be treated as being a binding 'precedent', that is to say, a binding statement of law. A statement of law in a particular case will only be a binding precedent when the statement forms part of the *ratio decidendi* of the judgment in that case, and when, if more than one judge heard the case, the statement of law supported the decision of them all or of the majority of them. The *ratio* of the case is that part of the judgment which expresses the judges' reasons for coming to the conclusion they came to on the questions of law in the case. In cases where there is more than one judge, the judges may agree upon the proper result, the decision in the case, but for different reasons. This can produce odd cases. Suppose an Appellant advances five grounds of appeal on an appeal to the House of Lords. It is quite possible for each of the five Law Lords hearing the case to accept one only of the five grounds, and to reject the others. That may not surprise us. The odd part is that each of the five Law Lords may have chosen to accept a different one of the five grounds of appeal. The *ratio decidendi* in such a case would be fivefold, and, thus, arguably, no *ratio* at all. (See, also, the answer to Question 20.)[7]

When citing a particular precedent to a court, it is a long accepted practice to refer to the precedent by the name of the case in which the binding statement of law was laid down. This is so even though it would be wrong to treat every statement of law in that case as having a binding precedental quality. Judicial statements which do not have binding precedental value include:

Findings of fact

It may have been in dispute that the defendant's negligent driving caused, as a matter of fact, the claimant's injuries. A court's conclusion on that question of fact will not oblige an inferior court to come to the same conclusion even where the evidence is virtually identical.

See the answer to Question 90 for the distinction between a judge's finding of fact and his or her decision on law.

---

6   As to whether a court is bound by the decisions of another court of equal status, see Question 87.

7   See, eg, *Esso Petroleum v Customs and Excise Commissioners* [1976] 1 WLR 1. In that case, four of their Lordships agreed in the result, but there was no real consensus as to the reason, ie, the *ratio*, why.

Obiter dicta

It is frequently the case that judges make statements of law merely 'by the way' (referred to as *obiter dicta*). Such statements have no direct relevance to determining the issues on the facts in the case, but usually express the judges' opinions as to how the case would have been decided, in the hypothetical, had the facts been somewhat different. If a case should arise in which the facts are indistinguishable from those envisaged by the judge who made the *obiter dictum* (see the answer to Question 89), the *obiter dictum*, whilst not binding, will nevertheless be of persuasive authority. The *obiter dictum* will be of strongly persuasive authority where it appeared in a superior court and the similar facts are now up for consideration in an inferior court (see the answer to Question 20).

Dicta per curiam

Occasionally, a judge will make statements which are not merely made 'by the way' as tangentially arising from the issues or facts in the case before him or her, but which are designed to clarify the law generally or to cure some judicial misunderstanding as to the true state of the law.

Dissentient *dicta*

Where a judge in an appellate court comes to a decision in a case which differs from the decision reached by the majority, the dissentient judge's legal reasons for reaching that decision will not form part of the *ratio* of the case. Dissentient *dicta* of this sort are of merely persuasive authority.

In our discussion of the doctrine of *stare decisis*, we have not yet considered the extent to which the doctrine applies to oblige a court to follow precedents set by courts of equal status. So, for instance, when is the present Court of Appeal bound by a precedent set by a previous Court of Appeal? The answer is that courts are *prima facie* obliged to follow the previous decisions of courts of equal status. In other words, courts should only exceptionally depart from their own decisions. The situations in which it is permissible so to depart are outlined in the answer to Question 87.

86 How can one escape from an inconvenient authority?

We observed in the answer to Question 85 that, in accordance with the doctrine of *stare decisis*, a court is bound to follow precedents set by other courts superior to it in the hierarchy of courts. So, for example, the Court of Appeal is bound to follow precedents set by the House of Lords. We further observed that a court is *prima facie* bound to follow its own precedents.

The present question is one frequently asked by students who, when hoping to advance a sophisticated line in legal reasoning before the moot court, wish first to avoid a troublesome case in which there are statements of law directly contradictory to their intended line of argument. In answering this question, we will consider the accepted modes of escaping such inconvenient authorities. (For less orthodox techniques for avoiding inconvenient authorities, see the answers to Questions 60 and 66.)

As we saw in the answer to Question 85, statements of law in a case may have a binding precedental quality or may be of merely persuasive authority. When the latter type of authority is used against you, you must raise an argument asking the court to be not persuaded by it – oxymoronic as that sounds. However, when faced with binding statements of law which run counter to your submissions you must ask the moot court to do one of two things. You must ask the court to overrule the inconvenient authority, or else you must ask the court to distinguish it on its facts from the present case (see the answer to Question 89). An authority cannot be overruled if it is an authority of a court superior in the hierarchy to the court in which the moot is hypothetically set. In such a case, the only option is to ask the court to distinguish the inconvenient authority on its facts. (One would only ask a court to *reverse* a decision where that decision had been made by an inferior court in the very same case.) *Overruling* cases is considered in the answer to Question 87. *Distinguishing* cases is considered in the answers to Questions 88 and 89.

87 In what circumstances can a case be overruled?

There is no difficulty in overruling an authority set by a court inferior to the court in which the moot is imagined to be set, and it is not possible to overrule an authority laid down in a court superior to the moot court. It follows that the difficulty will come when attempting to overrule a precedent set by a court of equal status to the court in which the moot is set. Accordingly, the following briefly sets out the situations in which the House of Lords and the Court of Appeal are able to depart from their own precedents.

House of Lords

According to *Practice Statement (Judicial Precedent)* [1966] 1 WLR 1234 (see Appendix 4), the House of Lords, 'while treating former decisions of the House as normally binding', will nevertheless 'depart from a previous decision when it appears right to do so.' Previously, the House had only departed from its own precedents where the precedents had been set *per incuriam* (in erroneous disregard of a statutory provision or other binding authority). It seems to follow from the 1966 *Practice Statement*, and the accompanying explanatory note for the press (again, see Appendix 4), that the House is now, in addition to the *per incuriam* exception, most likely to depart from its own precedents in the following situations. First, where the precedent was laid down in response to factors which no longer prevail and is accordingly unsuited to modern conditions. Secondly, where the precedent is inconsistent with developments in the superior courts of the Commonwealth, which developments the House sees fit to adopt.

The Practice Statement makes it very clear, however, that the House will remain most reluctant to disturb 'retrospectively the basis on which contracts, settlements of property and fiscal arrangements have been entered into'. The House will also remain mindful of the 'especial need for certainty as to the criminal law'.

Court of Appeal (Civil Division)

In 1944 six of the eight regular members of the Court of Appeal sat together in the matter of *Young v Bristol Aeroplane Co Ltd* [1944] 1 KB 718, to consider the application of the doctrine of *stare decisis* to decisions of the Court of Appeal in civil actions. The judgment of the court was delivered by Lord Greene MR, and its effect is accurately summarised in the headnote to the case, as follows:

> The Court of Appeal is bound to follow its own decisions and those of courts of co-ordinate jurisdiction, and the 'full' court is in the same position in this respect as a division of the court consisting of three members. The only exceptions to this rule are: (1) The court is entitled and bound to decide which of two conflicting decisions of its own it will follow; (2) the court is bound to refuse to follow a decision of its own which, though not expressly overruled, cannot, in its opinion, stand with a decision of the House of Lords; (3) the court is not bound to follow a decision of its own if it is satisfied that the decision was given *per incuriam*, for example, where a statute or rule having statutory effect which would have affected the decision was not brought to the attention of the earlier court.

More recently, in *Davis v Johnson* [1979] AC 264, the House of Lords took, in the words of Lord Diplock, the opportunity 'to re-affirm expressly, unequivocally and unanimously that the rule laid down in the *Bristol Aeroplane* case as to *stare decisis* is still binding on the Court of Appeal'.[8]

The doctrine of *stare decisis* was again reasserted by the Court of Appeal in the case of *Williams v Fawcett* [1986] QB 604 as being 'of the very greatest importance' in order to prevent fragmentation of the law. In the same case, it was held that a decision has certainly been reached *per incuriam* where it has been reached in ignorance or forgetfulness of a statute or other binding authority (the obvious example of the latter being a precedent set in the House

---

8   It should be noted that the Court of Appeal is of co-ordinate jurisdiction with the old Court of Exchequer Chamber and both courts are treated as being of equal status for the purpose of the doctrine of *stare decisis*.

of Lords). It was further held that there might also be other, albeit very rare, cases where a decision can be treated as having been reached *per incuriam*, but such cases must be dealt with on their special facts. For any authority to be treated as having been decided *per incuriam*, some part of the decision or step in the judicial reasoning in the authority must be demonstrably wrong. In fact, in *Williams v Fawcett*, the Court of Appeal took the view that even demonstrable error will not of itself be enough in every case, and sought to justify its conclusion that certain 'inconvenient' (to use our word) cases had been decided *per incuriam* by showing, further, that other exceptional features of those cases justified their being overruled. These exceptional features included the apparent growth of the error from case to case; the fact that the cases all concerned imprisonment and the fact that the cases were unlikely to reach the House of Lords and, therefore, would not be susceptible to overrule unless it be by the Court of Appeal.

Court of Appeal (Criminal Division)

The other division of the Court of Appeal will not consider itself quite so bound by its own decisions as does the Civil Division. For, as Lord Goddard CJ put it, in *R v Taylor* [1950] 2 KB 368:

> This court ... has to deal with questions involving the liberty of the subject, and if it finds, on reconsideration, that, in the opinion of a full court assembled for that purpose, the law has been either misapplied or misunderstood in a decision which it has previously given, and that, on the strength of that decision, an accused person has been sentenced and imprisoned it is the bounden duty of the court to reconsider the earlier decision with a view to seeing whether that person had been properly convicted. The exceptions which apply in civil cases ought not to be the only ones applied ... [see [1950] 2 KB 368, p 371].

88 How and when can a case be distinguished in law from another?

Before reading the answer to this question, you may like to refer back to the answer to Question 20 and the answers to Questions 85–87. In the answer to Question 20, we looked at techniques for determining the *ratio decidendi* of a case and looked at the significance of the distinction between the *ratio decidendi* and *obiter dicta* (see, also, Appendix 8).

As we shall repeat in the answer to Question 89, the process of distinguishing one case from another can take one of at least two forms. The first is referred to as *restrictive distinguishing*. This is distinguishing one case from another *in law*, a process which we discuss in this answer. The second form is *non-restrictive distinguishing*, a form of distinguishing which lawyers refer to as distinguishing one case from another *on its facts*. This is the form of distinguishing with which we are concerned in the answer to Question 89. As we stress in the answers to both this question and Question 89, whichever of these two forms the distinguishing takes, if you distinguish Case B from Case A successfully, then the *ratio decidendi* of Case A will not be binding in Case B (see the answers to Questions 85 and 86).

If you distinguish a case *in law*, that is, restrictively, you seek to cut down the *ratio* of the other case. This is different from *non-restrictive distinguishing*, discussed in the answer to Question 89. You are submitting that Case B should be distinguished from Case A, because the received formulation of the *ratio decidendi*, the rule of law on which the decision in Case A was based, is too widely stated. For this purpose, it could have been too widely stated by the judge or judges in Case A, by other judges, or even by your opponent in the moot. The words 'too widely stated' here simply mean that, in Case A, the court should have regarded as material a fact to which no importance seems to have been attached by it. There is no general formula for discovering when the *ratio* of a case has been too widely stated, although it is reasonably obvious when this is arguable, once you are familiar with the other cases in the area of law under consideration. The point to remember, for mooting purposes at least, is that, in a developing area of law, no one individual or group of individuals has had the last word on what the *ratio decidendi* of a case actually is. As with non-restrictive distinguishing, which we discuss in the answer to Question 89, everything depends on the particular facts of Cases A and B, viewed in relation to the legal context in which they are being considered.

The authors would suggest that it is the process of restrictive distinguishing which has brought discredit on the concepts of *rationes decidendi* and *obiter dicta*. As discussed in the answer to Question 20, although the concepts are regarded as fundamental to the reasoning of the common law by some commentators, many lawyers would regard the concepts as fallacious ones, or in need of formulation in different terms from the formulation stated above. Glanville Williams quotes a subversive extra-judicial comment of Pollock CB to Frederick Pollock, the distinguished academic lawyer who was his grandson:

> Even [Mr Baron] Parke, Lord Wensleydale (the greatest legal pedant that I believe ever existed) did not always follow even the House of Lords; he did not overrule – oh no ... but he did not act upon cases which were nonsense (as many are).[9]

The part of Glanville Williams's book where this quotation is footnoted is worth reading very closely,[10] since it discusses how the *ratio* of a simple case, *Wilkinson v Downton* [1897] 2 QB 57, can be successfully restrictively distinguished, in the way described above. Pollock CB's comments about Lord Wensleydale are,

---

9 Williams, G, *Learning The Law*, 11th edn, 1982, London: Stevens, p 77.

10 *Ibid*, Chapter 6.

incidentally, very interesting when read in the light of the quotation from Lord Wensleydale set out in the answer to Question 94, in relation to the *Golden Rule* of statutory interpretation.

You will need to distinguish one case from another *in law* where the doctrine of *stare decisis* means that it is otherwise binding on the moot court, and it is not possible to distinguish the two cases on their facts (see the answer to Question 89). We suggest that the need to distinguish one case from another in law is, together with the need to distinguish one case from another on its facts, one of the few situations in which, as Respondent in a moot, you should consider dealing with the Appellant's submissions before proceeding with your own submissions (see the answer to Question 15).

89 How and when can a case be distinguished on its facts from another?

Before reading the answer to this question, you may like to refer briefly to the answers to Questions 20 and 88. In the answer to Question 20 we looked at techniques for determining the *ratio decidendi* of a case and looked at the significance of the distinction between the *ratio decidendi* and *obiter dicta* (see, also, Appendix 8).

As we said in the answer to Question 88, the process of distinguishing one case from another can take one of at least two forms. The first is referred to as *restrictive distinguishing*. This is distinguishing one case from another in law, and is discussed in that answer. The second form is *non-restrictive distinguishing*,[11] the form of distinguishing which lawyers refer to as distinguishing one case from another on its facts. This is the form of distinguishing with which we are concerned in the answer to this question. Whichever of these two forms the distinguishing takes, if you distinguish Case A from Case B successfully, then the *ratio decidendi* of Case A will not be binding in Case B (see the answers to Questions 85 and 86).

If you distinguish a case on its facts, that is, non-restrictively, you do *not* seek to cut down the *ratio* of the other case, as you do with restrictive distinguishing. Instead, you are submitting that Case B should be distinguished from Case A, because the *facts* of Case B are materially different from those of Case A. The words materially different here simply mean *different in a way which is legally relevant*, as opposed to a way which is not legally relevant, that is, in a way which is merely incidental. There is no general definition of when the facts of one case are materially different from the facts of another, although it is reasonably obvious when a difference between the facts of one case and another case is not material. Take a very crude example first. You cannot, in the absence

---

11   *Op cit*, Williams, fn 9, p 76.

of some special reason, distinguish Case B from Case A, both cases of murder, on the basis that in Case B the murder had been committed with a knife, whereas in Case A, the murder was committed with a fork. We say 'in the absence of some special reason' because, in a certain context, the nature of the murder weapon *may* be legally relevant. Everything depends on the particular facts of Case A and Case B, viewed in relation to the legal context in which they are considered.

Take the following example, made well known by Lord Denning's famous discussion of it in his book, *The Discipline of Law*.[12] In Case A, an Act of Parliament provided that the validity of a compulsory purchase order could not be challenged in any proceedings more than six weeks after the order had been made. A compulsory purchase order was made against X by a Council. X challenged it six years after it had been made, on the ground that it had been made in bad faith. The House of Lords held that he was not entitled to do so. The Act meant *exactly* what it said: see *Smith v East Elloe Rural District Council* [1956] AC 736.

In Case B, an Act of Parliament provided that a decision by a Commission 'shall not be called in question in any court of law'. The Commission rejected A's claim for compensation. A challenged the decision, on the ground that it was a nullity. The House of Lords held that it was entitled to do so. The Commission's decision was indeed a nullity: see *Anisminic v The Foreign Compensation Commission* [1969] 2 AC 147.

Although Case B did *not* overrule Case A, Lord Wilberforce distinguished Case A (see [1969] 2 AC 147, p 210G). Lord Reid did not regard Case A as binding on Case B ([1969] 2 AC 147, p 171A–B), as also did not Lord Pearce ([1969] 2 AC 147, p 200H).

In Case C, an Act of Parliament provided that the validity of a compulsory purchase order could not be challenged in any proceedings more than six weeks after the order had been made. A compulsory purchase order was made against Y by a government department. Y challenged it a year after it had been made, on the grounds that it had been made in bad faith and in breach of natural justice. The *Court of Appeal* held that he was *not* entitled to do so.

Why did the Court of Appeal choose Case A, distinguishing Case B from Case C? (See *R v Secretary of State for the Environment ex p Ostler* [1977] QB 122.)

The Court of Appeal distinguished Case B from Case C, Case C being the case it was dealing with, on the following bases:

Lord Denning MR: (i) In Case B, the Act ousted the court's jurisdiction altogether but not in Case A (see [1977] 1 QB 122, p 135C); (ii) in Case B, the determination was a

---

12 Denning (Lord), *The Discipline of Law*, 1979, London: Butterworths, pp 108–09. The discussion in the text is adapted from the discussion in Bailey, SH and Gunn, MJ, *The Modern English Legal System*, 3rd edn, 1996, London: Sweet & Maxwell, pp 448–49.

judicial one, whereas in Case A, it was an administrative one (see [1977] 1 QB 122, p 135D–E); (iii) in Case B, the actual decision was under consideration, whereas in Case A it was the process by which it had been reached (see [1977] 1 QB 122, p 135F); and (iv) in Case C, the decision challenged was voidable, not void (see [1977] 1 QB 122, p 135G–H).

Goff LJ: (i) in Case B, the determination was a judicial one, whereas in Case A, it was an executive one (see [1977] 1 QB 122, p 138D–F); (ii) [see the answer to Question 88], the *ratio* in Case B was dealing simply with a question of jurisdiction, not bad faith (see [1977] 1 QB 122, pp 138H–39A) – his Lordship realised there were difficulties with this reasoning.

As mentioned above, Lord Denning MR later regretted, in *The Discipline of Law*, pp 108–09, basis (ii) of his distinction.

These three cases are a very striking illustration of the principles discussed in the answer to this question and the answer to Question 89. Whatever Lord Denning thinks of his own reasoning, the bases of his distinguishing one case from another are very clearly laid out in his Lordship's judgment indeed. Not all judges are as clear as this, obviously. You will need to distinguish one case from another *on its facts* where the doctrine of *stare decisis* means that it is otherwise binding on the moot court, and it is not possible to distinguish the two cases in law (see the answer to Question 88). We suggest that the need to distinguish one case from another on its facts is, together with the need to distinguish one case from another in law, one of the few situations in which, as Respondent in a moot, you should consider dealing with the Appellant's submissions before proceeding with your own submissions (see the answer to Question 15).

90   What is the distinction between a judge's finding of fact and his or her decision on the law?

The distinction is important in a number of mooting contexts. First, the grounds of appeal in moot problems must deal exclusively with areas of doubt in the *law* (see the answers to Questions 1 and 2). Secondly, when you are choosing your authorities, you need to bear in mind that only decisions of *law* may count as precedent for the purposes of supporting your submissions (see the answer to Question 20). You should briefly refer to the answers to those Questions in reading what follows. Obviously, we are not talking here about decisions of moot judges. Rather, we are talking about findings of fact and decisions of law in reported cases.

The question, therefore, is what the distinction is between a judge's finding of fact and his or her decision on law. As so often, generalisations are difficult. Moreover, the task of generalising is not helped by two factors. First, in reading an authority decided in, say, the Court of Appeal or the House of Lords, you may notice that the court is obviously straining to classify a point raised in the case as one of law rather than as one of fact. This is because the *statutory provision* under which an appeal has been made to that court will almost invariably have been restricted to questions of law. Secondly, the effect of a decision at first instance being one which *no person acting judicially and properly instructed as to the relevant law* could have reached, is to make its decision wrong as a matter of law rather than as a matter of fact. A decision will be such a decision, *inter alia*, if it is unsupported by any evidence.

Allowing for the effects of these two factors, certain tests are nonetheless helpful. Thus, if when reading an authority, you find that a judge has pronounced on something which is a question of 'degree', then that question will be one of fact. This test is of considerable use in analysing the decisions of the Special Commissioners of Income Tax in tax cases. In *Edwards v Bairstow and Harrison* [1956] AC 14, for example, the House of Lords had to decide whether a particular profit was a profit from an 'adventure in the nature of trade', so as to make it chargeable to income tax, in accordance with what is now s 18 of the Income and Corporation Taxes Act 1988. In that case, Lord Radcliffe said that the question was one of degree, '... in which the facts warrant a determination either way [that is, adventure in the nature of trade or no adventure in the nature of trade, and] ... it could not be said to be wrong to arrive at a conclusion either way'.[13] This question of degree is, of course, subject to the relevant finding being one which no person acting judicially and properly instructed as to the relevant law could have reached, in which case it will be wrong in law.

First, any finding by a court as to whether the conduct of an individual has matched up to a particular standard laid down by the law should be a finding of *fact* rather than a decision on law. Again, however, its status as a question of fact is subject to the qualification that the finding on whether the individual's conduct measured up to that standard was one which a person acting judicially and properly instructed as to the relevant law could have reached. If not, then whether a party acted reasonably or recklessly, and so on, becomes a question of *law*.

Secondly, if a layperson could have made the finding just as well as a trained lawyer, it will be a finding of fact. This is apparent from the following well known passage in the judgment of Denning LJ, as he then was, in *British Launderers' Association v Borough of Hendon*:[14]

> On this point it is important to distinguish between primary facts and the conclusions from them. Primary facts are facts which are observed by witnesses and proved by oral testimony or facts proved by the production of a thing itself, such as original documents. Their determination is essentially a question of fact for the tribunal of

---

13 [1956] AC 14, p 33.

14 [1949] 1 KB 462, pp 471–72.

fact, and the only question of law that can arise on them is whether there was any evidence to support the finding. The conclusions from primary facts are, however, inferences deduced by a process of reasoning from them. If, and in so far as, those conclusions can as well be drawn by a layman (properly instructed on the law) as by a lawyer, they are conclusions of fact for the tribunal of fact: and the only questions of law which can arise on them are whether there was a proper direction in point of law; and whether the conclusion is one which could reasonably be drawn from the primary facts ...

Again, however, the status of this finding as one of fact is subject to the qualification that the finding must be one which a person acting judicially and properly instructed as to the relevant law could have reached.

Finally, if the authority you are reading involved the application of ordinary words of the English language, the application of those words will be a finding of fact, subject to the same qualifications as for the three tests mentioned above. Thus, in criminal law, for example, in order for a person to be guilty of theft, he or she must dishonestly appropriate property belonging to another with the intention of permanently depriving that other of the property (see s 1(1) of the Theft Act 1968). Whether the person has dishonestly appropriated that property is generally a question of fact: see *R v Ghosh* [1982] QB 1053, since 'dishonestly' is an ordinary word of the English language.

91 What is the status of a judgment of the Divisional Court?

Let us take the Queen's Bench Division as our example: it is usually the case that a single High Court judge will preside over a hearing in the Queen's Bench Division of the High Court. In the Queen's Bench *Divisional Court*, however, the crucial distinction is that more than one judge will preside over the hearing of the matter. Consequently, a judge of the High Court sitting alone is bound by decisions of the Divisional Court: see *Huddersfield Police Authority v Watson* [1947] KB 842. Conversely, the Divisional Court will never consider itself to be bound by the judgment of a High Court judge sitting alone.

A Divisional Court is nevertheless bound by decisions of the Court of Appeal and House of Lords and, most interestingly, the Divisional Court will usually consider itself bound by its own decisions, in much the same way as the Court of Appeal generally considers itself to be bound by its own decisions: see *Younghusband v Luftig* [1949] 2 KB 354 (see the answer to Question 86). An exception may be where a Divisional Court is considering applications for judicial review. A later Divisional Court may, in such a case, consider itself bound much as a judge of the High Court would generally consider him or herself to be bound by previous decisions of individual judges of the High Court: *R v Greater Manchester Coroner ex p Tal* [1985] QB 67. This means that the

Divisional Court may refuse to follow a previous judgment of the Divisional Court if it is convinced that the earlier judgment was wrong.

92 Is a 'Jessel' better than a 'Kekewich'?

Obscure as it may seem, this is a question about judicial reputations. In other words, it is a question about the intellectual abilities of judges. This is because, by contrast with barristers' speeches which, according to Horace Rumpole, 'vanish quicker than Chinese dinners',[15] the doctrine of precedent means that not just the decisions, but also remarks of judges, made along the way can last for years (see the answer to Question 20). Moreover, it would not be an issue, were it not for the fact that the nature of mooting means that there may be two or more conflicting *obiter dicta* on one point of law, and you may wonder which of them will tend to be accorded more weight by the moot judge. Needless to say, you are not allowed to venture your own – or, indeed, anyone else's – opinion of a judge's reputation during a moot, unless it is an extremely favourable one. However, noted carefully, and with a degree of scepticism on your part, any information about how highly the abilities of a particular judge have stood or may still stand in the eyes of other lawyers can be very useful indeed. If the ability of a judge stands high in the estimation of other lawyers, the chances are that it will also do so in the eyes of the moot judge.

The 'Jessel' in the question refers, of course, to the 19th century Master of the Rolls, Sir George Jessel MR (1824–83, Master of the Rolls from 1873–83). His reputation as a judge, as a peerless legal reasoner, is great even today. One might go so far as to say that he is the judge's equivalent of Johann Sebastian Bach or Johannes Brahms in music – you cannot say anything credible against the ability of them or him! The 'Kekewich' refers to Kekewich J. Sir Arthur Kekewich (1832–1907) was a Chancery Division judge. He was known for the number of times his decisions were reversed. We are using Jessel MR and Kekewich J as contrasting examples. It may seem that we are being unnecessarily hard on the unfortunate Sir Arthur Kekewich. Even the *Dictionary of National Biography*, however, says that '... though he was occasionally avenged by the House of Lords, it was his lot to be reversed in the court of appeal to an extent which would have been disconcerting to a judge of less sanguine temperament'. You may have heard of – may even have heard – the operetta *Trial by Jury* by Gilbert and Sullivan, which was first performed in 1875 and which ridiculed the institutions of the Victorian legal system, by making fun of judges and barristers. Kekewich J was one of the many who had seen *Trial by Jury* and its writer, Sir WS Gilbert, who seems to have known Kekewich J personally, said that: 'He says he

---

15 Mortimer, J, 'Rumpole and the younger generation', in *The Best of Rumpole*, 1993, London: Viking, p 9.

likes all my plays except *Trial by Jury*. He seems to think that in holding the proceedings up to ridicule I was trenching on his prerogative.'[16]

By contrast with Kekewich J, you will know, if you have tried to read one of the famous judgments of Sir George Jessel, how his high reputation originated and has endured. Many of the famous equity cases from the 1870s and 1880s are decisions in which Jessel MR gave the only, or leading, judgment, for example, *Richards v Delbridge* (1874) LR 18 Eq 11, in which his Lordship enunciates the principle that the court cannot perfect an imperfect gift by construing it as a trust; *Re Hallett's Estate* (1880) 13 Ch D 696, in which he laid down the basic rules for the tracing of trust property; *Walsh v Lonsdale* (1882) 21 Ch D 9, in which he stated perhaps too widely the effect of an equitable lease after the Judicature Acts; and *Re Johnson* (1880) 15 Ch D 548, in which he discussed the exercise of a power of an executor to carry on the trade carried on by the deceased trader when the power was conferred by the deceased's will. What these cases have in common is the clarity of Jessel MR's explanation of the principles involved in the decision. In other words, when you read what he said, you understand it. Sir William Holdsworth, the eminent 19th century historian of English law, summarised Sir George Jessel's qualities thus: '... he was a profound equity lawyer with the mind of an acute juryman, who, by reason of that unique combination of qualities, was able to apply to the rules of equity the touchstone of common sense.'[17] Praise indeed! And it is all the more incredible that Jessel MR almost always gave judgment immediately, and was said to have reserved judgment on only two occasions, at the request of the judges sitting with him.[18]

Of course, it must be a truism that the judgments of judges vary widely in quality. The question is: how do you know whether the judgment you are reading is of a high standard? We would suggest the following approach. First, if as in the case of a 'Jessel', you read a judgment and find the discussion of the law particularly clear and concise, then this is a good indication of its quality. Lord Reid is often cited as an example of a judge capable of great clarity in this way. That said, a judge may be very highly regarded even though he is somewhat prolix and convoluted. We venture to suggest, with the utmost respect to his Lordship's memory, that the speeches of Lord Diplock might fall

---

16   Quoted in Ayre, L, *The Gilbert and Sullivan Companion*, 1986, London: WH Allen (although no source is given for Gilbert's comment). The learned judge in *Trial by Jury* is greeted with the rather pointed words: 'May each decree/As statute rank/And never be/Reversed *in banc* ... ' (See Gilbert, WS, 'Trial by jury', in Bradley, I (ed), *The Complete Annotated Gilbert and Sullivan*, 1996, Oxford: OUP, p 13, lines 98–101.) Maybe this was what Sir Arthur Kekewich found upsetting! It is rather ironic that his Lordship's judgment in one of the few surviving 'Kekewich cases' begins with the words: 'To prevent any misconception ...' (See *Fortescue v Lostwithiel and Fowey Railway* [1894] 3 Ch 621, p 636.)

17   Holdsworth, W (Sir), *A History of English Law*, in Goodhart, AL and Hanbury, HG (eds), 1965, London: Methuen, Vol 16, p 122.

18   *Ibid*, p 123.

into this category since, despite their invariably high quality,[19] they can be extremely long and indigestible.

Secondly, you may like to consult a very useful book by AWB Simpson called a *Biographical Dictionary of the Common Law*.[20] This contains short biographies of many English judges and eminent lawyers down through the ages, all arranged alphabetically. These short biographies usually contain some discussion of the qualities and other characteristics of the judges to which reference is being made. Opening the volume at random, for example, we find that, Walmesley J, a 16th century justice of Court of Common Pleas, is described as 'the most conservative judge in a conservative court [that is, the court of Common Pleas]' and his judgments as being 'characterised by well argued justifications of doctrines regarded by many of his contemporaries as outdated'.

Thirdly, you may chance upon a statement of the qualities of a judge by another judge. For example, discussing whether particular payments were revenue in nature or instalments of a capital sum for income tax purposes, Lord Wilberforce in *Inland Revenue Commissioners v Church Commissioners* [1977] AC 329, p 342H, said this about the judgments of Lord Greene MR:

> [The authorities] rest upon the basis that there are two alternatives, instalments of capital, or production of an annual payment, and that the task of the court is to find which it is. That this basis is a solid one is borne out by the fact that most of these decisions ... bear the authority, or contain the judgment of, Lord Greene – a hallmark of gold.

This type of effusion occurs comparatively rarely, it should be said!

Fourthly, in the case of very recent judgments only, you may consult *Legal Business*, a modern periodical read by the legal profession, which has, at least once, contained evaluations of today's judges by members of the profession.[21] Whichever of these routes you choose in ascertaining how high a judge stands or has stood in the eyes of other lawyers, be sceptical. Lord Hewart CJ, described extrajudicially by Lord Devlin as 'a horror',[22] was the judge who uttered that classic of English legal rhetoric in *R v Sussex Justices ex p McCarthy* [1924] 1 KB 256, p 259:

> ... a long line of cases shows that it is not merely of some importance but is of fundamental importance that justice should not only be done, but should manifestly and undoubtedly be seen to be done.

Make your own evaluation of the ability of a judge from his or her judgments – it may just be that you need to rely on a passage from a judgment of Kekewich J!

---

19 The judgment of Diplock LJ in the tax case of *London and Thames Haven Oil Wharves Ltd v Attwooll* [1967] Ch 772 has been described as 'limpidly clear' (see Morse, G, Williams, D and Salter, D (eds), *Davies: Principles of Tax Law*, 3rd edn, 1996, London: Sweet & Maxwell, p 79).

20 Simpson, AWB, *Biographical Dictionary of the Common Law*, 1984, London: Butterworths.

21 Eg, *The Good, the Bad and the Bench*, April 1994.

22 Devlin (Lord), *The Judge*, 1979, Oxford: OUP, p 24.

93 When is a change in the law a matter for Parliament and when is it a matter for the courts?

As a mooter, you could easily be asked this question by a moot judge. Both as Appellant and Respondent, your submissions may involve arguing for a change in the law. You will have to consider whether that change will be one which you could, as a real advocate, argue for. The question is one about the function of the appellate judges in the English legal system. Interestingly, it was a Scottish judge, Lord Reid, who once famously said:[23]

> We do not believe in fairy tales any more. So we must accept the fact that for better or worse judges do make law, and tackle the question how do they approach their task and how they should approach it.

This is in fact the question we also need to ask ourselves. What Lord Reid was challenging, in the address from which this quotation comes, was the *declaratory theory of English law*. This is the ancient theory that the function of the judges of the appellate courts in the English legal system is to apply a pre-existing legal principle to new factual situations, and not to create new legal principles. As Francis Bacon said: 'Judges ought to remember that their office is *jus dicare* and not *jus dare*; to interpret the law, and not to make law or give law.'[24] One of the main implications of the declaratory theory is that the creation of new legal principles is the function of Parliament. However, it is only a theory and, as we shall see, at various times, significant erosions to it have occurred. As we shall also see, the power of the judges to change the law can depend on the area of law with which they are concerned. It follows that there is no all-embracing definitive answer to this question. The best we can do is to suggest some general arguments in each direction.

In the discussion below, therefore, we have divided the answer to the question into two parts. The assumption is that what you, the mooter, have done – or need to do – is to ask the moot judge to make a change in the law, as part of your submissions on the relevant ground of appeal. What, then, are the arguments *for* this, and what are the arguments *against* it?

Arguments for

The arguments in favour of judges changing the law are necessarily mirrored, to some extent at least, in the arguments against it. As you are reading the points listed here, therefore, you should briefly refer to the *arguments against*, which are listed below:

---

23   Reid (Lord), 'The judge as lawmaker' (1972) 12 JSPTL 22.

24   Bacon, F, 'Of judicature', in Hawkins, M (ed), *Essays*, 2nd edn, 1973, London: JM Dent, p 162.

- No legal system can remain static. The law must change to reflect changes in social and economic conditions.

- The court cannot avoid making a decision in the case before it. If all relevant case law is distinguishable from that case and no statutory provision applies to it either, it is inevitable that the court must change the law.

- Changes in the law made by judges do not militate against certainty in the law (see below). Although there must be consistency between the case before the court and the case law on the subject matter of the case before the court, the decision in the case before the court may merely result in some *qualification* to the rules established in the previous case law.

- Even if certainty in the law is as important as the previous point suggests, its importance may vary according to the area of law under consideration in a particular case. In cases involving, for example, criminal law, certainty may be less important than in cases involving property or commercial law.

- Justice must be done between the parties to the case before the court.

- It is not the case that judges have no accurate way of researching the issues involved in the case before the court (see below). They have the means of judging the state of current opinion from many sources, including newspapers, textbooks, articles, and so on, as well as with the assistance of counsel's researches.

Arguments against

Conversely, the arguments *against* judges changing the law are mirrored, to some extent at least, in the arguments *in favour* of it. As you are reading the points listed under this heading, therefore, you should again briefly refer to the *arguments for*, which are listed above:

- The *declaratory theory of English law* (see, for example, *Launchbury v Morgans* [1973] AC 127). In his *Commentaries on the Laws of England*, Sir William Blackstone considered this to be demonstrated by the rationale under which previous decisions are overruled if found to be wrong:[25]

  For if it be found that the former [that is, the older] decision is manifestly absurd or unjust, it is declared not that such a sentence [that is, decision] was bad law, but that it was not law, that is, that it is not the established custom of the realm, as has been erroneously determined.

- Judges can only pronounce on the arguments put by the parties to a case.

---

25 Blackstone, W (Sir), *Commentaries on the Laws of England*, Coleridge, JT (ed), 16th edn, 1825, London: T Cadell & J Butterworth, Vol 1, p 70.

- If the judges make new law, the *power* to do so will be taken away from them. This was a reason for not changing the law advanced by Lord Scarman in *Duport Steels Ltd v Sirs* [1980] 1 All ER 529, p 521:[26]

  ... if people and Parliament come to think that the judicial power is to be confined by nothing other than the judge's sense of what is right (or, as Selden put it, by the length of the Chancellor's foot), confidence in the judicial system will be replaced by fear of it becoming uncertain and arbitrary in its application. Society will then be ready for Parliament to cut the power of the judges. Their power to do justice will become more restricted by law than it need be, or is today.

- The way in which litigation raises issues for the courts to adjudicate on are sometimes an unsuitable basis for changes in the law by judges. To take one example out of many, for the House of Lords in *Rhone v Stephens* [1994] 2 AC 310 to have changed the rule that the burden of covenants in freehold land does not run with the land would, because of the way in which the issue was raised by the case, have resulted in widespread interference with pre-existing property rights.[27]

- Changes in the law made by judges, by the very nature of the forum in which they make them, tend to violate the presumption against retrospective changes in the law (see *Rhone v Stephens*, above).

- Changes in the law made by judges militate against *certainty* in the law, since there must be consistency between the case before the court and previously decided cases.

- Although justice must be done between the parties to the case, on their appointment, judges are sworn to do *justice according to law*.

- Intervening parliamentary silence: 'I accept the submission of Mr Mitchell QC who appeared for the appellants, that if Parliament had though *R & O* ---s wrongly decided, it has had plenty of opportunity to put the matter right since then, but has declined to do so, for the obvious reason, in my v ⌐w, that it is plainly right.'

- On the basis of the case presented to the court, judges have no way of researching the wider issues involved in the case before the court.

---

26 *Op cit*, Bailey and Gunn, fn 12, p 256. In note 58, the authors point out that, 'when Roger Parker QC made a similar prediction in his submissions to the Court of Appeal in *Congreve v Home Office* [1976] QB 629, Lord Denning MR stated: "We trust that this was not said seriously, but only as a piece of advocate's li ⌐nce." Mr Parker subsequently apologised if anything he said sounded like a threat' (see (19 5) *The Times*, 6 and 9 December).

27 Snape, J, 'The burden of positive covenants' [1994] Conv ʻ77.

To some extent, at least, the points summarised here overlap with those dealt with in the answer to Question 74.

94 How do I know what a statute means?

Mr Haddock: ... The Act under which I am indicted does not apply in the House of Commons.

The Judge: Again, Mr Haddock – if it is not impertinent, why not?

Mr Haddock: My Lord, the Act contains elaborate provisions for the suppression of the sale and distribution of unlawful lottery tickets. If it is suspected that any premises are being used for the purpose of the commission of an offence under Part 2 of the Act, that is, in connexion with a lottery, a magistrate may grant a search warrant to any constable authorising him to enter those premises, if necessary by force, my Lord: s 27, my Lord. But obviously no magistrate would grant a warrant to enter by force and search the House of Commons for lottery tickets. In other words, the Act does not apply there: and therefore I cannot be convicted of an act committed there ...[28]

In the answer to this question, we can only draw the outlines of what is a vast area of case law and learning. For detailed consideration of the area, reference should be made to the works listed in the notes below. As you can see, whole books have been devoted to the question of what statutes mean, and we venture a few comments on those books at the end of the answer to this question. Having said all of this, however, we can give a pretty clear indication here of the issues with which you will be concerned when asking yourself this question in the context of mooting. We shall consider exclusively UK statutes. However, we comment also on EC legislation, again at the end of the answer to the question. We have derived enormous assistance from Bailey and Gunn's *The Modern English Legal System*, and we record our indebtedness here to that work. In addition, whenever tackling any moot problem involving statutory interpretation, we recommend most strongly that you consult the *All England Law Reports Annual Review*. As its title suggests, this is published annually, and the section headed 'Statute Law', by Francis Bennion, includes a detailed discussion of recent decisions involving statutory interpretation under helpful headings.

The effect of the Human Rights Act 1998 on the material contained in the answer to this question is yet to be felt. See, generally, Appendix 11 which contains some thoughts on how your mooting might take the Act into account.

The question of what a statute means is most likely to arise in mooting where you are making submissions on a ground of appeal in a moot problem which is designed to reflect the doubts which have been raised by legal commentators on

---

28 Herbert, AP, *Uncommon Law*, 4th edn, 1942, London: Methuen, pp 414–15.

whether the provisions of a particular statute might apply to a particular set of facts. The statute could be a real one or it could be one designed by the author of the moot problem to contain a similar form of wording to that of a statute which has caused doubts. The particular set of facts, the application of the provision to which is in doubt is, of course, the one in the moot problem itself. There is an example of this type of ground of appeal in Appendix 1. There, as you will see, the relevant statutory provision is the much debated s 30(1) of the Trustee Act 1925. In your submissions on the ground of appeal in such a moot problem, you will be arguing for a particular meaning to be given to the wording of the statutory provision and, in support of those submissions, you may have to invoke one or more of the *rules of interpretation or construction, aids to interpretation or presumptions* which are discussed below.

Aids to interpretation and presumptions

We begin with *aids to interpretation and presumptions*. We shall consider these fairly briefly since, given the nature of grounds of appeal in moot problems, *rules of interpretation or construction* are arguably of more importance in a mooting context than these two are. Any of the works referred to in the footnotes to this question, and in the Bibliography, will contain a more detailed discussion of them.

Aids to interpretation

Aids to interpretation of a statute fall into three categories: *internal aids to interpretation, external aids to interpretation* and *rules of language*. Each of these three categories has a somewhat mystical ring but, briefly, they are as follows.

Internal aids to interpretation are those found within the statute under consideration itself. The most obvious *internal aid* to interpretation is a definitions section in the statute (see, for example, s 205 of the Law of Property Act 1925 or s 832 of the Income and Corporation Taxes Act 1988). Other, less obvious, internal aids to interpretation include the *long title* of the statute and its *short title*. You may wonder what the difference is between the two. All modern statutes have a similar format,[29] and the long title and the short title appear at the top, short title first. One example would be the statute 1990 Chapter 1, a taxation statute. Its short title is 'The Capital Allowances Act 1990'. Its long title is 'An Act to consolidate certain enactments relating to capital allowances'.

Another example would be the statute 1996 Chapter 47, a property statute. Its short title is 'The Trusts of Land and Appointment of Trustees Act 1996'. Its long title is:

---

29   *Op cit*, Bailey and Gunn, fn 12, pp 280–85.

An Act to make new provision about trusts of land including provision phasing out the Settled Land Act 1925, abolishing the doctrine of conversion and otherwise amending the law about trusts for sale of land; to amend the law about the appointment and retirement of trustees of any trust; and for connected purposes [24 July 1996].

The long title is an aid to interpretation (see *Fielding v Morley Corporation* [1899] 1 Ch 34; *Black-Clawson International Ltd v Papierwerke Waldhof Aschaffenburg AG* [1975] AC 591, p 647). The short title should not generally be so used (see *Vacher & Sons Ltd v London Society of Compositors* [1913] AC 107, *per* Lord Moulton, p 128).[30]

Other items capable of qualifying as internal aids to interpretation are: (a) the preamble (see *Attorney General v Prince Ernest Augustus of Hanover* [1957] AC 436, p 467, *per* Lord Normand); and (b) headings, marginal – or side – notes and punctuation (see *Director of Public Prosecutions v Schildkamp* [1971] AC 1, p 10, *per* Lord Reid (headings)); *Stephens v Cuckfield Rural District Council* [1960] 2 QB 372 (side notes); *Tudor Grange Holdings v Citibank NA* [1992] Ch 53 (side notes); *Hanlon v The Law Society* [1981] AC 124, p 198, *per* Lord Lowry (punctuation).

The most obvious *external aid* to interpretation is perhaps that of parliamentary materials, especially, perhaps, *Hansard*. (The term 'parliamentary materials' covers drafts of Bills, reports, and so on.) The general rule, in *Davis v Johnson* [1979] AC 264, is that a court may not interpret statutes by reference to parliamentary materials. However, this rule was relaxed in *Pepper (Inspector of Taxes) v Hart* [1993] AC 593,[31] where the House of Lords (consisting of *seven* Law Lords, no less) held that, provided the statute and the parliamentary materials fulfilled the conditions set out below, statutory materials *could* be referred to in the interpretation of a statute. The conditions under which parliamentary material could be referred to, as laid down by Lord Browne-Wilkinson, were as follows:

> I therefore reach the conclusion, subject to any question of parliamentary privilege, that the exclusionary rule [that is, the general rule in *Davis v Johnson*] should be relaxed so as to permit reference to parliamentary materials where: (a) legislation is ambiguous or obscure, or leads to an absurdity; (b) the material relied upon consists of one or more statements by a minister or other promoter of the Bill together if necessary with such other parliamentary material as is necessary to understand such statements and their effect; (c) the statements relied upon are clear.
>
> Further than this, I would not at present go.[32]

---

30 But see Bailey and Gunn, *op cit*, fn 12, p 375, notes 90 and 91.

31 [1993] AC 593, p 640C.

32 See now also *Practice Direction for the Court of Appeal, Civil Division* [1999] 2 All ER 490, pp 521h–22c (para 10.2).

Reference to parliamentary material was denied in the tax case of *Inland Revenue Commissioners v Willoughby* [1995] STC 143.

Other *external aids to interpretation* are: related statutes on the same subject matter as that under consideration (*Attorney General v Prince Ernest Augustus of Hanover*, above); certain statutory antecedents to the provision under consideration (*Beswick v Beswick* [1968] AC 58); considering the historical setting of the statutory provision under consideration (see *Chandler v Director of Public Prosecutions* [1964] AC 763, p 791, *per* Lord Reid); referring to dictionaries (see *Eglen (Inspector of Taxes) v Butcher* [1988] STC 782); referring to textbooks (see *Re Castioni* [1891] 1 QB 149); and usage or practice prior to the passing of the statute under consideration, subject to significant caveats (see *United Dominions Trust Ltd v Kirkwood* [1966] 2 QB 431; *Campbell College Belfast (Governors) v Commissioners of Valuation for Northern Ireland* [1964] 1 WLR 912).

Finally, among aids to interpretation, are *rules of language*. Sensibly enough for rules of the English language, their names are tastefully rendered in Latin. they include *noscitur a sociis* (see Appendix 8); *ejusdem generis* (see the answer to Question 36); and *expressio unius est exclusio alterius* (see, again, Appendix 8).

Presumptions

The reader may fast be gaining the impression that the answer to this Question is attaining the complexity of a medieval science! Nonetheless, besides presumptions of general application, such as the one that a person is to be presumed innocent until proven guilty (see, for example, *Woolmington v Director of Public Prosecutions* [1935] AC 462, pp 481–82, *per* Viscount Sankey LC), there is a non-exhaustive list of presumptions which will be applied in cases of doubt, unless the contrary is stated with special clarity.

These presumptions include the following: the presumption that the Crown is not affected by a statute (see *British Broadcasting Corporation v Johns* [1965] Ch 32, p 78, *per* Diplock LJ); the presumption that a retrospective operation is not to be given to a statute (see *Re Athlumney* [1898] 2 QB 547, pp 551–52, *per* RS Wright J, but see *L'Office Cherifien des Phosphates v Yamashita-Shinnihon Steamship Co Ltd* [1994] 1 AC 486, pp 524–25, *per* Lord Mustill); the presumption where there is ambiguity that '... the legislature does not intend to limit vested rights further than clearly appears from the enactment' (see *Re Metropolitan Film Studios Application* [1962] 1 WLR 1315, p 1323, *per* Ungoed-Thomas J; *Secretary of State for Defence v Guardian Newspapers Ltd* [1985] AC 339); the somewhat controversial presumption that the statute does not change the common law (see *Black-Clawson International Ltd v Papierwerke Waldhof-Aschaffenburg AG* [1975] AC 591, p 614, *per* Lord Reid, and see *Beswick v Beswick*, where the House of Lords refused to hold that s 56 of the Law of Property Act 1956 had abolished privity of contract); the presumption that Parliament is not ousting the jurisdiction of the courts, so important to the development of administrative law (see *Anisminic Ltd v Foreign*

Compensation Commission [1969] 2 AC 147; *R v Secretary of State for the Environment ex p Ostler* [1977] QB 122 (see answer to Question 89)); and the presumption that, if a statute imposes penalties, and two reasonable interpretations of it are possible, the more lenient one will be the one to which effect is given (see *Tuck & Sons v Priester* (1887) 19 QBD 629, p 638, *per* Lord Esher).[33]

Rules of interpretation or construction

So much for *aids to interpretation and presumptions*. We mentioned above that, given the nature of grounds of appeal in moot problems, *rules of interpretation or construction* are arguably of more importance in a mooting context.

Over a period of four centuries or so, the courts have evolved the following rules: the *Literal Rule* (also referred to as 'the Ordinary Meaning Approach'), the *Golden Rule*, the *Mischief Rule* and the *Unified Approach*. We discuss each of these in turn.

The Literal Rule

The classic articulation of this rule was in the *Sussex Peerage Case* (1844) 11 Cl & Fin 85. The case seemed to indicate that the rule applied unless the provision under consideration was ambiguous, in which case the *Mischief Rule* was to be applied. *Per* Tindal CJ, p 143:

> My Lords, the only rule for the construction of Acts of Parliament is, that they should be construed according to the intent of the Parliament which passed the Act. If the words of the statute are in themselves precise and unambiguous, then no more can be necessary than to expound those words in their natural and ordinary sense. The words themselves alone do, in such a case, best declare the intention of the lawgiver. But if any doubt arises from the terms employed by the Legislature, it has always been held a safe means of collecting the intention, to call in aid the ground and cause of making the statute, and to have recourse to the preamble, which, according to Chief Justice Dyer ... is 'a key to open the minds of the makers of the Act, and the mischiefs which they intend to redress'.

The Literal Rule was strongly favoured by Victorian judges, who would apply it regardless of whether the result of so doing was to produce an unjust result. Although occasionally used by appellate courts in recent times (see *Puhlhofer v Hillingdon London Borough Council* [1986] AC 484), it is open to criticism in at least three respects: (a) it takes no account of whether the result of applying it is unjust; (b) its application is an abdication of judicial responsibility, since it implies too restricted a view of the judicial function; and (c) the concept of the 'natural and ordinary sense of a word' is a meaningless one.

33　This is not an exhaustive list. *Op cit*, Bailey and Gunn, fn 12, pp 379–94.

The Mischief Rule

The classic articulation of this rule was in *Heydon's Case* (1584) 3 Co Rep 7a. The *Mischief Rule* is a more liberal approach to the interpretation of statutory provisions than the Literal Rule, in the sense that it acknowledges a wider view of the judicial function. It is, perhaps, no accident that it dates from an earlier period in the constitutional history of this country. The Mischief Rule enables a judge to consider the common law prior to the statute under consideration, and the common law 'mischief' for which the statute under consideration was intended to be a remedy. The judge may then construe the statute in order to advance the remedy and suppress the mischief. In *Heydon's Case*, Sir Edward Coke tells us, the Barons of the Exchequer resolved as follows:

> ... that for the sure and true interpretation of all statutes in general (be they penal or beneficial, restrictive or enlarging of the common law), four things are to be discerned and considered:
>
> 1st What was the common law before the making of the Act?
>
> 2nd What was the mischief and defect for which the common law did not provide?
>
> 3rd What remedy the Parliament hath resolved and appointed to cure the disease of the commonwealth?
>
> 4th The true reason of the remedy; and then the office of all the judges is always to make such construction as shall suppress the mischief, and advance the remedy, and to suppress subtle inventions and evasions for continuance of the mischief, and *pro privato commodo*, and to add force and life to the cure and remedy, according to the true intent of the makers of the Act, *pro bono publico*?

Couched in archaic language and very old though it is, the Mischief Rule has commended itself to judges in recent times. In modern guise, it is spoken of as the *purposive approach* to statutory interpretation. Following *Pepper (Inspector of Taxes) v Hart*, see above, it is now possible for judges to consult parliamentary materials, in using the Mischief Rule or purposive approach, subject to the closely worded conditions set out by the Law Lords in that case.

The Golden Rule

The original articulation of this rule was in *Grey v Pearson* (1857) 6 HL Cas 61. The *Golden Rule* is again a more liberal approach to the interpretation of statutory provisions than the Literal Rule. However, it was not clear whether, in order for a judge to be able to use it, the words in the provision under consideration had to be *ambiguous* or whether it could be used where there was *no ambiguity* but, nevertheless, the ordinary meaning of the words produced absurdity. In *Grey v Pearson*, Lord Wensleydale said ((1857) 6 HL Cas 61, p 106):

> I have been long and deeply impressed with the wisdom of the rule, now, I believe, universally adopted, at least in the Courts of Law in Westminster Hall, that in construing wills and indeed statutes, and all written instruments, the grammatical and ordinary sense of the words is to be adhered to, unless that would lead to some

absurdity, or some repugnance or inconsistency with the rest of the instrument, in which case the grammatical and ordinary sense of the words may be modified, so as to avoid that absurdity and inconsistency, but no farther.

A well known example of judges using the Golden Rule to interpret statutory provisions occurs in the case of *Adler v George* [1964] 2 QB 7. In that case, Lord Parker CJ, who gave the only judgment of the Divisional Court of the Queen's Bench Division, used the Golden Rule to avoid what he ventured to think was an 'absurd' result, by interpreting s 3 of the Official Secrets Act 1920 as though it contained two extra words, 'in or'. It is worth comparing the approach taken by Lord Parker CJ in this case with the approach taken by him in the famous contract law case of *Fisher v Bell* [1961] 1 QB 394.

The Unified Approach

This approach was suggested, not by a judge, but by a leading academic lawyer, Sir Rupert Cross, in his book *Statutory Interpretation*.[34] The *Unified Approach* consists of four rules, as amended by subsequent editors of the book (text in square brackets):

1   The judge must give effect to the [grammatical and] ordinary or, where appropriate, the technical meaning of words in the general context of the statute; he must also determine the extent of general words with reference to that context.

2   If the judge considers that the application of the words in their [grammatical and] ordinary sense would produce [a result which is contrary to the purpose of the statute], he may apply them in any secondary meaning which they are capable of bearing.

3   The judge may read in words which he considers to be necessarily implied by words which are already in the statute and he has a limited power to add to, alter or ignore statutory words in order to prevent a provision from being unintelligible or absurd or totally unreasonable, unworkable, or totally irreconcilable with the rest of the statute.

4   In applying the above rules the judge may resort to [certain] aids to construction and presumptions ...

It is increasingly difficult to see which, if any, of the Literal Rule, the Mischief Rule and the Golden Rule judges are using today. Certainly, the approach of most judges would seem to correspond most closely to the purposive approach implied by the Mischief Rule.

As we mentioned at the beginning of the answer to this question, whole books have been devoted to the question of what statutes mean. Pre-eminent are Sir Rupert Cross's *Statutory Interpretation*, referred to above, as well as FAR

---

34   Cross, R (Sir), *Statutory Interpretation*, Bell, JS and Engle, G (Sir) (eds), 1995, London: Butterworths.

Bennion's *Statute Law*.[35] However, there is also an excellent detailed discussion of all of the issues which we have discussed in the answer to this question – and more – in Bailey and Gunn, *The Modern English Legal System*, Chapter 6.[36] You will find each of these texts extremely useful in preparing submissions on grounds of appeal dealing with matters of statutory interpretation.

Everything we have said so far has related to the interpretation of UK statutes. It is necessary to comment briefly on EC legislation before leaving this question. The substance and form of EC legislation is quite different from the substance and form of UK legislation. As such, it needs to be interpreted by The Court of Justice of the European Communities, as well as by the UK courts. As we emphasise throughout this Guide, a moot could be set in the European Court just as easily as in, say, the Court of Appeal or the House of Lords. So far as the European Court is concerned, it employs a *purposive or teleological* interpretation of EC legislation and, in doing so, often uses so called 'general principles of law'. The use of the general principles of law is justified by it by reference to the fact that the principles are apparent from the laws of the Member States. Thus, for example, there are principles of *equality, audi alterem partem, legal certainty, legitimate expectation* and *proportionality*. It is interesting to note that, in *R v Secretary of State for the Home Department ex p Brind* [1991] AC 696, the House of Lords declined to hold that the principle of proportionality was part of the domestic law of the UK.

So far as UK courts interpreting EC law are concerned, the approach to be taken was stated in *Bulmer v Bollinger* [1974] Ch 401, by Lord Denning MR:[37]

... English courts must follow the same principles as [The Court of Justice of the European Communities] ... No longer must they examine the words in meticulous detail. No longer must they argue about the precise grammatical sense. They must look to the purpose or intent. To quote the words of the European Court in the *Da Costa* case [see [1963] CMLR 224, p 237] they must deduce 'from the wording and the spirit of the treaty the meaning of the community rules'. They must not confine themselves to the English text. They must consider, if need be, all the authentic texts ... They must divine the spirit of the treaty and gain inspiration from it. If they find a gap, they must fill it as best they can. They must do what the framers of the instrument would have done if they had thought about it. So we must do the same. Those are the principles, as I understand it, on which the European Court acts.

---

35 Bennion, FAR, *Bennion on Statute Law*, 3rd edn, 1990, London: Longman.

36 *Op cit*, Bailey and Gunn, fn 12, Chapter 6, note 2.

37 [1974] Ch 401, pp 425–26. See the discussion of this area in Bailey and Gunn, *op cit*, fn 12, pp 404–12.

95   What are inter-university competitive moots?

Inter-university competitive moots are moots in which students represent their universities against students from other universities. The following are the more established competitions in which UK universities are eligible to compete. Full details of the various organisers of these competitions are to be found in the answer to Question 96.

The English-Speaking Union National Mooting Competition

This competition is based on the law common to England, Wales and Scotland and virtually all UK law schools take part. In the 1996–97 academic year, for instance, there were a total of 65 law schools competing. The competition is run on a knock-out basis and for each round there is a different moot problem. There are two persons per team appearing as Lead Appellant and Junior Appellant, with the home side always acting for the Appellants and the away side always acting for the Respondents.

The Philip C Jessup International Law Moot Court Competition

This competition is based on public international law and is competed for by law schools throughout the world. (Fourty-five countries entered for the 1997 Jessup Moot.) Full details of the competition are available on the internet (see the answer to Question 96).

The competition has a national round and the winners of the national round represent their countries in the world finals which are usually held in Washington, DC.

Members of the four person team take the roles of advocates appearing in a hypothetical case involving issues of public international law before the International Court of Justice. Two of the team appear for the applicant country and the other two members of the team appear for the respondent country. The rules of the Jessup Moot require skeleton arguments (called *memorials*) to be submitted in addition to the presentation of arguments.

The Telders International Law Moot Court Competition

This is a public international law moot organised by the University of Leiden, in the Netherlands, on virtually identical lines to the Jessup Moot, the main difference being that there is an English round, rather than a UK round (thus,

Scotland is separately represented) and only undergraduates are eligible to compete. The finals take place in the International Court of Justice in the Peace Palace in The Hague, before actual judges of the International Court of Justice.

The European Law Moot Court Competition

The European Law Moot Court Competition is based on European Union law and, thus, the hypothetical court in which the moot is held is the European Court of Justice. It is run by the University of Stockholm and requires each team to submit full written pleadings on behalf of the Appellant and Respondent as well as a written brief on behalf of the Advocate General. The 1997 regional finals took place in Brussels, Copenhagen, Vienna and Warsaw and the all-European final is held in the European Court of Justice in Luxembourg, before real judges of that court.

Extra marks are awarded to mooters that have their skeleton arguments in one European language and plead orally in another European language.

The United Kingdom Environmental Law Association Prize Moot

This is an environmental law moot competition run by the UK Environmental Law Association (UKELA). There are two competitions: one for undergraduates and one for postgraduates, who have yet to complete their professional training (their pupillage if they are at the Bar, their training contract if they are to be solicitors). The finalists are chosen on the basis of their written skeleton arguments and the finals (in which oral presentations are made to defend the written skeleton arguments) are held at Lincoln's Inn (see the answer to Question 4 for the history of mooting in the Inns of Court). The presiding judge at the finals since 1994 has been Lord Slynn of Hadley.

96 How do I acquire more detail on inter-university competitive moots?

We set out some relevant contact details below. These details, correct at the time of going to press, may of course differ from year to year.

The English-Speaking Union National Mooting Competition

Jonathan Hills
The English-Speaking Union
Dartmouth House
37 Charles Street
London W1X 8AB

Tel: 020 7493 3328
Fax: 020 7495 6108
Email: centre@esu.org
Internet: http://www.esu.org

(There is also a National Adjudicator, appointed annually, who is usually a member of the faculty of a UK university law school.)

The Philip C Jessup International Law Moot Court Competition

Jessup Administrator
2223 Massachusetts Avenue, NW
Washington, DC
20008-2864
USA

Tel: (001) 202 939 6030
Fax: (001) 202 265 0386
Email: ilsaed@universe.digex.net

The full details of the Jessup Moot may be downloaded from the internet. The materials, which includes the moot problem and the rules, are posted at http://www.ilsa.org.

The European Law Moot Court Competition

European Law Moot Court Society
c/o Law Faculty, University of Copenhagen
Studiestraede 6
1455 Copenhagen K
Denmark

Tel: (0045) 35 32 31 94
Fax: (0045) 35 32 40 00
Email: ot@jur.ku.dk
Internet: http://www.elmc.org

Concours Europeen des Droits de L'Homme Rene Cassin

(This competition, dating from 1984, is conducted entirely in French.)

Association Juris Ludi
17 rue de la Haute Montee 67000
Strasbourg
France

Tel: (0033) 3 88 37 18 78
Fax: (0033) 3 88 52 19 75
Email: jurisludi@mail.sdv.fr
    or   juris@concourscassin.org

The United Kingdom Environmental Law Association Prize Moot

Gregory Jones, Master of the Moot
2 Harcourt Buildings
Temple
London EC4Y 9DB

Tel: 020 7353 8415
Fax: 020 7353 7622

The full details of the UKELA Prize Moot are published in the December edition of the *United Kingdom Environmental Law Association Law Journal*. The details include the following year's moot problem and the rules of the competition.

Willem C Vis International Commercial Arbitration Moot

Professor Eric E Bergsten
Schimmelgasse 16/14
A-1030 Vienna
Austria

Tel: (0043) 1 713 5408
Fax: (0043) 1 713 5408
Email: ebergsten@law.pace.edu
    or   eric.bergsten@chello.at

Internet: http://www.cisg.law.pace.edu/cisg/moot

The moot involves 'a dispute arising out of a contract of sale between two countries that are party to the United Nations Convention on Contracts for the International Sale of Goods'.

97   Do I need to be a specialist to participate in an inter-university competitive moot?

The names of the various mooting competitions may suggest that you need to be a specialist in one of the areas of law covered by them, for example, public international law, EC law, and so on. In principle, this should not be the case. As a mooter, you should be able to argue any issue of doubt in the law by researching the arguments on it thoroughly. This, after all, replicates fairly closely one aspect of the work of any advocate.

Having said this, however, there may be rules of selection of mooters in your law school which require you to be studying one of the subject areas covered by the mooting competitions before you are eligible for selection.

98 How do I take part in inter-university moots?

There is a very wide range of practice in respect of how students are chosen to take part in competitive mooting.

Some universities regard competing in such moots as an extra-curricular activity to be arranged by the student mooters themselves or by their law society. Other universities take the view that students are officially representing their universities when they take part in such competitive moots and accordingly select the students on the basis of their performances in internal moots and their general academic ability. Indeed some universities, such as The Nottingham Trent University, award academic credits to students who take part in those inter-university moots which require written pleadings. These credits count towards the students' final degree classification.

Where students moot competitively on their own initiative, they will ordinarily be invited to compete by election by their student law society or by the drawing of lots. Where students moot competitively as official representatives of their university, it is far more likely that they will be selected according to the marks that they have already achieved in moots held within their law school. It may also be that the general level of academic performance of the various candidates for mooting competitively will be a factor in deciding whether they are eligible to moot competitively or not.

99 If I am organising a moot, where can I get a moot problem from and do I need permission to use it?

There are a number of prerequisites to a good moot problem. First, each moot point (usually expressed in the form of a ground of appeal) should be chosen so as to raise arguments of roughly equal strength on both sides. Secondly, every moot point (there are usually two in each moot) should arise naturally from the same hypothetical fact situation. Thirdly, it is ideal to moot issues which have a certain topicality. It may be that a particular issue is the subject of current academic debate, popular news items or a law commission working paper or report. Such topicality can only serve to enhance the mooting exercise. In view of the constantly changing nature of law it is not surprising, therefore, that moots generally have a short shelf-life. So, where will you find a good moot problem?

In view of our preceding description of the ideal moot problem it follows that our best advice is to draft your own. If you are a member of the academic staff at a law school, you will no doubt have a particular expertise and will be able to draft a challenging moot arising from issues of debate within your field. If you are a student, you may find the exercise rather more challenging, but you have the advantage of studying at the 'cutting edge' of a number of different legal disciplines at the same time. There is no reason to suppose that you will not be able to draft a stimulating and workable moot problem. At The Nottingham Trent University, small groups of final year students are required to draft a moot problem as part of their course. The exercise is academically challenging, and tests research and drafting skills (see, by way of illustration, the moot problem reproduced as Appendix 3). So, if you can, do attempt to draft a topical moot problem. Ideally, a number of students at your law school will be keen to test out each others' moot problems in a moot court setting.

If you do decide to draft a moot problem, the following approach may simplify your task. First, choose a topic, the facts or law of which you find interesting – genuine intellectual curiosity is the best fuel for any sort of research. Secondly, search textbooks for areas where the author admits that the law is currently unresolved and doubtful, and where it is not clear what the courts will next decide when they come to consider the issues. The author might refer you to cases decided in the House of Lords or Court of Appeal in which the judges were not unanimous in their opinions on the law. Thirdly, to establish the facts of your moot problem choose a decided case in the relevant area and change the facts so as to give rise to some genuine doubt as to whether the decided case can be said to cover the facts of the moot problem. Be careful, however. In a good moot problem, the facts are crystal clear. It is only the law relating to those clear facts which should be in doubt. Fourthly, set out a brief judgment on the facts of the case, set the judgment in a lower court, then draft two grounds of appeal against that judgment. The grounds of appeal should be tightly drafted so as to raise only the narrow issues of law, principle, and policy which you believe remain unresolved at the present time. Fifthly, choose a setting for the moot. Sometimes the House of Lords is not as appropriate a setting as the Court of Appeal for mooting questions of 'black letter' law, precisely because the House will depart from its own previous decisions where there is good reason to do so (see the answer to Question 86); it does, however, make an excellent forum for arguing conflicting policy considerations and issues of principle. However, where there is an existing House of Lords authority relating to the moot point, it may be that you will have no realistic debate on the law unless you set the moot in the House of Lords. Finally, a good technique for narrowing down the range of legitimate arguments in a moot is to introduce concessions into the wording of your moot problem. So, for example, if you want the mooters to discuss self-defence, but do not wish them to discuss provocation, simply add the words: 'The defendant conceded that he or she had not been provoked.'

If you do not have the time or the inclination to draft your own moot problem you should approach the 'master' or 'mistress' of moots at your institution. ('Master of Moots' or 'Master of the Moot' is the title traditionally used exclusively at the Inns of Court, and now more widely used, to describe the staff or student member of the law school who has special responsibility for mooting.) If you make a polite request, your 'master' or 'mistress' of moots will probably be able and pleased to provide you with a moot problem for your use. They will generally have a collection of tried and tested moots left over from previous years' competitive mooting. Take one gratefully, but make sure that you choose one which has not been rendered unmootable by recent developments in the law.

If nobody at your law school admits to having responsibility for mooting, and if those who do have responsibility are unable or unwilling to assist you, do not give up just yet in your quest for a moot problem. You are welcome to moot any of the moot problems included in Appendices 2 and 3. There are, in addition, books available which contain a wide selection of moot problems. *The Observer Book of Moots* [38] is now out of print but there may be a copy in your law library. Before using a moot from that collection, however, check that it has not become obsolete and check that the terminology used (for example, 'claimant' for 'plaintiff') complies with recent developments in the law (for example, the Civil Procedure Rules 1998). The more recent *Blackstone's Book of Moots* [39] also contains a wide range of moot problems covering a variety of areas of law. Before using a moot problem from these or other sources, check also that they are not subject to copyright restrictions on their use. In fact, the publishers of the various sources of moot problems usually expressly waive any copyright restrictions.

The moot problems for the Jessup and Telders moots are, however, copyright protected. Having said that, permission is granted to any university to use them for internal moots, in order to assist the election of teams to take part.

100 How do I judge a moot?

All the questions which we have answered so far have been questions which, as we said in our preface, are ones which *students* have asked, might ask, or ought to ask, about mooting. It might seem rather odd to finish up with this question, therefore. This question might be asked by a *postgraduate* law student who has been asked to judge a moot for the first time. It is, however, far more likely to be

---

38 Dobson, P and Fitzpatrick, B (eds), *The Observer Book of Moots*, 1986, London: Sweet & Maxwell.

39 Kaye, T and Townley, L, *Blackstone Book of Moots*, 1996, London: Blackstone.

asked by the member of staff or the legal practitioner who has been asked to sit as a moot judge for the first time. Who knows, perhaps even real judges need some guidance in sitting in the capacity of a moot judge for the first time!

The first rule to remember is that you, no less than the mooters, must be completely familiar with the authorities which both moot teams intend to cite. This almost goes without saying. Having said this, however, it is not necessary to be a specialist in the area of law covered by the moot problem. Lawyers speak the language of lawyers and, in principle, a non-specialist should be able to appreciate the issues in an area of law outside his or her specialism.

The second rule to remember is that, as a moot judge, you are discharging a different function from a real judge. It is true that a moot judge has a judicial function, but the matters upon which he or she must adjudicate are different from those upon which a real judge must adjudicate. In addition, the mooters who appear before you are in a fundamentally different position from advocates in a real court. This is both because they are students and because there are no real life clients whose interests are represented by them. The reason why these points are important is that, unless you bear them in mind, your attitude towards and behaviour in the role of the moot judge will simply be a rather grotesque parody of the attitude and behaviour of some real judges. A real judge might choose to reject the arguments of counsel on both sides.[40] A moot judge will be discouraged from taking that approach.

The third rule to remember is that you must treat the moot as a game. Obviously, it is a highly formalised game, with clear rules relating even to matters of etiquette. Nonetheless, it is still a game. It follows from this that it is imperative to create a formal but relaxed and pleasant atmosphere in which the mooters can demonstrate their skills to the best advantage. In this, your role is very much a subsidiary one to the mooters. Thus, whilst you may by all means introduce a certain amount of humour into the proceedings, it should only be for the purpose of creating the formal but relaxed and pleasant atmosphere referred to above. You should resist the temptation to indulge in any behaviour – jibes, anecdotage, and so on – during the mooters' presentations which detracts from the mooters' opportunity to demonstrate their skills to their best advantage. Any form of judicial rudeness or intimidation is necessarily unacceptable.

The fourth rule to remember is that, whilst you should question the mooters thoroughly on the submissions made in the course of their presentations, you must not over-question them. This is, as is said, a matter of degree. The best general guide which the authors can offer, each of them being experienced moot judges, is

---

40 See *Rabin v Gerson Berger Association* [1986] 1 WLR 526, p 539, where Balcombe LJ held that, 'in a given case, the judge might speculate, and he might come to a conclusion different from that which counsel intended – which only means no more than this, that counsel, in a particular case, got it wrong ...'.

to confine your questions to complete propositions within the submissions made by the mooters. The pauses in what a mooter is saying will tend to fall naturally and, to some extent at least, invite questions at natural intervals. What you should avoid at all costs is the temptation to interrupt. Not only moot judges, but real judges also have been censured for this in the past. It was Francis Bacon who said, centuries ago, that 'Patience and gravity of hearing is an essential part of justice; and an over-speaking judge is no *well tuned cymbal*'.[41] Likewise, it was Lord Denning who, commenting on the resignation of Hallett J after the latter's censure by the Court of Appeal in *Jones v National Coal Board* [1957] 2 QB 55, said laconically:

> It was a poignant case; for [Hallett J] was able and intelligent – but he asked too many questions ... Let others take heed.[42]

The fifth rule is to remember that most moots – competitive or otherwise – have performance criteria, or criteria of assessment. Depending on the moot, you may be required to attach greater importance to the law than the moot (or vice versa: see the answer to Question 8). You should consider this carefully before going into the moot court. Make sure that the questions you do ask are in some way directed to eliciting information on the basis of which you can adjudicate on these criteria. The moot which you are judging will probably have its own criteria. If not, we have included as Appendices 6 and 7, two specimen Assessment Sheets. These are considered in detail in the answer to Question 8. If you have an opportunity of considering the mooters' presentations after the moot, as where a moot forms part of a course of legal study, complete the form of assessment which you use as quickly as possible after the mooters have made their presentations. It is a truism that a moot judgment delayed is a moot judgment denied.

We should also suggest a number of other non-exhaustive tips:

- First, look at the answers to the other questions in this book to see what exactly as a judge you will be looking for in the areas covered by them.

- Secondly, have a look at the courtroom before you judge the moot: you will find it uncomfortable, for instance, if the mooter making a presentation is so close to your desk that he or she can see you noting your comments on his or her moot presentation.

- Thirdly, make sure you take pen, paper and, if available, enough assessment sheets for all mooters, into the moot court with you.

---

41   *Op cit*, Bacon, fn 24, pp 162–63. See, also, Question 18, fn 42.

42   Denning (Lord), *The Due Process of Law*, 1980, London: Butterworths, p 62.

- Fourthly, dress soberly, to reflect the mode of dress adopted by the mooters (see the answer to Question 50).

- Finally, be aware of the passage of time, and take a watch into the moot. In principle, the time taken by you in questioning a mooter should not be taken into account in judging the length of his or her moot presentation and, although you may have the *clerk of the court* to assist you, make sure that the mooters' presentations do not overrun. The fact that a moot ends punctually is another important difference between a moot court and a real court (see the answer to Question 3)!

Appendix 1[1]

In the Court of Appeal
Re Porter's Will Trusts, Smithson et al v Dearing and Holmes

1.1 Daphne Porter died in 1990. Under the trusts of her will, she appointed an old friend, Nicholas Dearing, to be the sole executor and trustee of her personal estate. The estate comprised approximately £200,000 worth of shares in public limited companies. A clergyman by vocation, Nicholas Dearing professed little familiarity with matters of financial investment. Accordingly, he enlisted the assistance of a stockbroker, Mr Holmes, to advise him as to a prudent course of investment. On the broker's advice, Mr Dearing invested one-third of the trust fund in property development projects of a more or less speculative nature. Mr Dearing did not realise that investments of this type were unauthorised according to the terms of the trust instrument. Mr Holmes was aware that the investment was unauthorised and appears to have been motivated by a personal interest in the scheme.

1.2 Mr Dearing deposited the other two-thirds of the trust fund with the broker to be sold and reinvested in more profitable stock of a similar kind. In the event, the broker used the proceeds of sale of that part of the trust fund to feed his addiction to cocaine. Mr Dearing should have been suspicious when the broker failed to furnish details of the new investments at the appointed time. Instead, he naively accepted the broker's dishonest explanations for the delay. By the time Mr Dearing's suspicions were fully aroused, the broker had entirely exhausted two-thirds of the trust fund. To make matters worse, the speculative property investments were a complete failure, and that third of the fund was also lost.

1.3 The beneficiaries, Albert and Elizabeth Smithson, brought this action against the trustee for, *inter alia*, breach of trust in failing adequately to supervise that part of the fund which had been deposited with the stockbroker. They

---

1 This Appendix comprises a moot problem and the full transcript of the moot presentations of four mooters. It is not necessarily intended to epitomise mooting at its best, but you could certainly do worse than to try to emulate the clarity and composure of the mooters. We hope that you will read the transcript with a critical eye, marking with your pen any phrase you would have put differently, and any points you would have added or omitted. We hope, if nothing else, that a quick read through the transcript in advance of your next moot presentation will put you in a mooting frame of mind.

also sought to recover damages from the broker on the basis, *inter alia*, that he had committed the tort of procurement of a breach of trust in advising the trustee to invest in speculative property developments (applying the principle in *Lumley v Gye* (1853) 118 ER 749).

1.4   In the Chancery Division of the High Court of Justice, Risky J held that:

(a)   According to s 30(1) of the Trustee Act 1925, a trustee will not be liable for the defaults of any agent with whom trust moneys are deposited, unless the same happens through the trustee's own 'wilful default'. Following *Re Vickery* [1931] 1 Ch 572, it is clear that 'wilful default' must involve some conscious or deliberate wrongdoing; accordingly, Mr Dearing was not liable for losses caused through the defaults of Mr Holmes.[2]

(b)   The principle in *Lumley v Gye* has no application to the procurement of a breach of trust. Accordingly, Mr Holmes did not commit any such tort in advising the trustee to make the speculative investments.

2   The beneficiaries, Albert and Elizabeth Smithson, now appeal against the judgment of Risky J on the following grounds:

(a)   Where a trustee is merely impudent, he or she may nevertheless be liable to make good losses caused by the defaults of an agent with whom trust moneys have been deposited. It is not necessary that the trustee be shown to have consciously or deliberately breached his trust in order to be in 'wilful default' for the purposes of s 30(1) of the Trustee Act 1925.

(b)   It is possible for the agent of a trust to commit the tort of procurement of a breach of trust, and Mr Holmes committed such a tort when he advised Mr Dearing to make unauthorised investments (see the answer to Question 6).

3   [*In the typical undergraduate moot, there will be only one moot judge on the bench. For certain competitive moots, the number of judges in the moot court may be more realistic. Three Lord Justices of Appeal for a moot set in the Court of Appeal lends the exercise an air of authenticity. Five Law Lords for a moot set in the House of Lords is, however, an almost unheard of luxury. For the purposes of our example moot, we have only one Lord Justice of Appeal, Scales LJ. The authorities exchanged by the mooters, at the date and time set for the exchange, were as follows:*]

---

2   The reader may be interested to note that the Law Commission Consultation Paper, *Trustees' Powers and Duties* (No 146, 1997), considers academic and judicial reactions to *Re Vickery* at paras 4.39–4.49. A number of the recommendations made in the subsequent Law Commission Report, *Trustees' Powers and Duties* (No 260, 1999) appear, at the time of writing, in a Trustee Bill which had its first reading in the House of Lords on 20 January 2000.

4.1 For the *Lead Appellant: Re Briers* (1884) 26 Ch D 238; *Re City Equitable Fire Assurance Co* [1925] 1 Ch 407; *Bartlett v Barclays Bank (No 2)* [1980] Ch 515; *Speight v Gaunt* (1883) 22 Ch D 727.

4.2 For the *Junior Appellant: Royal Brunei Airlines Sdn Bhd v Tan Kok Ming* [1995] 3 WLR 64; *Law Debenture Corporation v Ural Caspian* [1993] 2 All ER 355; *Boulting v Association of Cinematograph, Television and Allied Technicians* [1963] 2 QB 606; *Prudential Assurance Co v Lorenz* (1971) 11 KIR 78.

4.3 For the *Lead Respondent: Re Trusts of Leeds City Brewery* [1925] Ch D 532; *Re Lucking's Will Trusts* [1968] 1 WLR 866; *Bartlett v Barclays Bank (No 2)* [1980] Ch 515.

4.4 For the *Junior Respondent: Royal Brunei Airlines Sdn Bhd v Tan Kok Ming* [1995] 3 WLR 64; *Metall und Rohstoff AG v Donaldson Lufkin and Jenrette Inc* [1990] 1 QB 391; *Barnes v Addy* (1874) 9 Ch App 244.

5 [*Before the moot judge enters the moot court, the four assembled mooters are seated. They rise as he enters. Upon reaching the bench, the judge bows his head to the mooters. They bow with him. As his Lordship sits, the mooters also sit. The* Lead Appellant *waits until the judge has indicated that he is ready to hear the submissions before standing.*]

6 *Scales LJ:*   [*Looking down at his papers*] Yes?

7.1 *Lead Appellant:*   [*Stands up, then leads in the case*] May it please your Lordship, my name is Miss Felicity Fowler and I appear in this case with my learned friend Mr Neil Wright for the Appellant. My learned friend Mr Amir Khan appears for the Respondent, Mr Dearing, and my learned friend Miss Sally James appears for the Respondent, Mr Holmes.

7.2 *Scales LJ:*   [*Writes down names*] Thank you.

7.3 *Lead Appellant:*   My Lord, in the instant case, there are two grounds of appeal. First, the issue whether the Respondent trustee, Mr Dearing, is liable to make good losses caused to the trust fund through the defaults of his agent, Mr Holmes; and secondly, the issue whether Mr Holmes can himself be said to have committed the tort of procurement of a breach of trust in advising Mr Dearing to make unauthorised investments. My Lord, I shall be dealing with the first ground of appeal and my learned junior will be dealing with the second ground of appeal.

7.4 *Scales LJ:*   Yes, thank you Miss Fowler. Before you proceed, I must tell you that the second ground of appeal intrigues me.

		This tort, the existence and application of which you claim, has never, until the instant case, been argued before any court, has it?

7.5   *Lead Appellant*: My Lord, my learned junior will be contending that the issue has been before the courts on a number of occasions. Indeed, he will also be arguing that the existence of such a tort is consistent with principle.

7.6   *Scales LJ*: I am always open to persuasion. In practice, I very much doubt that such an argument would be advanced very often but I realise that you are bound by the moot problem. But, anyway, please continue.

7.7   *Lead Appellant*: My Lord, I don't know whether your Lordship would find a brief summary of the facts of the instant case helpful?

7.8   *Scales LJ*: I have, of course, read the moot problem, but please refresh me as to the salient points, Miss Fowler.

7.9   *Lead Appellant*: The facts are briefly these: Mr Nicholas Dearing, the executor and trustee of the personal estate of Mrs Daphne Porter, appointed Mr Robert Holmes, a stockbroker, to advise him upon matters of trust investment. Mr Holmes advised Mr Dearing to invest, and Mr Dearing did invest, one-third of the fund in certain speculative property development schemes in which Mr Holmes had a personal interest. Mr Holmes was aware that such an investment did not lie within Mr Dearing's investment powers. Mr Holmes also persuaded Mr Dearing to deposit with him the remaining two-thirds of the trust fund. It was established in the court below that Mr Holmes dissipated these moneys to his own ends.

7.10 *Scales LJ*: Mr Holmes is, or was, addicted to cocaine. The trust moneys were spent on that drug.

7.11 *Lead Appellant*: My Lord, yes ...

7.12 *Scales LJ*: Do continue.

7.13 *Lead Appellant*: It was found in the court below that Mr Dearing should have been suspicious when the broker failed to account for the moneys upon request, but that Mr Dearing nevertheless failed to take action in time to save the trust fund.

7.14 *Scales LJ*: [*Addressing the Lead Respondent, who has stood up during the Lead Appellant's summary (see the answer to*

		Question 63)] Is your seat uncomfortable Mr Khan, or do you have a good reason for taking to your feet?
7.15	*Lead Respondent:*	[*Lead Appellant sits down as Lead Respondent addresses the judge*] If your Lordship will indulge me ... for completeness your Lordship should know that there is no evidence to show that prompt action by Mr Dearing would in fact have prevented loss.
7.16	*Scales LJ:*	I take your point, but to embark upon that discussion would take us away from the major legal issues.
7.17	*Lead Respondent:*	I am grateful your Lordship.
7.18	*Scales LJ:*	Very well, please be seated. Now, Miss Fowler, please conclude your summary of the facts. You say that Mr Dearing failed to take prompt action ...
7.19	*Lead Appellant:*	Yes, my Lord. It seems that Mr Holmes gave Mr Dearing certain dishonest explanations for his failure to account for the two-thirds part of the trust fund, and that Mr Dearing at first accepted these explanations. By the time Mr Dearing's suspicions had been fully aroused, that part of the trust fund had been lost. As to the other one-third part of the trust fund, that was also lost, due to the failure of the property development schemes.
7.20	*Scales LJ:*	Thank you.
7.21	*Lead Appellant:*	My Lord, if I may turn to my submissions.
7.22	*Scales LJ:*	Please do.
7.23	*Lead Appellant:*	My Lord, in relation to the first ground of appeal, I have two submissions to make. First, that according to the authorities the phrase 'wilful default' in s 30, sub-s (1) of the Trustee Act 1925 was never intended to have the meaning attributed to it by Mr Justice Maugham in *Re Vickery*, and does in fact cover innocent, but imprudent behaviour such as that exhibited by the Respondent. Secondly –
7.24	*Scales LJ:*	[*Busy writing*] Slow down please –
7.25	*Lead Appellant:*	I apologise, my Lord [*waits for moot judge to finish writing*]. My second submission is that, if, in the alternative, the authorities are against me ... they are not binding upon this court ... and I will argue that according to fundamental principles of the law of trusts ... imprudent trustees should not be protected ... even in cases where they have not been dishonest.

7.26 *Scales LJ*:	The law should not protect honest fools!
7.27 *Lead Appellant*:	I am much obliged, my Lord. That is my argument.
7.28 *Scales LJ*:	Thank you.
7.29 *Lead Appellant*:	As to my first submission, might I immediately take your Lordship to the case of *Re Vickery*, which is to be found in the first volume of the *Chancery Law Reports* for 1931, page 572.
7.30 *Scales LJ*:	[*Having found the reference*] Yes.
7.31 *Lead Appellant*:	Is your Lordship familiar with the facts of this case?
7.32 *Scales LJ*:	Yes, thank you. In that case the trustee was a missionary, ignorant of business affairs, who failed adequately to supervise a stockbroker with whom he had deposited the trust fund.
7.33 *Lead Appellant*:	My Lord, yes ... Mr Justice Risky relied upon this case at first instance for the proposition that a trustee will only be liable for 'wilful default' under s 30, sub-s (1) of the Trustee Act 1925 if the trustee has consciously or deliberately been at fault. I intend to show that the *Re Vickery* interpretation of the phrase 'wilful default' is at odds with the orthodox interpretation and should not be followed. The passage to which I wish to direct your Lordship's attention is from the judgment of Mr Justice Maugham, at the very top of page 582, starting with the words 'I have now to consider'.
7.34 *Scales LJ*:	Yes.
7.35 *Lead Appellant*:	[*Quoting*] 'I have now to consider s 30, sub-s (1), of the Trustee Act 1925, a section which replaces s 24 of the Trustee Act 1893, which in its turn re-enacted Lord Cranworth's Act, s 31'. My Lord, I refer to this brief *dictum* merely to show that s 30, sub-s (1) of the Trustee Act 1925 is a provision of long standing authority. Accordingly, judicial interpretation of the phrase 'wilful default' in relation to s 24 of the 1893 Act and s 31 of Lord Cranworth's Act, should equally well apply to s 30, sub-s (1) of the 1925 Act. It is my submission that Mr Justice Maugham in *Re Vickery* did not attach sufficient weight to earlier judicial interpretations of the phrase 'wilful default'.
7.36 *Scales LJ*:	Are you arguing that *Re Vickery* was decided *per incuriam*?

7.37	*Lead Appellant*:	My Lord, I might have argued that, but I need not do so. Your Lordship could not in any event be bound by the first instance judgment of Mr Justice Maugham, I therefore merely urge your Lordship to prefer the cases which he ignored, and other cases which have been decided since *Re Vickery*.
7.38	*Scales LJ*:	I see. Perhaps you had better take me to those cases.
7.39	*Lead Appellant*:	The first of the cases to which I wish to refer your Lordship is the case of *Re Brier*, reported in the twenty-sixth volume of the *Law Reports for the Chancery Division* for 1884, page 238 [*waits ...*].
7.40	*Scales LJ*:	I have it.
7.41	*Lead Appellant*:	My Lord, in this case the Lord Chancellor, Lord Selborne, considered facts very similar to those of the instant case. It was a case where a trustee (an executor, to be precise) appointed an agent to receive trust moneys in circumstances where some of those moneys were lost (due, in that case, to the agent's insolvency). His Lordship, in applying the precursor section to the modern s 30, sub-s (1) of the Trustee Act 1925, at no time entertained the view that 'wilful default' might necessitate deliberate or conscious wrongdoing.
7.42	*Scales LJ*:	What alternative definition of 'wilful default' did the Lord Chancellor prefer?
7.43	*Lead Appellant*:	His Lordship did not in express terms lay down any definition, my Lord. Rather, his Lordship's *dictum* is most notable for what he did *not* say! It is clear from the law report that the Appellants argued that the question to be asked in determining whether there had been 'wilful default' was whether the trustee had been negligent. If I might refer your Lordship to page 242 of the report, near the very top of the page, where the Appellants argue that 'the burden is on the other side to show that the principal's negligence led to the loss'. It is clear that the Lord Chancellor accepted this analysis. At the top of page 243, his Lordship says to counsel for the Respondent, 'I am disposed to think that the onus is on you to show that the executors were negligent'.
7.44	*Scales LJ*:	But, Miss Fowler, you cannot rely upon statements not appearing in the judgment.

7.45 *Lead Appellant*:	My Lord is perfectly correct when your Lordship says that such statements are of no authority in themselves. However, they do show, I submit, that the Lord Chancellor's omission to consider expressly the standard of care in his judgment was no oversight. The judgment focused upon another issue, namely that of the *onus probandi*, precisely because it went without saying that the trustee would be liable if found to have been negligent, that is, imprudent.
7.46 *Scales LJ*:	Was *Re Brier* considered in *Re Vickery*?
7.47 *Lead Appellant*:	Only in the most cursory manner, my Lord. As I recall, Mr Justice Maugham merely noted that the trustees in *Re Brier* were not found to have been in wilful default. His Lordship did not discuss the interpretation of wilful default that had been implicit in *Re Brier*.
7.48 *Scales LJ*:	Thank you Miss Fowler, your recollection corresponds with mine.
7.49 *Lead Appellant*:	My Lord, the second case to which I wish to refer your Lordship is *Bartlett v Barclays Bank (No 2)* which is to be found in the *Law Reports of the Chancery Division* for 1980, page 515. The passage to which I wish to refer your Lordship is taken from the judgment of Lord Justice Brightman, page 546 ... [*waits*] ... between the marginal letters E and F ... beginning 'during the course of the argument ...'
7.50 *Scales LJ*:	Thank you, I have it.
7.51 *Lead Appellant*:	... during the course of the argument at the trial the defendant's counsel disclaimed the proposition that wilful default involved conscious wrongdoing in the context of a claim against a trustee for an account on the footing of wilful default. For reasons which I have indicated I think that that concession was rightly made'. His Lordship's own interpretation of wilful default appears on the same page at B, where he says: '... wilful default by a trustee in this context means a passive breach of trust, an omission by a trustee to do something which, as a prudent trustee, he ought to have done, as distinct from an active breach of trust.'
7.52 *Scales LJ*:	In both *dicta*, his Lordship makes it clear that his comments are specific to the context he was considering. He was not considering s 30, sub-s (1).

7.53 *Lead Appellant*:	My Lord, I am grateful. I merely urge your Lordship to adopt this interpretation of 'wilful default', taken as it is from another trust context, and consistent as it is with *Re Brier*, in preference to the *Re Vickery* interpretation, which was taken, not from a trust context at all, but from a company law context. Would your Lordship wish me to refer to the relevant passage from *Re Vickery*?
7.54 *Scales LJ*:	No, that won't be necessary. It is clear, I think, that Mr Justice Maugham was strongly persuaded by the case of *Re City Equitable Fire Life Assurance Co* in formulating his view of 'wilful default', and I accept that in that case the liability of directors and not trustees was being considered.
7.55 *Lead Appellant*:	My Lord, I am grateful. [Lead Appellant *had cited* Re City Equitable Fire Life Assurance Co *but now wisely decides not to make use of it, as the judge has already accepted the submission to which that authority related.*]
7.56 *Scales LJ*:	Yes, very good. Now Miss Fowler, I am concerned that time may be somewhat against you. Would you please conclude your first submission and move to your second.
7.57 *Lead Appellant*:	Certainly, my Lord. To conclude my first submission I would invite your Lordship to hold that the authorities show that before 1926 the phrase 'wilful default' was understood to mean 'negligence' or 'a want of ordinary prudence', and that even after 1925 and the enactment of s 30, sub-s (1) that phrase should still be given the same meaning. Accordingly, I invite your Lordship to hold Mr Dearing liable for breach of trust, for the facts clearly show that he was *negligent* in being unaware of the terms of the trust and naively accepting Mr Holmes's excuses for failing to account for the trust fund.
7.58 *Scales LJ*:	Thank you.
7.59 *Lead Appellant*:	I now turn to my second submission. Namely, that, if your Lordship is of the view that the authorities are against me, then in accordance with fundamental trust principles your Lordship should decline to follow those authorities, their effect being to exonerate foolish trustees at the expense of innocent beneficiaries.
7.60 *Scales LJ*:	Yes, I follow that.
7.61 *Lead Appellant*:	May I refer your Lordship to the case of *Speight v Gaunt*, a judgment of this court. It is to be found in the twenty-second volume of the *Law Reports of the Chancery Division* for 1883, page 727.

7.62 *Scales LJ*:	[*The clerk of the court having passed the volume to the judge*] I have it. Why are you taking me to this case?
7.63 *Lead Appellant*:	I intend to show that the standard of care to be expected of trustees is an objective one, and that it is no excuse for a trustee to show that their default was not deliberate, if it be shown objectively that they acted imprudently.
7.64 *Scales LJ*:	I see, but what is the link between 'wilful default' and whether a duty of care exists, and the nature of that duty of care?
7.65 *Lead Appellant*:	My Lord, it is my submission that to approve the interpretation given to 'wilful default' in *Re Vickery* would be wrongly to replace the usual objective standard of care expected of trustees with a subjective standard of care. If Parliament, in enacting s 30, sub-s (1), had really intended such a dramatic change in the law, I submit that such intention would have been expressed far more clearly.
7.66 *Lead Appellant*:	Would your Lordship require a brief summary of the facts of *Speight v Gaunt*?
7.67 *Scales LJ*:	No, thank you, I presume you will be taking me to the well known passage of Sir George Jessel where he sets down the standard of care to be expected of trustees.
7.68 *Lead Appellant*:	My Lord, yes. If I may take you to that passage ... [*judge nods approval*] ... the Master of the Rolls says, page 739, 'on general principles a trustee ought to conduct the business of the trust in the same manner that an ordinary prudent man of business would conduct his own'. My Lord, the standard of care expected of trustees is an objective standard of 'prudence'. They are not to be relieved of the consequences of their imprudence merely because they acted honestly, or because they, through their own folly, did not appreciate that what they were doing was imprudent. As your Lordship succinctly put it, the courts should not protect honest fools. Why, my Lord, should foolish trustees be preferred to innocent beneficiaries?
7.69 *Scales LJ*:	Thank you.
7.70 *Lead Appellant*:	In conclusion, I would invite your Lordship to overrule the case of *Re Vickery* and to hold that 'wilful default' includes any breach of the trustees' usual objective standard of prudence, and accordingly to reverse the

decision of Mr Justice Risky and to allow this appeal. My Lord unless your Lordship has any further questions, that concludes my submissions on this ground of appeal.

7.71 *Scales LJ*: Thank you, I have no further questions.

[*The* Lead Appellant *sits down, and the* Junior Appellant *rises.*]

8.1 *Junior Appellant*: May it please your Lordship, as has already been indicated, my name is Neil Wright and I appear for the Appellant on the second ground of appeal. On this ground, the Appellant's case is that it is legitimate to extend the principle in *Lumley v Gye* so as to hold the Respondent liable for committing the tort of procuring a breach of trust. [*Here the* Junior Appellant *has usefully paraphrased the actual words used in the ground of appeal.*] In support of this ground, I have two submissions to make. First, that there are authorities to support the existence of such a tort. Secondly, that the existence of such a tort is consistent with principle. My Lord, if I may turn to my first submission?

8.2 *Scales LJ*: Before you do, I have a burning question I must let fall … The rule in *Lumley v Gye* is a long established rule of common law which states that it is a tort to procure the breach of another's contract. That is all very well for we know that the common law acknowledges the binding nature of legal contracts, and thus must treat as a tort any attempt by a third party to induce a breach of contract, but the common law is supposedly blind to trusts. How can it be a legal tort to procure the breach of a purely equitable right? Put another way, the common law does not acknowledge a breach of trust to be a wrong, so how can it treat as a legal wrong the procurement of a breach of trust?

8.3 *Junior Appellant*: My Lord, I am grateful. Might I refer your Lordship to a recent judgment of this court which I submit will answer the point?

8.4 *Scales LJ*: By all means.

8.5 *Junior Appellant*: The passage to which I wish to refer your Lordship is taken from the judgment of Lord Justice Hoffman, as he then was, in *Law Debenture Corporation v Ural Caspian Ltd*

183

		which is reported in the second volume of the *All England Law Reports* for 1993, page 355.
8.6	*Scales LJ*:	I have it. Is this the best report of the case?
8.7	*Junior Appellant*:	My Lord, I believe it is. It does not appear in the *Law Reports*.
8.8	*Scales LJ*:	That is true, but unfortunately, Mr Wright, I know that this case is reported in the first volume of the *Weekly Law Reports* for that year. I would prefer the 'Weeklies', but you may proceed nevertheless with the report in the *All England Law Reports*, otherwise we shall all become terribly confused.
8.9	*Junior Appellant*:	My Lord, I am most grateful.
8.10	*Scales LJ*:	In which court was this case heard?
8.11	*Junior Appellant*:	The High Court, my Lord. The Chancery Division of the High Court.
8.12	*Scales LJ*:	But I thought you said Lord Justice Hoffman.
8.13	*Junior Appellant*:	I did my Lord, the present Lord Hoffman, Lord Justice Hoffman as he then was, was sitting as an additional judge of the Chancery Division.
8.14	*Scales LJ*:	Is it usual for a Lord Justice of Appeal to sit in the High Court?
8.15	*Junior Appellant*:	No, my Lord, it is most unusual. The reason why it happened in the *Law Debenture* case is that when Sir Leonard Hoffman first began to hear the case in March 1992 he was Mr Justice Hoffman, but there was a long adjournment until the case resumed in November 1992. In that interval, he had been appointed to the Court of Appeal and had become Lord Justice Hoffman. However, for convenience, his Lordship finished hearing the case and then delivered the judgment to which I wish to refer.
8.16	*Scales LJ*:	Before you do that, Mr Wright, I would like you to explain to me what weight this authority has, given that this court went on to reverse his judgment, did it not?
8.17	*Junior Appellant*:	Yes, your Lordship is correct. However, the case was reversed on other grounds. There is nothing in the Court of Appeal's decision in the case to cast any doubt on that aspect of Lord Justice Hoffman's analysis upon which I rely, and therefore there is nothing in the Court of Appeal's decision to deter your Lordship from approving my submission.

8.18 *Scales LJ*:	Thank you, do proceed.
8.19 *Junior Appellant*:	I'm grateful. My Lord, the facts of the case are not directly relevant. The case concerned the procurement of an interference with a contract and the question whether the secondary stage of procurement of interference with remedies for breach of contract could be an actionable wrong. The *dictum* to which I wish to refer your Lordship commences on page 368, the first paragraph, with the words:

> Although *Lumley v Gye* (1853) 2 E & B 216; [1843–60] All ER Rep 208 usually appears under the rubric 'procuring breach of contract' or the like, the principle was formulated in wider terms. Earle J said (2 E & B 216, p 232; [1843–60] All ER Rep 208, p 214): 'It is clear that the procurement of the violation of a right is a cause of action in all instances where the violation is an actionable wrong ...' There are thus three elements to the tort: (1) a right in the plaintiff; (2) violated by an actionable wrong; (3) procured by the defendant ...

> My Lord, it is clear that *Lumley v Gye* has broad application and that the three constituent elements of the rule in that case are present in the facts of the instant case.

8.20 *Scales LJ*:	I see.
8.21 *Junior Appellant*:	My Lord, the passage continues:

> ... there has been an extension of at least the first and third of these elements in the tort. First, the rights capable of being violated have been held to include ... fiduciary obligations imposed in equity ...

> It is clear from this passage that *Lumley v Gye* has already been extended to cover the procurement of the breach of fiduciary obligations of a purely equitable nature. Therefore, I submit that there can be no good reason to deny its application to cases where a person has procured the breach of equitable rights existing under a trust.

8.22 *Scales LJ*:	Yes, I see. And can you direct me to any cases, apart from the *Law Debenture Corporation* case, to support your submission?
8.23 *Junior Appellant*:	I have two cases. The first concerns a company director's duty of fidelity to his company. It is *Boulting v Association of Cinematograph, Television and Allied*

Technicians which is reported in the second volume of the *Law Reports of the Queen's Bench* for 1963, page 606. The second is the case of *Prudential Life Assurance Co v Lorenz*, which is to be found in the eleventh volume of *Knight's Industrial Reports* for 1971, page 78, which case concerned an agent's duty of confidence to his principal. My Lord, if I may turn to the first of those authorities?

8.24 *Scales LJ*:	Please do. I have them.
8.25 *Junior Appellant*:	As to the *Boulting* case, the passage to which I wish to refer your Lordship is taken from the judgment of Lord Denning, the then Master of the Rolls, page 627, about half way down the first paragraph:

> It is contrary to public policy that any director should be made to deny his trust and throw over the interests of those whom he is bound to protect ... An officer of a trade union, too, is in a fiduciary position towards the members, and no employer would be justified in seeking, by promises or threats, to induce him to act disloyally towards them. In each one of these cases, the reason is simple: it is wrong to induce another to act inconsistently with the duty of fidelity which he has undertaken by contract or trust to perform ...

8.26 *Scales LJ*:	Thank you.
8.27 *Junior Appellant*:	May I now turn to the *Lorenz* case?
8.28 *Scales LJ*:	Time is too pressing, I am afraid. Be assured that I have read that case and accept that it could be read as providing some support for your submission. Thank you for your arguments on the authorities, Mr Wright, which have been very eloquently put. Now I must ask you how you intend to deal with the authorities which I see the Respondents will put before the court. In particular, the recent case of *Royal Brunei Airlines v Tan*. Without wishing to second-guess the Respondents' arguments unduly, I anticipate that they will say that the procurement of a breach of trust is already an actionable equitable wrong according to that recent case, and that this case leaves no room for a common law tort of procuring a breach of trust.
8.29 *Junior Appellant*:	My Lord, if I might refer your Lordship once again to the judgment of Hoffman LJ in the *Law Debenture* case. His Lordship expressly considered the possibility of a tort of procuring a breach of trust, and noted that the 'only' reason the courts had not yet acknowledged such a tort was because the area was already adequately covered by

the well known case of *Barnes v Addy*. If I might refer your Lordship to page 368 F, where his Lordship says: 'It is true that in *Metall und Rohstoff AG v Donaldson Lufkin and Jeanrette Inc* [1989] 3 All ER 14; [1990] 1 QB 391, the Court of Appeal refused to extend the *Lumley v Gye* principle to create a tort of inducing breach of trust, but that was *only* because the ground was already adequately covered by the equitable doctrine of knowing assistance, as formulated in *Barnes v Addy* (1874) LR 9 Ch App 244.' One aspect of the advice of the Judicial Committee of the Privy Council in *Royal Brunei* was to disapprove the very view that *Barnes v Addy* adequately covered this area. Indeed, their Lordships considered *Barnes v Addy* to have been afforded far too much weight over the last hundred years or more.

8.30 *Scales LJ*:	Yes, yes. But that argument does not get you very far, for is it not now the case that the *Royal Brunei* case adequately covers this area?
8.31 *Junior Appellant*:	My Lord, no. I submit, my Lord, that having restricted *Barnes v Addy*, their Lordships in the Judicial Committee of the Privy Council missed an opportunity to extend *Lumley v Gye* to recognise a tort of procuring a breach of trust. It is that opportunity which remains open to your Lordship today, and I would urge your Lordship to seize it.
8.32 *Scales LJ*:	Am I not bound to follow *Royal Brunei*?
8.33 *Junior Appellant*:	My Lord, no. As it was an advice of the Judicial Committee of the Privy Council, that case is of merely persuasive authority in this court.
8.34 *Scales LJ*:	Mr Wright, you would have profited from pointing that fact out without my prompting. Now perhaps you would kindly turn to your second submission.
8.35 *Junior Appellant*:	My Lord, my second submission is that there are sound reasons of principle for acknowledging the existence of a tort of procuring a breach of trust. The first of these reasons is that the wrong, the essential turpitude, the 'tort', is essentially the same whether or not the wrong is to procure a breach of trust or a breach of contract or, indeed, a breach of any legal or equitable right. The second reason is that where equity finds an accessory liable for procuring a breach of trust the accessory is made personally liable as if they were a constructive trustee. In my submission, it is excessively artificial to treat an

accessory to a breach of trust as if they were a trustee, for they will often (as in the present case) have never held or controlled trust property.

8.36 *Scales LJ*: I see, well thank you Mr Wright, that is clear. However, I am afraid that time appears to be somewhat against you. Please would you briefly conclude your submissions.

8.37 *Junior Appellant*: In conclusion, I invite this court to follow the judgment of Lord Justice Hoffman in *Law Debenture Company* and the line of authority upon which his Lordship based his judgment and, consequently, to acknowledge a tort of procuring a breach of trust and to hold that Mr Holmes was guilty of that tort, which conclusion the facts (as found by the judge at first instance) clearly support. To do so would be consistent with principle and end the illogicality of treating wrongdoers, such as Mr Holmes, who have never held trust property, as if they were constructive trustees. I, therefore, invite the court to allow this appeal and, if your Lordship has no further questions, that concludes my arguments on this ground of appeal.

8.38 *Scales LJ*: I have no further questions, thank you. You may sit down.

9.1 *Lead Respondent*: If it pleases your Lordship, my name is Mr Amir Khan and I represent the Respondent together with my learned junior, Miss Sally James. I shall be arguing against the first ground of appeal, namely that, where a trustee is merely impudent, he can be liable to make good losses caused through the default of an agent with whom trust moneys have been deposited. I have two submissions to make. First, that the authorities make it clear that mere imprudence will not make a trustee liable for the defaults of an agent with whom trust moneys have been deposited. Secondly, if your Lordship is against me on my reading of the authorities, then I will submit that there are good reasons of principle why a trustee should not be held liable in such circumstances. As to the authorities, I would first like to respond briefly to one of the authorities presented by the leading counsel for the Appellant.

9.2 *Scales LJ*: Yes, you may proceed ...

9.3	*Lead Respondent*:	May I also refer your Lordship to the case of *Speight v Gaunt*, which is to be found in the twenty-second volume of the *Chancery Law Reports* 1883, page 727.
9.4	*Scales LJ*:	Thank you, I have it.
9.5	*Lead Respondent*:	It is my submission that the facts of that case bear a remarkable resemblance to the case before your Lordship today. The trustees of a will trust employed a stockbroker to sell part of the estate and to reinvest the proceeds in new equities ... . The trustees made enquiries on many occasions as to when the new securities would be handed over to the trust. The broker gave excuses on those occasions ... . Eventually, the broker's firm was declared bankrupt and the beneficiary of the will trust brought an action against the trustees. My Lord, this action failed. If I may take your Lordship to the judgment of Sir George Jessel, the Master of the Rolls, page 746 and the second major paragraph 'You are to endeavour ... '
9.6	*Scales LJ*:	Yes, I have it.
9.7	*Lead Respondent*:	[*Quoting*] 'You are to endeavour as far as possible, having regard to the whole transaction, to avoid making an honest man who is not paid for the performance of an unthankful office liable for the failure of other people from whom he receives no benefit.'
9.8	*Scales LJ*:	Yes, Mr Khan, but as I understand it your opponent would not disagree with that statement. She relies upon the argument that honesty alone is not enough to exonerate the trustee and, upon the finding of fact at first instance, that Mr Dearing did not act prudently in relation to his dealings with Mr Holmes.
9.9	*Lead Respondent*:	My Lord, I am grateful. I merely intend to respectfully submit that if your Lordship were to allow the appeal today the report of this case may sit somewhat uneasily with *Speight v Gaunt*, the facts of both cases being so similar.
9.10	*Scales LJ*:	I thank you for your concerns, but I am inclined to think that the two cases are quite different. In the present case, it is not disputed that Mr Dearing acted imprudently; in *Speight v Gaunt*, the question whether Mr Gaunt had acted imprudently was the very essence of the case. The

question before us today is a narrower one, it is whether, on the basis of mere imprudence, Mr Dearing can be said to be in 'wilful default' for the purposes of s 30, sub-s (1) of the Trustee Act 1925.

9.11 *Lead Respondent:* I will argue that Mr Dearing cannot be said to be in 'wilful default' on the basis of mere imprudence. To that end, may I refer your Lordship to the case of *In re Trusts of Leeds City Brewery Ltd* reported in note form in the *Chancery Division Law Reports* for 1925, page 532 [*the judge reads*]. The action in that case was brought against, *inter alia*, the trustees for the debenture holder of a company. It was a case in which King's Counsel, Mr Maugham as he then was, appeared as counsel. On page 533 ... [*waits*] ... Lord Sterndale interpreted the phrase 'wilful default' in a relieving clause in the trust instrument as connoting 'some wilful misconduct' covering cases where the trustees 'have failed to do their duty purposely and wilfully'. My Lord, 'wilful default' means default 'on purpose', that is deliberate or conscious default.

9.12 *Scales LJ:* Yes, I follow that.

9.13 *Lead Respondent:* My Lord, that case was followed with approval in *Re Vickery* itself. By which time Mr Justice Maugham had been elevated to the bench. My Lord, I need not remind the court of Mr Justice Maugham's understanding of the phrase wilful default as it appears in s 30, sub-s (1) of the Trustee Act 1925 ...

9.14 *Scales LJ:* No thank you, I am familiar with it.

9.15 *Lead Respondent:* My Lord, *Re Vickery* has never been overruled, even where it has been considered. If I might refer your Lordship to the case of *Re Lucking's Will Trusts*, reported in the first volume of the *Weekly Law Reports* for 1968, page 866.

9.16 *Scales LJ:* That won't be necessary, for it is clear, isn't it, that, in the case of *Re Lucking's Will Trusts*, Mr Justice Cross did all he could to avoid applying *Re Vickery*?

9.17 *Lead Respondent:* My Lord, I would respectfully submit that Mr Justice Cross did no more than Mr Justice Maugham had done himself, which was to restrict his interpretation of 'wilful default' to that very narrow class of cases which fall within s 30, sub-s (1) of the Trustee Act 1925. If I might refer your Lordship to the relevant passages of both judgments. [Lead Respondent *then expands upon the authorities further*.]

9.18 *Scales LJ*: Your arguments on the authorities are well put, but none of your authorities are binding on this court. Do you have any argument of principle to support the application of your interpretation of 'wilful default' to cases where trust moneys have been deposited with an agent?

9.19 *Lead Respondent*: My Lord, it might be that in such cases the defendant trustee would have most difficulty in controlling the fund, and should therefore be relieved of liability unless losses were caused through 'wilful default' in the sense of deliberate or conscious wrongdoing.

9.20 *Scales LJ*: Thank you, Mr Khan. Your arguments may nearly have persuaded me.

9.21 *Lead Respondent*: Might I seek to persuade your Lordship further by referring to the actual wording of s 30, sub-s (1) of the Trustee Act itself.

9.22 *Scales LJ*: Yes, I have that section ...

9.23 *Lead Respondent*: The section reads as follows:

> A trustee shall be chargeable only for the money and securities actually received by him notwithstanding his signing any receipt for the sake of conformity, and shall be answerable and accountable only for *his own* acts, receipts, neglects or defaults, and not for those of *any other* trustee ... banker, broker or other person with whom any trust money or securities may be deposited, nor for any insufficiency or deficiency of any securities, nor for any other loss, unless the same happens through *his own* wilful default.

My Lord, I have emphasised certain phrases in the section to show that the section was designed to relieve the trustee of liability for another's default precisely because the section applies to situations where the trustee is not in a position to control the actions of that other. I concede that a trustee can be liable for mere imprudence where his own defaults are at issue. However, that concession does not touch a case such as the present where the defaults are those of another with whom trust moneys have been deposited and over whom the trustee must have less control than he would have over his own actions.

9.24 *Scales LJ*: Yes, I follow that. You submit that s 30, sub-s (1) has a somewhat narrow application, and that within its proper sphere of operation it is appropriate to interpret 'wilful default' as connoting deliberate or conscious wrongdoing ...

9.25 *Lead Respondent*: My Lord, I am obliged.

9.26 *Scales LJ*: However, the difficulty, as I see it, for your submission is that the principal authorities in support of that interpretation are not binding on this court. How, then do you respond to the argument of principle, submitted by leading counsel for the Appellant, that your proposed interpretation of 'wilful default' must be wrong because it tends to relieve foolish trustees at the expense of innocent beneficiaries?

9.27 *Lead Respondent*: As to principle, may I refer your Lordship once again to the *dictum* of Sir George Jessel, the then Master of the Rolls, in *Speight v Gaunt* where he said that

> ... you are to endeavour as far as possible, having regard to the whole transaction, to avoid making an honest man who is not paid for the performance of an unthankful office liable for the failures of other people from whom he receives no benefit.

> If the instant case is to be disposed of on the basis of principle, it would be my respectful submission that there can be no better principle than to avoid making honest, unremunerated trustees liable for the dishonesty or negligence of their carefully chosen agents. I submit, my Lord, that s 30, sub-s (1) and its precursors reflect that principle in statutory form.

9.28 *Scales LJ*: Thank you, Mr Khan, that is all very clear.

9.29 *Lead Respondent*: If your Lordship has no further questions that concludes my submissions on this ground of appeal.

9.30 *Scales LJ*: I have no further questions.

9.31 *Lead Respondent*: Then I invite the court to follow the definition of 'wilful default' laid down by Mr Justice Maugham in *Re Vickery* and accordingly to dismiss the appeal.

10.1 *Scales LJ*: Thank you Mr Khan ... [*Mr Khan sits down.*] ... Now then, Miss James, you have some submissions on the second ground of appeal?

10.2 *Junior Respondent*: Indeed, my Lord. I have a number of arguments, and a number of remarks to make in response to the arguments put by my learned friend Mr Wright for the Appellant.

10.3 *Scales LJ*:	Shall we hear your responses first, and then your other submissions? It may be that if your responses fully address the grounds of appeal you will win on the law without any need to go into further submissions.
10.4 *Junior Respondent*:	My Lord, I may be reluctant to be so successful!
10.5 *Scales LJ*:	Quite. Well let us hear your responses anyway.
10.6 *Junior Respondent*:	Mr Wright submitted that there are a number of authorities in support of the existence of a tort of procuring a breach of trust. My Lord, I am not aware of any. The instant case concerns the express will trust of Mrs Daphne Porter. Not one of the authorities to which your Lordship was referred by the Appellant actually concerned an express trust. The *Law Debenture* case concerned covenants between Russian companies. The *Boulting* case concerned a dispute as to membership fees of a trade union. The *Royal Brunei* case concerned the liability of the controlling director of a corporation. My Lord, junior counsel for the Appellant has raised no authority which directly supports his case. Then, in addition to his arguments on the authorities, my learned friend sought to persuade your Lordship that there are compelling arguments of principle to support the Appellant's case. My learned friend argued that it would be contrary to principle to make a defendant personally liable as a trustee in a case where they have never held or controlled trust property. It is my submission, my Lord, that there is no illogicality in treating a defendant as if he or she were a trustee. Liability as a trustee is merely a convenient shorthand to describe the extent of the defendant's liability, it says nothing as to the status of the defendant. Liability as a trustee is onerous. It is therefore quite logical to make a defendant so liable who has dishonestly assisted in or procured a breach of trust. It is my respectful submission that the Appellant's arguments of principle are not convincing. On the other hand, there is in support of the Respondent, as your Lordship has observed, a most fundamental principle of English law that the courts of common law do not recognise the trust concept.
10.7 *Scales LJ*:	I must stop you there Miss James. Your learned friend for the Appellant, Mr Wright, could have argued (he chose not to, or neglected to) that the common law is not

totally blind to trusts, but that it merely refuses to enforce them. Surely, since the fusion of the administration of the courts of equity and common law by the Supreme Court of Judicature Act of 1875, the common law has at least recognised trusts!

10.8 *Junior Respondent*: My Lord, I am grateful. I appreciate your Lordship's point. I would still submit, however, that this court should not take the wholly novel step of granting a common law right of action to persons, the beneficiaries of the trust in the instant case, whose *locus standi* derives solely from an equitable entitlement.

10.9 *Scales LJ*: Very well, I shall note what you say. Please will you now take me to your main submissions.

10.10 *Junior Respondent*: My Lord, I have only one submission. It is, as your Lordship anticipated, that the authorities show that the procurement of a breach of a trust is already an actionable equitable wrong and that there is therefore no need to invent a common law tort of procuring a breach of trust.

10.11 *Scales LJ*: Thank you, Miss James.

10.12 *Junior Respondent*: May I refer your Lordship to the Court of Appeal decision in the case of *Metall und Rohstoff AG v Donaldson Lufkin and Jenrette Inc*, which is reported in the first volume of the *Law Reports of the Queen's Bench Division* for 1990, page 391. This was a case concerning an agreement unlawfully to convert the property of a Swiss company by the use of an agent of that company, but the question of whether or not the court should recognise a tort of procurement of a breach of trust came up for consideration. The passage to which I wish to refer your Lordship is taken from the judgment of Lord Justice Slade and can be found on page 481 of the report at G, commencing with the words 'The principles of the law of trusts ...'.

10.13 *Scales LJ*: Yes, I have it.

10.14 *Junior Respondent*: 'The principles of the law of trusts, in particular those expounded by Lord Selborne LC in *Barnes v Addy* ... are quite sufficient to deal with those persons who incite a breach of trust. We know of no authority supporting the existence of the alleged tort [being the tort of procuring a breach of trust] and can see no sufficient justification for the introduction of a new tort of this nature.'

10.15 *Scales LJ*: Yes, it is a *dictum* which appears to assist you greatly. On the other hand it is merely an *obiter dictum*, and the Appellant has in any event argued that as a result of the recent case of *Royal Brunei Airlines v Tan* it is now clear that *Barnes v Addy* is far from sufficient to deal with persons who incite a breach of trust!

10.16 *Junior Respondent*: My Lord, one can see the attraction in the Appellant's argument, but the substantial truth of the matter is that *Royal Brunei* is merely the latest step in a long line of authorities starting with *Barnes v Addy* (if it did not start earlier) which have sought to develop and refine the nature of the equitable liability which should attach to persons who incite or assist in breaches of trust. It is of the greatest assistance to my client, Mr Holmes, that even the Appellant admits that *Royal Brunei* is a compelling authority. For the advice of the Judicial Committee of the Privy Council in that case leaves no room for a common law tort of procuring a breach of trust. If I might refer your Lordship to a most pertinent passage in the *Royal Brunei* case?

10.17 *Scales LJ*: Please do.

10.18 *Junior Respondent*: The passage is on page 71, at the marginal letters C and D, where Lord Nicholls, delivering the opinion of the Board, says, 'A person who knowingly procures a breach of contract, or knowingly interferes with the due performance of a contract, is liable to the innocent party. The underlying rationale is the same.' It is clear from this passage that his Lordship was fully aware of the principle in *Lumley v Gye* that there can be common law liability for procurement of a breach of contract. It is surely no accident that his Lordship, nevertheless, resisted the obvious temptation to extend that principle to create tortious liability for the procurement of a breach of trust.

10.19 *Scales LJ*: I have no doubt that junior counsel for the Appellant regrets that he is unable to argue that Mr Holmes has committed an equitable wrong (I need not comment as to what might have been Mr Holmes' expectations of success had equitable liability been argued), but it is clear from the grounds of appeal that the Appellant's hands are tied and that he must argue that Mr Holmes has committed a common law tort. Nevertheless, Mr Wright observes that the *Royal Brunei* case is not binding on this court. What do you say to that?

10.20 *Junior Appellant*:	My Lord, the *Royal Brunei* case is indeed of persuasive authority only. I submit, however, that it is of the strongest possible persuasive authority. The advice of the Judicial Committee of the Privy Council comprised a single opinion delivered by Lord Nicholls, in which their other Lordships concurred. Lord Nicholls is, of course, a Lord of Appeal in Ordinary, and his opinion should therefore be afforded the greatest respect in your Lordship's court. Furthermore, the Judicial Committee in *Royal Brunei* was considering matters of English law, not least the status of the long standing English authority, *Barnes v Addy*. With great respect, I submit that your Lordship should be most reluctant to depart from the decision in *Royal Brunei v Tan*.
10.21 *Scales LJ*:	Has *Royal Brunei* been followed in any English case since?
10.22 *Junior Respondent*:	My Lord, yes. My Lord will see that I have cited on my list of authorities the case of *Brinks v Abu Saleh*. *Royal Brunei* was applied and approved in that case. Does your Lordship wish me to direct the court to that case?
10.23 *Scales LJ*:	That will not be necessary. It is only one very recent first instance decision, it cannot claim to set any precedent binding on this court. I do note, however, that Mr Justice Rimer did, as you say, apply and approve *Royal Brunei*. Miss James, I think your case has been clearly made out. Does that conclude your submissions?
10.24 *Junior Respondent*:	If your Lordship pleases, it does. If I may conclude ...
10.25 *Scales LJ*:	By all means ...
10.26 *Junior Respondent*:	For over 100 years it has been clearly established that the principle in *Lumley v Gye* has no application to the procurement of a breach of trust. It has been equally well established during the same period that the wrong of procuring a breach of trust gives rise to a form of equitable liability. In *Barnes v Addy*, this liability was based upon knowing assistance in another's fraudulent or dishonest design. More recently, in *Royal Brunei v Tan* the concept has been somewhat refined so as to lay greater emphasis upon the dishonesty of the person who it is alleged has procured the breach of trust (Mr Holmes in the instant case), and so as to remove the requirement that the breach of trust so procured must itself have been dishonestly carried out by the trustee (Mr Dearing in the instant case). With these refinements

there can be no doubt that the form of equitable liability laid down in *Royal Brunei* adequately covers the instant case. It is equally clear that there is, therefore, no scope for the invention of the tort of procurement of a breach of trust for which the Appellant contends. I, therefore, invite your Lordship to follow the case of *Royal Brunei v Tan* and to dismiss the appeal. If your Lordship has no further questions that concludes my submissions on this ground of appeal.

10.27 *Scales LJ*:   I have no further questions. Thank you for your submissions, Miss James.

10.28 *Junior Respondent*:   [*The Junior Respondent sits.*]

10.29 *Scales LJ*:   We now come to that part of the case where it falls to me to give a judgment ...[3]

---

3   In some competitive moots, the Lead Appellant would, in addition, be given the option to take five or 10 minutes before the judgment to reply to the arguments of both Lead and Junior Respondent (see the answer to Question 13).

Appendix 2[1] – Example Moot Problems

In the House of Lords – Criminal Law Moot
R v Bones (Indiana)

Sir Indiana Bones, an eminent antiquarian, had a special interest in the relics of English saints. He travelled to Bugthorpe Manor in Berkshire, to make the acquaintance of its owner, Lady Bugthorpe, an impoverished elderly widow. Lady Bugthorpe had an outstanding collection of religious relics, including what purported to be the finger bone of St George, the patron saint of England.

Lady Bugthorpe was overwhelmed at the honour of being visited by such an eminent figure. Not lacking in considerable personal charm, Sir Indiana persuaded Lady Bugthorpe to give her the relic. In what she later described to the police as a 'moment of madness', she handed the relic over to him 'as a present'. Sir Indiana thanked her and left with the relic as quickly as politeness allowed.

The day after Sir Indiana's visit, on suddenly coming to her senses, Lady Bugthorpe telephoned the police. They quickly arrested Sir Indiana and charged him with dishonestly appropriating property, namely the finger bone, belonging to another, namely Lady Bugthorpe.

At his trial, counsel for the defendant argued that the acceptance of a gift could not be an appropriation, within the meaning of the Theft Act 1968, and that, even if it could, a human finger bone was incapable of 'belonging to another' within the meaning of the Act. No question arose as to the defendant's dishonesty.

The trial judge, her Honour, Judge Phalange QC, directed the jury *inter alia* that, in order for them to convict the defendant of theft:

(1) It was immaterial that the victim, Lady Bugthorpe, gave the relic to the defendant, since a person who receives a gift may appropriate the property which is the subject matter of the gift.

(2) The expression 'property belonging to another' as used in the 1968 Act, could apply to a relic of this kind, since the common law rule that there was no property in a body applied only to a corpse awaiting burial.

The defendant appealed to the Court of Appeal on the ground that the trial judge had erred in directing the jury in this way. The Court of Appeal, however, affirmed the trial judge's direction in its entirety.

---

1   See above, p x.

The defendant now appeals to the House of Lords on the grounds that:

(1)   A person who receives a valid gift from another cannot be held, within the meaning of s 3 of the Theft Act 1968, to be a person who 'appropriates' the property which is the subject matter of the gift.

(2)   A relic consisting of a human bone cannot be 'property belonging to another', as that expression is used in the Theft Act 1968, since the common law rule that there was no property in a body applied, not only to a corpse awaiting burial, but to human bodies and human body parts generally.

(This moot problem is a version of a moot problem originally prepared by Professor Diane Birch of The University of Nottingham. The authors extend their thanks to Professor Birch for allowing the use of this version of the problem here.)

In the Court of Appeal (Civil Division) – Public Law Moot

R v The Bird Preservation Commission ex p English Country Holidays

Following growing evidence that numerous species of British birds are under threat of extinction from farming and tourism, the Bird Preservation Commission (BPC) is set up by the (fictitious) Birds Act. Under s 1 of the Act, the BPC is given power to acquire areas where there is 'a substantial threat of serious harm to the local bird population' by compulsory purchase. Section 2 states that, if the BPC considers that a given area should be compulsorily purchased, it shall publish details of the proposed compulsory purchase order, and unless no objections are received, shall arrange for a public local inquiry to be conducted by an inspector appointed by the Department of the Environment. Section 3 provides that, 28 days prior to the enquiry, the BPC and any objectors shall disclose to each other the substance of the evidence that each side proposes to rely on at the inquiry. Section 4 provides that, following the inquiry, the inspector will make a report and a recommendation to the BPC, which will then decide whether or not to make the final purchase order. The Act contains no provision as to the procedure to be followed at or after the inquiry, a matter which it should be assumed is not covered by any other statutory provision.

In May 1999, the BPC gave notification that it proposed to compulsorily purchase the Parkland Leisure Area in Sussex, which is owned by English Country Holidays (ECH). ECH objected to the purchase. Each side disclosed its evidence to the other, in accordance with the Act; this included summaries of the evidence of a number of expert witnesses as to the threat to bird life in the Parkland area, which was sent to ECH. The inquiry was chaired by Dr Hawk, the inspector appointed by the Department of the Environment. During the inquiry, Dr Hawk ruled that an expert witness (Dr Eagle), whose evidence had not been disclosed in advance, should be permitted to give evidence about the recent destruction of birds' nests and eggs by children visiting the picnic site with their families. Cross-examination of all witnesses by a lawyer for this purpose was turned down by him. Dr Hawk's report strongly recommended that the Parkland area be subject to compulsory purchase, a recommendation which was accepted by the BPC.

After the hearing, and the BPC's decision, it subsequently transpired that Dr Hawk was at the time of the inquiry, and still is, an active member of and part time campaigner for the Royal Society for the Protection of Birds (RSPB).

ECH sought judicial review of the decision to compulsorily purchase the Parkland Leisure Area in the High Court.

At the trial, Giles J refused the application for judicial review on the following grounds:

(1) Applying the test in R v Gough [1993] AC 646, there was no real danger of bias on the part of Dr Hawk; the case did not fall within the automatic disqualification rule set out in R v Pinochet [1999] 1 WLR 272.

(2) The requirement to disclose the evidence to the other side prior to the inquiry was, on its proper construction, a directory one only; therefore, although there had been a technical breach of the statute in allowing Dr Eagle to give evidence which had not been so disclosed, this was not grounds for overturning the decision of the BPC. Similarly, the denial of legal representation provided no such grounds: whilst there might, in cases of grave threat to the applicant's liberty, be a discretion to permit him or her to have legal representation, this was not such a case and Dr Hawk's discretion on the matter had not been incorrectly exercised.

ECH now appeals to the Court of Appeal, contending that the ruling of Giles J should be reversed, and the decision of the BPC quashed, on the following grounds:

(1) Dr Hawk's membership of the RSPB and the work it did meant that in conducting an inquiry which turned principally upon the preservation of bird life, he was, in effect, acting as a judge in his own case and, therefore, under the rule set out in Re Pinochet [1999] 1 WLR 272, he should be treated as having been automatically disqualified from acting as inspector; alternatively, there was real danger that he had been biased, under the test in R v Gough [1993] AC 646.[2]

---

2   See, now, *Locabail (UK) Ltd v Bayfield Properties Ltd* [2000] 1 All ER 673.

(2) The requirement to disclose the expert's reports prior to the inquiry was clearly intended to be mandatory but had been breached, resulting in prejudice to ECH and unfairness at the inquiry; moreover the ECH had been wrongfully denied the right to make use of legal representation. Consequently, the inquiry had suffered from fundamental procedural defects.

[The authors would like to thank the English-Speaking Union for permission to reprint this moot problem.]

In the Court of Appeal – Contract Law Moot
Salisbury's plc v Derek Wilton

A poster in the window of Salisbury's self-service supermarket stated:

> Free carving knife to any shopper purchasing a minimum of £150 worth of goods in this store this week.

During the relevant week Derek Wilton visited the store and placed £160 worth of goods in a shopping trolley and went to the check-out. The check-out operator recorded all the purchases on the computerised till and asked Derek for £160. When Derek asked for the free carving knife he was told by the operator that the store had run out of them, but that he could have a tea-towel instead. Derek refused to accept a tea-towel and also refused to pay for the £160 worth of goods. He started to replace those goods on the shelves. The manager was called and he refused to allow the goods to be replaced, claiming Derek had already purchased the goods and was liable to pay for them. Derek refused to pay and left the store without the goods.

Salisbury's brought a claim against Derek asserting that Derek was in breach of a contract of sale and claimed for the lost profit on the £160 worth of goods.

Derek counterclaimed for the value of the carving knife.

At first instance her Honour Judge Pennyworth allowed Salisbury's claim, holding that Derek had entered a legally binding contract when the goods were recorded on the till at the cash point, but dismissed Derek's counterclaim[3] on the grounds that the poster in the window was merely an advertising puff and, that in any case, there was no intention on the part of Salisbury's to create legal relations in respect of the carving knife.

Derek now appeals to the Court of Appeal on the following grounds:

In respect of Salisbury's claim:

---

3   Now, strictly, referred to as a 'Part 20 claim', under the CPR 1998.

(a) there was no contract for the £160 worth of goods since no payment had been made.

In respect of his counterclaim:

(b) that, in the alternative, if the court were to hold that there was a contract for £160 worth of goods, there was an offer of a carving knife and that that offer had been accepted.

In the House of Lords – Evidence Moot
R v Smith

Mr Simon Smith was convicted of causing an explosion, on 15 February 1997, by the use of a bomb, contrary to s 3(a) of the Explosive Substances Act 1883.

Expert forensic evidence showed that the bomb in question involved a particular and unusual construction and a similarly unusual timing device. The prosecution was granted leave to prove that another bomb (similar in all respects) had caused the death of two persons on an earlier occasion (in January 1995). A thumb print identified as Mr Smith's was found on part of that earlier bomb.

Mr Smith's defence was that while it was not denied (nor was it admitted) that the bomb was constructed from the circuit board mechanism of a 'fruit machine', as he was employed by the largest manufacturer of fruit machines in the UK the presence of his print was not significant in the case against him. Mr Smith was at no time charged with an offence relating to the earlier bomb.

The only other evidence against Mr Smith was a photofit picture which had been compiled by a police officer from the description of an eye witness to the bombing. That witness is now dead. At trial the judge, Brown J, rejected a defence submission that the photofit was inadmissible evidence.

The jury found Mr Smith guilty and his appeal against conviction was dismissed by the Court of Appeal. He now appeals to the House of Lords on the following two certified points of law:

(1) Whether a photofit compiled by a description from an eye witness is hearsay and inadmissible; or whether, if hearsay, it falls within the exceptions to the hearsay rule.

(2) If the photofit evidence were to be found inadmissible, whether there must be evidence directly or indirectly connecting an accused person with the present offence(s) before evidence of similar facts can be admitted on behalf of the prosecution.

In the House of Lords – Trusts Law Moot
Re Hythe (Fawcett v Bannister)

On 13 May 1996, Amanda Hythe died. By cl 4 of her will, drafted by herself, she left:

> ... £250,000 to my close friend Jennifer Bannister UPON TRUST to invest the same and to distribute the income thereof for the maximum period permitted by the law among such of my relatives as the said Jennifer Bannister should, in her absolute discretion, think fit.

The residue of Ms. Hythe's estate was left to Sarah Fawcett absolutely. Nowhere in the will was the expression 'my relatives' defined. Sarah Fawcett challenged the validity of cl 4 on the basis that the word 'relatives' was uncertain.

In the Chancery Division of the High Court of Justice, Fearless J held that cl 4 was sufficiently certain and therefore valid. Her Ladyship said that she was bound, by a combination of the decision of the House of Lords in *McPhail v Doulton* [1971] AC 424 and the decision of the Court of Appeal in *Re Baden's Deed Trusts (No 2)* [1973] Ch 9, so to hold.

Sarah Fawcett, the residuary legatee, now appeals to the House of Lords, all formalities having been complied with for a 'leapfrog' appeal. She contends that:

(1) Contrary to the decision of the Court of Appeal in *Re Baden's Deed Trusts (No 2)*, the word 'relatives' fails the test for the certainty of objects laid down by the House of Lords in *McPhail v Doulton*.

(2) In the alternative, since the test for the certainty of objects of discretionary trusts laid down in *McPhail v Doulton* is defective, it is right for the House of Lords now to depart from it, by holding that the objects of a discretionary trust are uncertain unless the whole range of potential beneficiaries of the trust is ascertainable with certainty.

Appendix 3[1]

In the House of Lords – Tort Moot
Smith and Davies v Chemco Ltd

Chemco Ltd is a chemical manufacturing company which manufactures chemicals for commercial use. The chemicals are dangerous and are accordingly stored underground. However, due to a crack in the container tanks (which can in no way be attributed to fault on the part of Chemco Ltd) chemicals escape into the mains water supply of a neighbouring house owned by Mrs Davies. Chemco Ltd is fully aware of the inherent dangers of grave physical injury being caused by direct human contact with the chemicals.

Mrs Smith lives with her daughter, Mrs Davies, in Rose Cottage, an old workman's cottage which is adjacent to the chemical plant. Whilst sitting in the garden one summer's afternoon, Mrs Smith poured her daughter a glass of iced water. Shortly after drinking the water Mrs Davies suddenly started to suffer serious convulsions and collapsed. On seeing her daughter collapse, suspecting the worst, Mrs Smith panicked.

Mrs Davies was rushed to hospital where she was treated for serious internal injuries caused by drinking the contaminated water. Since the incident, Mrs Smith has been unable to sleep due to recurring nightmares. She has been diagnosed as suffering post-traumatic stress disorder.

Mrs Smith and Mrs Davies took legal action against Chemco Ltd in respect of the personal injuries they sustained.

The Court of Appeal upheld the decision of Acid J at first instance who found that:

(1)   In relation to Mrs Davies, there can be no claim for personal injury under the rule in *Rylands v Fletcher*.

(2)   As to Mrs Smith, there can be no liability for psychiatric injury founded on *Rylands v Fletcher* liability.

---

1   This moot problem was originally prepared by Caroline Jackson, Collette Jolly, Marie Jones, Colin Makin and Faye Maxted, who were then students at the Nottingham Law School, The Nottingham Trent University.

Mrs Davies and Mrs Smith now appeal to the House of Lords on the following two grounds:

(1) In relation to Mrs Davies, there can be a claim for personal injury under the rule in *Rylands v Fletcher*.

(2) As to Mrs Smith, there can be liability for psychiatric injury under the rule in *Rylands v Fletcher*.

Appendix 4

Practice Statement (Judicial Precedent) [1966] 1 WLR 1234

Before judgments were given in the House of Lords on 26 July 1966, Lord Gardiner LC made the following statement on behalf of himself and the Lords of Appeal in Ordinary:

> Their Lordships regard the use of precedent as an indispensable foundation upon which to decide what is the law and its application to individual cases. It provides at least some degree of certainty upon which individuals can rely in the conduct of their affairs, as well as a basis for orderly development of legal rules.
>
> Their Lordships nevertheless recognise that too rigid an adherence to precedent may lead to injustice in a particular case and also unduly restrict the proper development of the law. They propose, therefore, to modify their present practice and, while treating former decisions of this House as normally binding, to depart from a previous decision when it appears right to do so.
>
> In this connection they will bear in mind the danger of disturbing retrospectively the basis on which contracts, settlements of property and fiscal arrangements have been entered into and also the especial need for certainty as to the criminal law.
>
> This announcement is not intended to affect the use of precedent elsewhere than in this House.

Explanatory Note for Press

Since the House of Lords decided the English case of *London Street Tramways* [*sic*] *v London County Council* in 1898, the House have considered themselves bound to follow their own decisions, except where a decision has been given, *per incuriam*, in disregard of a statutory provision or another decision binding on them.

The statement made is one of great importance, although it should not be supposed that there will frequently be cases in which the House thinks it right not to follow their own precedent. An example of a case in which the House might think it right to depart from a precedent is where they consider that the earlier decision was influenced by the existence of conditions which no longer prevail, and that in modern conditions, the law ought to be different.

One consequence of this change is of major importance. The relaxation of the rule of judicial precedent will enable the House of Lords to pay greater attention to judicial decisions reached in the superior courts of the Commonwealth, where they differ from earlier decisions of the House of Lords. That could be of great help in the development of our own law. The superior courts of many other countries are not rigidly bound by their own decisions and the change in the practice of the House of Lords will bring us more in line with them.

Appendix 5

Extracts from the Official Handbook for the English-Speaking Union National Mooting Competition 1999–2000

COMPETITION RULES

The competition is to be known as 'The ESU National Mooting Competition, sponsored by Lovell White Durrant'. The competition is administered by Jonathan Hills at the English-Speaking Union (ESU). The National Adjudicator, Laura Macgregor, is responsible for the setting of moot problems and any matters of a legal nature relating to the competition.

Entry to the competition is open to all universities or higher education colleges involved in the teaching of law in the UK. To qualify for entry, an institution must:

- send an entry fee of £20 to the ESU; and
- submit a moot problem, as described below.

A participating institution may enter a team consisting of two eligible students at that institution. The members of the team may be varied between rounds; however, the members of a team that wins a competition semi-final must also represent the institution in the final. Students are regarded as eligible if they are registered students at the participating institution and are not graduates in law. Similarly, students are not eligible if they hold or are studying for professional legal qualifications (that is, the Legal Practice Course, Bar Vocational Course or ILEX courses).

There shall be no appeal on any grounds from the decision of a judge or upon the conduct of the moot itself at any round. Any complaints about, or problems with, the conduct of teams during a round, must be made in writing to the National Adjudicator, who may then investigate and resolve the problem as she thinks fit in the best interests of the competition. The National Adjudicator and the ESU have the discretion to disqualify at any stage any institution that fails to comply with these rules or with the spirit of the competition. An institution may be disqualified either on the basis of its own acts or omissions, or on the basis of the conduct of the team representing it in a given round.

Any questions regarding the interpretation of these rules shall be submitted to the National Adjudicator who may, in consultation with the ESU, resolve the problem in her absolute discretion ...

MOOT FORMAT

All moot problems are set as a case on appeal to the Court of Appeal or the House of Lords, represented by a single judge. Each round consists of two teams, with the Home team in each case representing the Appellant and the Away team representing the Respondent. Three judges will sit at the National Final. Teams participating in the final will be allocated sides at random.

Each team consists of two speakers, a leader and a junior. The leader takes the first ground of appeal; the junior takes the second. The four speakers will be heard in the following order and for the following times:

Leader for the Appellant:	20 minutes
Junior for the Appellant:	15 minutes
Leader for the Respondent:	20 minutes
Junior for the Respondent:	20 minutes
Appellant's Right to Reply:	5 minutes (not obligatory)

On an occasion where the moot takes the form of an appeal and cross-appeal, the order and timing of speeches shall be as follows:

Leader for the Appellant:	20 minutes
Leader for the Respondent:	20 minutes
Junior for the Cross-Appellant:	15 minutes
Junior for the Cross-Respondent:	15 minutes
Reply by the Appellant:	5 minutes
Reply by the Cross-Appellant:	5 minutes

The order may be changed with the consent of all concerned. No team may concede a point of law identified in the problem as one to be argued except with the express prior consent of the other team and the judge of that round.

PROBLEMS

Every participating institution must submit a moot problem, which must be of a *sufficient standard for university students*. Each moot problem submitted must be approved by at least one member of staff in the faculty or department concerned, other than the person who devised the problem.

A moot problem must be on a 'core' legal subject that does not require specialist knowledge. Examples of core subjects are criminal law, contract, tort (or delict), company and commercial law, constitutional law, employment law, consumer protection law, EC law and any area of law based on a UK statute.

Problems should be on legal issues that are common to all the legal jurisdictions of the UK. If, however, two Scottish teams are drawn against each other, they may substitute the set problem with one from Scottish law

The moot problem shall be solely concerned with points of law. It shall be a case heard on appeal by the Court of Appeal or the House of Lords and must have no less and no more than two grounds for appeal clearly stated.

No objection to any moot problem will be sustained unless communicated to the National Adjudicator within seven days of the receipt of the problem. If the National Adjudicator is satisfied with the objection, she may direct that another problem be used.

AUTHORITIES

A team may rely on no more than eight authorities of its own choosing, which it must cite in a list of authorities. All authorities cited may be used by either the Appellants or the Respondents for any purpose. If an authority is cited as part of the moot problem, it is classed as a court authority which may be used by either team and which need not be included in either side's list.

A single case which has been decided in more than one court (for example, a case that has started in the High Court and then gone to the Court of Appeal and then to the House of Lords) counts as one authority, although all references must be cited if a team wishes to use them.

For the purpose of this competition, only cases count as authorities. However if it is intended to cite statutes, texts or other legal literature then, notwithstanding that these do not count in the lists of eight, they must be disclosed to the opposing team at the time of the exchange of authorities.

Both lists of authorities must be exchanged by fax at least 48 hours before the moot. Forty-eight hours is calculated on the basis of ordinary working days, and does not include weekends or bank holidays. Their arrival and contents must be confirmed by the sender by telephone. No variation of authorities will be allowed unless the opposing team agrees.

Cases should be cited as authorities in the following descending order of priority:

> *Law Reports;*
> *Weekly Law Reports;*
> *All England Law Reports;*
> others.

A team that cites an 'obscure' authority (an authority which cannot within reason be located by their opponents) is responsible for providing copies of that authority for their opponent and the Moot Court.

SKELETON ARGUMENTS

A team must also submit a skeleton argument setting out the main propositions and submissions in support of their case. This skeleton argument must also be exchanged by fax at least 48 hours before the Moot. Its arrival must be confirmed by the sender by telephone. Forty-eight hours is again based on ordinary working days, and does not include weekends and bank holidays. **The skeleton argument should not be longer than one side of A4, and should be typed, word processed, or hand written in block capitals.** The main grounds of argument should be set out concisely, together with the authorities relied on to support the argument. Apart from the Final, it is not necessary for judges to be sent skeleton arguments in advance of the moot.

Both teams may, by consent, dispense with the need for skeleton arguments if such a course is agreed upon at least seven days before the Moot is due to take place.

TEAMS IN THE FINAL

The teams participating in the Final are required to produce skeleton arguments, lists of authorities and three copies (bundles) of all their authorities in advance of the Final for use by the Judges. These must be delivered to the ESU no later than **Thursday 15th June 2000**. The requirement for skeleton arguments for the Final may not be dispensed with.

HOST RESPONSIBILITIES

The English-Speaking Union greatly appreciates the warm hospitality of the institutions that host the rounds of the competition. All participating institutions undertake to host a round, if allocated the position of 'Home' team. A host institution has a number of responsibilities:

- to locate a judge who meets the criteria described below in Selection of Judges. The 'Away' team must give their consent to the judge, whose identity and background should be made known to them with as much notice as possible;

- to provide the judge with a copy of the moot problem and this handbook, drawing their attention to these rules and the marking sheets;

- to provide the judge with the lists of authorities prior to the moot;

- to provide the ESU with copies of the completed judges' marksheet, where possible, so that a record can be kept in case of appeal;

- to ensure that copies of the skeleton arguments are produced for the judge at the time of the moot;

- to ensure sufficient copies of all authorities cited by both parties are available for production in the Moot Court;

- to communicate details of the round venue, date and time to the Away team, and to confirm that they have been received;

- to prepare a Moot Courtroom and provide water for the judge and speakers' use;

- to provide a clerk to the Moot Court, who is required to keep time. The clerk shall inform the judge when the time periods have elapsed, preferably by means of a note. Mooters should also be alerted, through the display of a card, when they have five minutes left to speak and also one minute left. The clerk should use a stopwatch to keep time. **Please note that the clock is not stopped for interruptions by judges.**

SELECTION OF JUDGES

Judges shall be qualified legal practitioners (barristers, solicitors or advocates) or lecturers in law, and must be experienced in the judging of moots. Unless agreed in advance by both competing institutions and the National Adjudicator, the judge in a given round other than the National Final (for which a panel of judges must be arranged before the finalists are known) may not be an employee, former employee, student or former student of either competing institution. An employee of a neighbouring institution is an appropriate judge.

Judges should be selected who have some relevant experience of the fields of law upon which the moot is set. For example, a practitioner or academic who has acted solely in the area of civil law would be an inappropriate judge in a criminal moot problem.

GUIDANCE FOR JUDGES

A judge has the following duties:

- to give judgement on the various points of law argued by the speakers;
- to give a reasoned judgment as to the merits and faults of the participants;
- to decide upon and announce the winning team.

The winning team of the round is at the sole discretion of the judge. The decision of the judge on any point cannot be appealed.

It is suggested that, in order to ensure an element of consistency throughout the competition, the judge should use three criteria to decide upon each team's performance: Content; Strategy and Style. It is hoped that these criteria can best evaluate each team's relative strengths. A scoring sheet has been provided to assess mooters' individual marks. In the end, however, it is the overall impression of which team made the most convincing presentation of their case that will determine the outcome. The better team will not necessarily be the team for whom judgement is given on the points of law. The following areas can be considered as relevant guidelines for assessment of the mooters:

Content

- the insight into and analysis of the moot problem and grounds of appeal;
- the relevance of the authorities cited and the fluidity with which they are adduced;
- the ability to summarise facts, cases or law where appropriate.

Strategy

- the presentation and structure of the legal arguments, including skeleton arguments, where used (rigidly scripted speeches, in particular, should be penalised);
- the rebuttal of opponents' arguments;
- the ability of the two individuals to work as a team;
- the effective use of the speaker's limited time;
- the ability to answer questions from the bench.

Style

- the speaker's skill as an advocate;
- the proper use of court etiquette.

The judge may retire to consider the decision. Since this is a team competition, it is expected that the best all-round team will be chosen. When announcing the decision, it is greatly appreciated if, in addition to the questions of law, the judge makes some comment on the merits of the mooters' performances. This advice is always listened to very carefully and the mooters will value such balanced assessments.

Judges are encouraged to interrupt speakers at any time where the judge requires clarification of the legal argument being presented; interruptions also test the mooter's ability to respond as an advocate. **However, the clock is not stopped during interruptions by judges so they are asked to treat all four mooters equitably.** Questions should not be unduly difficult at this level. None of the stated grounds of appeal should be thought to be unarguable by counsel or the judge, and judges should not refuse to hear an argument for that reason. However, if a team fails to produce cited authorities, the judge has the discretion to render the citation inadmissible. Finally, judges should not ask so many questions that mooters are unable to complete the points raised in their skeleton arguments. Although it is proper for judges to assess the quality and appropriateness of arguments, mooters should not be prevented from putting forward arguments in their own way.

Appendix 6

THE ESU NATIONAL MOOTING COMPETITION 1999–2000

SPONSORED BY

LOVELL WHITE DURRANT

JUDGE'S SCORE SHEET

Appellants: *Respondents:*

APPELLANTS

Speaker Name	Content	Strategy	Style	Total	Comment
Leader	20	20	10	50	
Junior	20	20	10	50	
Reply Speech					
Total	**40**	**40**	**20**	**100**	

RESPONDENTS

Speaker Name	Content	Strategy	Style	Total	Comment
Leader	20	20	10	50	
Junior	20	20	10	50	
Total	**40**	**40**	**20**	**100**	

The Official Handbook for the ESU National Mooting Competition, sponsored by Essex Court Chambers, is published by the English-Speaking Union Centre for Speech and Debate, tel: 020 7493 3328.

Appendix 7

Specimen moot assessment sheet

Name of judge: **Moot problem details:**

Name of student: **Date:**

1   Ability to moot without reading from a prepared script, and to maintain eye contact with the moot judge.

F ☐   3 ☐   2.2 ☐   2.1 ☐   1 ☐

2   Posture, that is, the ability to sit still whilst other mooters are making their submissions and (subject to physical capacity) to stand still without fidgeting or making unnecessary gestures when making submissions.

F ☐   3 ☐   2.2 ☐   2.1 ☐   1 ☐

3   Use of language, for example, grammar and sentence construction.

F ☐   3 ☐   2.2 ☐   2.1 ☐   1 ☐

4   Quality of speech, that is, speed, pronunciation and voice protection.

F ☐   3 ☐   2.2 ☐   2.1 ☐   1 ☐

5   Court etiquette, in particular, the ability to refer to the judges by their correct titles and their decisions by their correct names, for example, judgment, speech or opinion.

F ☐   3 ☐   2.2 ☐   2.1 ☐   1 ☐

6   Courtesy towards the judge, for example, waiting until he or she has found the place in the law report or has finished making a written note and your ability to recognise when a submission is being well or poorly received by the judge and to adapt accordingly.

F ☐   3 ☐   2.2 ☐   2.1 ☐   1 ☐

7   Confidence of mooter's delivery.

F ☐   3 ☐   2.2 ☐   2.1 ☐   1 ☐

8   Persuasiveness of mooter's delivery.

F ☐   3 ☐   2.2 ☐   2.1 ☐   1 ☐

9   Clarity of initial submissions.

F ☐   3 ☐   2.2 ☐   2.1 ☐   1 ☐

10   Logical structure of legal argument.

F ☐   3 ☐   2.2 ☐   2.1 ☐   1 ☐

11   Recognition of legal issues raised by moot problem.

F ☐   3 ☐   2.2 ☐   2.1 ☐   1 ☐

12   Apparent depth of research and preparation.

F ☐   3 ☐   2.2 ☐   2.1 ☐   1 ☐

13   Ability to argue within the ground of appeal.

F ☐   3 ☐   2.2 ☐   2.1 ☐   1 ☐

14   Application of law to the facts of the moot problem.

15   Ingenuity of the legal argument, for example, ability to utilise or adopt apparently unconnected areas of law.

F ☐   3 ☐   2.2 ☐   2.1 ☐   1 ☐

16   Understanding and application of English legal method.

F ☐   3 ☐   2.2 ☐   2.1 ☐   1 ☐

17   Familiarity with the authorities cited, including the ability to cite from the judges in those authorities and not headnotes or counsel's argument.

F ☐   3 ☐   2.2 ☐   2.1 ☐   1 ☐

18   Ability to withstand judicial questioning and to respond to questions logically.

F ☐   3 ☐   2.2 ☐   2.1 ☐   1 ☐

19   Ability to respond to the moot judge's questions by reference to appropriate law.

F ☐   3 ☐   2.2 ☐   2.1 ☐   1 ☐

20   Clarity of your invitations to the court, for example, that you are inviting the court to overrule case A or to distinguish case B or telling the court that it is bound by the decision in case C.

Penalties

- There is a maximum of five penalty marks for failing to give your list of authorities to your opponents and to the judge on time.
- There is a maximum of five penalty marks for citing an authority not appearing on the lists of authorities.

Appendix 8

Latin and law-French Glossary

A pronunciation guide is included. It is not set out in any internationally recognised phonetic script, instead we have opted for a literal pronunciation guide. Glanville Williams in *Learning the Law* (see Bibliography) provides a good example when he advises the student to pronounce *cestui que trust* as "settee key trust". In our guide we amplify this guidance thus: settee key trust. The underlining denotes the use of a standard English word as a guide to pronunciation. Some of the phrases in this glossary can be pronounced other than in the way we recommend. Where there is a legitimate choice, use the pronunciation you feel most comfortable with.

ab initio	Ab in-ish-ee-<u>oh</u>: from the beginning. For example, a trust set up by a trader, with the intention of defrauding his creditors will be void *ab initio*.
actus non facit reum nisi mens sit rea	<u>Act</u>-uss Non fakkit <u>ray</u>-um <u>Nigh</u>-<u>sigh</u> menz <u>sit</u> <u>ray</u>-ah: the act does not become a wrong without a wrongful intent, hence *actus reus* and *mens rea*.
ad litem	Ad <u>light</u>-em: for the purpose of litigation. For example, a guardian *ad litem* is appointed by the court to defend the interests of infants in litigation. On and after 26 April 1999, under the Civil Procedure Rules, guardians *ad litem*, as next friends, are together referred to as 'litigation friends'.
amicus curiae	a-meek-uss <u>cure</u>-ee-<u>eye</u>: friend of the court (see the answer to Question 11).
a priori	ae <u>pry</u>-or-<u>eye</u>: from first principles. Deductive reasoning. For example, if all Romans are men, and if Caesar is a Roman, then *a priori* Caesar is a man (see the answer to Question 31).
audi alteram partem	ow-<u>die</u> al-<u>tare</u>-emm <u>part</u>-emm: hear the other side.
autrefois acquit/convict	out-rer fwar <u>a</u>-<u>quit</u>/<u>convict</u>: previously acquitted/convicted [law-French]. A defence to a criminal prosecution where the defendant pleads that he has already been acquitted/convicted of the offence.

autre vie	<u>out</u>-rer vee: the life of another [law-French]. For example, a gift of land can be made to X *pur autre vie* (that is, to be X's as long as another person, Y, shall live).
bona fide	<u>bone</u>-a fyde (or: bonna fye-dee): good faith. For example, under the *bona fide* purchaser rule, the *bona fide* purchaser who purchased a legal interest without notice of equitable encumbrances on the title was not bound by those encumbrances.
bona vacantia	<u>bone</u>-a vak-ansh-ee-a (or: bonna vak-<u>ant</u>-ee-a): vacant goods, that is, ownerless property. In England and Wales ownerless property will usually pass to the Crown or the Duchy of Lancaster.
causa causans	co-<u>czar</u> co-sanz (or: <u>core</u>-<u>czar</u> <u>core</u>-sanz): the effective cause. If X sells a bullet, Y sells a gun and Z shoots and thereby kills somebody with the bullet from the gun, we would say that Z's action was the *causa causans* of the victim's death.
causa sine qua non	co-<u>czar</u> <u>sigh</u>-<u>nigh</u> kwarr <u>none</u>: continuing the above example, we would say that the actions of X and Y were *causae sine qua non* of the killing. That is, actions without which the killing would not have taken place.
caveat emptor	kav-ee-at empt-<u>or</u>: let the buyer beware. This is the ancient rule that a purchaser of goods must satisfy himself of their quality before purchase or else be bound by the consequences. Largely superseded by the Sale of Goods Act 1979, although it still applies to land.
certiorari	<u>sir</u>-<u>she</u>-<u>err</u>-<u>rare</u>-<u>eye</u> (or: <u>sir</u>-<u>she</u>-<u>err</u>-<u>rare</u>-ee): an administrative law prerogative order, whereby the decision of an inferior court or tribunal is quashed (for example, where decision made *ultra vires*).
certum est quod certum reddi potest	<u>sir</u>-tumm esst <u>quad</u> <u>sir</u>-tumm <u>red</u>-dee poh-<u>test</u>: that is certain which can be made certain. A good maxim to produce next time a moot judge tells you that your arguments are too vague!
cestui que trust	<u>settee</u> <u>key</u> <u>trust</u>: the one who trusts, that is, the beneficiary of a trust (see the answer to Question 47).
chose in action	<u>shows</u> <u>in</u> <u>action</u>: the right to proceed for a remedy in a court of law.
compos mentis	kommp-oss <u>meant</u>-iss: of sound mind.

contra proferentem	kontra <u>prow</u>-<u>far</u>-ent-em: against the one who benefits. Where, for instance, a term of a trust instrument purports to limit or exclude the trustees liability for breach of trust, such a clause will be construed, where ambiguous, in favour of the beneficiaries and against the trustee.
cujus est solum ejus est usque ad coelem et ad infernos	coo-juss esst <u>sole</u>-um esst uss-<u>key</u> <u>add</u> <u>sea</u>-lem ett <u>add</u> in-<u>fair</u>-noss: whoever is the owner of the soil is owner also up to heaven and down to hell. An ancient rule of land law, now much curtailed by the public interest in air travel, mining, and so on.
curia advisari vult	<u>cure</u>-<u>ear</u> <u>advise</u>-<u>airy</u> vulltt: the court wishes to be advised. In a case where the court postpones the giving of its judgment until some time after the hearing, the report will contain the following abbreviation: *cur adv vult*, or *cur ad vult*.
cy-près	<u>sea</u>-<u>pray</u>: the nearest thing [law-French]. Where a charitable gift fails it is often possible for the gift to be applied *cy-près* to benefit another charity with similar aims.
decree nisi	decree <u>nigh</u>-<u>sigh</u>: the interim decree which precedes the decrees absolute of, *inter alia*, divorce and foreclosure.
de facto/de jure	dee (or <u>day</u>) <u>fact</u>-<u>owe</u> / dee (or <u>day</u>) <u>jury</u>: in fact / in law. For example, the big boss was in *de facto* control of the company even though he was not a director of it.
delegatus non potest delegare	<u>dell</u>-<u>leg</u>-<u>art</u>-uss <u>none</u> poh-<u>test</u> <u>dell</u>-<u>leg</u>-<u>are</u>-ee: the one to whom power is delegated may not delegate this power to another.
de minimus non curat lex	dee (or <u>day</u>) <u>mini</u>-muss <u>none</u> <u>cure</u>-<u>at</u> lecks: the law does not concern itself with trifles. A trifle is a trivial matter – avoid the obvious pun!
devise	<u>devise</u>: a testamentary (that is, by will) gift of land.
donatio mortis causa	<u>dough</u>-naysh-ee-owe (or <u>dough</u>-nar-<u>tea</u>-<u>owe</u>) <u>more</u>-tiss co-<u>czar</u> (or <u>core</u>-<u>czar</u>): a gift made because of the donors impending death from some known cause.
ejusdem generis	ay-<u>juiced</u>-emm jenner-iss: of the same nature. A rule of construction and statutory interpretation which applies where the general follows the particular. So, for example, if the eating of apples, pears, oranges, bananas and other food is prohibited by a rule, the eating of fish is not (see the answers to Questions 36 and 94).
en ventre sa mère	on vonnt-rah <u>Sam</u>-<u>err</u>: in his or her mother's womb [law-French], that is, unborn.

ex abundanti cautela   <u>eggs</u> a-<u>bun</u>-<u>dan</u>-tay co-<u>tea</u>-la: from excess of caution.

ex parte   <u>eggs</u> <u>party</u>: without the party. Used in two contexts: (1) where an action is brought at the behest of a party which does not itself appear as a party, for example, *R v Secretary of State for the Home Department ex parte Brind* [1991] AC 696. Usually abbreviated *ex p* in this context; and (2) where an action is brought by one party in the absence of the other party. Usual in applications for emergency injunctions to restrain domestic violence. On and after 26 April 1999, under the Civil Procedure Rules 1999, *ex parte* applications are referred to as applications made without notice.

expressio unius   <u>eggs</u>-<u>press</u>-<u>she</u>-<u>owe</u> <u>you</u>-<u>knee</u>-uss esst <u>eggs</u>-<u>clue</u>-zee-
est exclusio alterius   <u>owe</u> ollt-<u>err</u>-ee-uss: express reference to one, excludes implied reference to another. A rule of language. For example, if the eating of apples, oranges, bananas and pears is expressly prohibited, the eating of fish is presumed not to be (see the answer to Question 94).

ex tempore   <u>eggs</u> temmp-<u>ore</u>-ee: At the time. For example, an *ex tempore* judgment is one which is delivered immediately upon the conclusion of the hearing of the matter (contrast the *reversed* judgment, which is a judgment delivered some time after the hearing, allowing the judge more time to consider the phrasing of the judgment).

ex turpi causa   <u>eggs</u> <u>tare</u>-<u>pay</u> <u>co</u>-<u>czar</u> <u>none</u> <u>ore</u>-retter ack-<u>she</u>-<u>owe</u>: no
non oritur actio   action can lie from a wrongful cause. The usual example given is that of the burglar who blows a safe negligently, injuring his partner in crime. The injured party cannot sue the safe-blower. The maxim has the potential to apply to moral wrongs as well as crimes.

habeas corpus   <u>hay</u>-<u>bee</u>-<u>ass</u> (or hab-<u>bee</u>-<u>ass</u>) <u>core</u>-<u>puss</u>: have the body. A writ by which the court requires a person to be produced to court out of custody.

ibid/ibidem   ibb-idd / ibb-idd-demm: in the same place as something else, usually a quotation from a text.

ignorantia   <u>ignore</u>-ansh-<u>ear</u> <u>jaw</u>-riss <u>none</u> <u>eggs</u>-<u>cue</u>-zat: ignorance of
juris non excusat   the law is no defence.

in banc   <u>inn</u> <u>bonk</u>: before the 1873–75 Judicature Acts, these were sittings of the judges of Exchequer, Queen's Bench and Common Pleas, for the determination of questions of law, as opposed to questions of fact (see the answer to Question 92).

in camera/curia	inn <u>camera</u> / <u>cure</u>-ear: in closed/open court. On and after 26 April 1999, *in camera* hearings are referred to simply as hearings in private.
in extenso	in <u>eggs</u>-<u>tents</u>-<u>so</u>: in full.
in lieu	inn lyuw: in the place of, ie instead of. For example, it is possible for a claimant to accept damages *in lieu* of specific performance.
in loco parentis	inn <u>low</u>-co <u>pair</u>-entiss: in the parent's place. A guardian is said to stand *in loco parentis* to the child in his or her care.
in pari delicto	inn <u>parry</u> <u>day</u>-<u>licked</u>-<u>toe</u>: equally at fault.
in pari materia	inn <u>parry</u> <u>mat</u>-ee-<u>rear</u>: in a case which is analogous.
in personam	inn <u>purse</u>-<u>own</u>-em: personally. For example, to say that X brought an in personam claim against Y, means that X brought the claim against Y personally. Normally contrasted with the claim *in rem*, which is a claim against property held by the defendant.
in rem	inn remm (or inn raym): see *in personam*.
in specie	inn spee-<u>she</u>-ee (or inns <u>pea</u>-<u>sea</u>): in its own species, for example, a dividend *in specie* of shares. This is a dividend paid on shares which takes the form of other shares.
inter alia	inn-<u>tare</u> <u>ale</u>-<u>lee</u>-yerr: among other things.
inter vivos	inn-<u>tare</u> <u>vie</u>-voss (or vee-voss) (or vee-vowz): between living people. A gift made *inter vivos* should be contrasted with a testamentary gift (one that is made by will and is effective from the death of the testator/testatrix).
intra vires	inn-tra <u>vie</u>-reez (or vee-reez): see *ultra vires*.
ipso facto	ipp-<u>so</u> <u>fact</u>-<u>owe</u>: by this very fact. For example, if Romans are never Greeks then *ipso facto* Greeks are never Romans.
lex posterior derogat priori	lecks <u>posterior</u> derr-<u>rogue</u>-att <u>pry</u>-<u>or</u>-<u>eye</u>: a later law overrules an earlier one.
locus standi	<u>low</u>-cuss <u>stand</u>-<u>eye</u>: the place of standing. The right to be heard before a court.
mala fides	malla <u>fie</u>-deez (or <u>fee</u>-<u>dies</u>): bad faith. See *bona fide*.
mandamus	man-<u>day</u>-muss: we command. A prerogative order of the court ordering the performance of a public duty (for example, compelling an inferior tribunal to re-hear a case).

mens rea	menz <u>rear</u>: a state of mind which the law considers criminal, literally a 'guilty mind', occasionally – possibly incorrectly – extending to concepts involving the absence of a state of mind, for example, recklessness (see *actus non facit reum, nisi mens sit rea*).
mutatis mutandis	<u>mute</u>-tay-tiss <u>mute</u>-<u>and</u>-iss: the necessary changes made.
nec vi, nec clam, nec precario	<u>neck</u>-vee <u>neck</u>-<u>clam</u> <u>neck</u> <u>pray</u>-<u>car</u>-<u>Rio</u>: without violence, stealth or permission. For a person successfully to claim adverse possession of another's land, or to claim an easement or profit by prescription as of right, they must show that they have acquired their right without force, concealment or permission.
nemo dat quod non habet	nemmo datt <u>quad</u> <u>none</u> habbet: nobody gives what they do not have. One cannot sell better title than the title which was sold to one.
nisi prius	<u>nigh</u>-<u>sigh</u> <u>pry</u>-uss: a trial with a jury and single judge, for example, on assize.
noscitur a sociis	noss-<u>set</u>-ur <u>so</u>-<u>sea</u>-iss: knowledge from its society. A rule of language that meaning can be deduced from context (see the answer to Question 94).
novus actus interveniens	<u>no</u>-vuss <u>act</u>-uss <u>inn</u>-<u>tare</u>-venn-ee-enz: a new act intervening. The intervening act of another person may break the chain of causation otherwise linking one to a result. Here is a poser: A man has enough water to survive a desert crossing but one night X poisons his water with poison certainly strong enough to kill him. Later that night, Y steals the traveller's water. The next day the traveller dies in the desert heat. Can you spot the *novus actus interveniens*? It might assist you to ask, who killed the traveller?
obiter dictum	<u>oh</u>-<u>bit</u>-<u>err</u> <u>Dick</u>-tumm: a saying which is 'by the way' in a judgment (see the answer to Question 20).
onus probandi	<u>oh</u>-nuss pro-<u>band</u>-<u>eye</u>: the onus (burden) of proof (convincing). In a criminal trial, the *onus probandi* is almost always on the prosecution in relation to all matters alleged by it. (See, for instance, *Woolmington v Director of Public Prosecutions* [1932] AC 462.)
pari passu	<u>parry</u> <u>pass</u>-<u>you</u> (or pass-oo): a fund divided *pari passu* is divided equally.
per curiam	<u>pair</u> <u>cure</u>-ee-amm: by the court (see the answer to Question 36).

per incuriam	pair ink-<u>cure</u>-ee-amm: without the court's knowledge (see answer to Question 36).
per stirpes	pair <u>stair</u>-<u>pea</u>s: by branches. Division of property by branches or stocks of descent, as on an intestacy.
pro bono publico	pro <u>bone</u>-<u>owe</u> <u>pub</u>-<u>leak</u>-<u>owe</u>: for the public good.
profits à prendre	<u>profits</u> a prond-rer: rights to take [law-French]. In land law, the right to take from another's land something which occurs there naturally. There are *profits à prendre* of pescary (fish), turbary (turf) pasture (grass) and estover (wood), to name but a few.
pro privato commodo	pro priv-art-<u>owe</u> kom-<u>oh</u>-<u>dough</u>: for private convenience.
pro rata	pro rar-<u>tar</u>: proportionally, rateably.
puisne	*puny*: lesser [law-French, pronounced 'puny']. A *puisne mortgage* is a legal mortgage which is not protected by a deposit of deeds and which must be registered to be protected. Judges of the High Court of Justice are sometimes referred to as *puisne* judges.
quantum meruit	kwont-umm <u>may</u>-<u>rue</u>-<u>it</u>: the sum merited. For example, a court may award money on a *quantum meruit* basis to a person who has worked for another's benefit under the legitimate expectation that they would be paid.
quicquid plantatur solo, solo cedit	<u>quick</u>-<u>quid</u> <u>plant</u>-a-<u>tour</u> <u>so</u>-<u>low</u>, <u>so</u>-<u>low</u> seed-<u>it</u>: that which is attached to soil accedes to the soil. The rule of fixtures, which states that land includes not only the soil, but all fixtures (for example, buildings and trees) on it.
quid pro quo	<u>quid</u> pro kwow: something for something else. For example, contractual consideration is a *quid pro quo*.
ratio decidendi	<u>ray</u>-<u>she</u>-<u>owe</u> dess-id-<u>den</u>-<u>dee</u> (or <u>den</u>-<u>die</u>): the reason given for a judgment (see the answer to Question 20).
re	ree (or <u>ray</u>): in the matter of.
rebus sic stantibus	ree-<u>bus</u> <u>sick</u> stann-<u>tea</u>-<u>bus</u>: matters standing thus. Where an authority is laid down *rebus sic stantibus*, it is said to be a binding authority only so long as those relevant conditions continue to prevail which existed at the time the authority was laid down. It is a term more usually applied in public international law as a means by which one nation State will, often unilaterally, purport to avoid the binding effect of a treaty (see the answer to Question 41).
Regina	rej-ine-a: the Queen (abbreviated to 'Reg' or 'R'). Note, however, that this may be pronounced 'the Crown'.

res ipsa loquitur	<u>ray</u>-<u>zip</u>-ssa <u>lock</u>-<u>quitter</u>: the thing speaks for itself. For example, if a collision occurs between two cars driven by strangers on an otherwise deserted road, the facts speak for themselves: one of the drivers was negligent.
Rex	<u>wrecks</u>: the King (abbreviated to 'R'). Note, however, that this may be pronounced 'the Crown'.
salus populi est suprema lex	sall-uss <u>pop</u>-<u>you</u>-<u>lie</u> esst <u>supreme</u>-<u>alex</u>: the welfare of the people is the highest law. (From the Roman Law of the Twelve Tables): A moot winning maxim?
stare decisis	<u>stay</u>-ree (or <u>starry</u>) <u>decease</u>-iss: to stand by things decided (see the answer to Question 85).
sui generis	ss-<u>you</u>-ee (or swee) jenner-iss: in a class of its own. Very useful in a moot when seeking to persuade the judge that your case, or another case, is peculiar to its facts.
sub judice	<u>sub</u> <u>Judy</u>-<u>sea</u> (or <u>dew</u>-<u>decay</u>): in the course of a trial.
sui juris	ss-<u>you</u>-ee (or swee) <u>jaw</u>-riss: having legal capacity. That is, being adult and of sound mind.
testator/testatrix	<u>test</u>-<u>ate</u>-<u>or</u> / <u>test</u>-a-<u>tricks</u>: male and female forms to describe a person who makes a will.
ultra vires	ull-tra <u>vie</u>-reez (or vee-reez): beyond the power. Acts of governmental bodies may be subjected to judicial review if made *ultra vires*. (The opposite of *ultra vires* is *intra vires*.)
verbatim	verr-<u>bait</u>-imm: word for word.
volenti non fit injuria	voll-en-<u>tea</u> <u>none</u> <u>fit</u> <u>in</u>-<u>your</u>-ee-<u>a</u>: a person who voluntarily submits to harm has suffered no legal wrong.

Appendix 9

Suggested moot court layout

The diagram below is no more than a suggestion as to the layout of a typical moot court.

As you can see, mooters and judge face each other. The Clerk of the Court sits in front of the judge, facing the mooters (see the answer to Question 11). Since the Clerk has the task of indicating timings to the mooters, it is essential that he or she can be clearly seen by them. Ideally, the moot judge should therefore be on a raised dais – a bench – so that he or she can also easily be seen by the mooters.

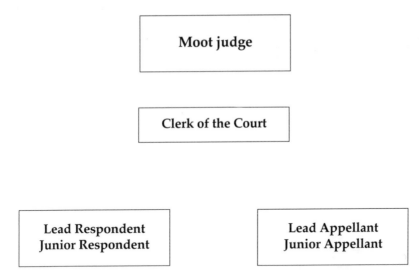

Note that the moot judge needs to be able to complete a moot assessment sheet in relation to each of the moot presentations without the mooters being able to see what he or she is writing. The master/mistress of moots should allow for this point in setting up the moot court (see 'The master or mistress of moots', in the answer to Question 11).

Appendix 10

A short essay on the future of mooting

There are a number of reasons for supposing that mooting may enjoy a future every bit as illustrious as its past (for an outline of the history of mooting see the answer to Question 4).

The future of mooting in the legal academy

This book is first and foremost a guide to student mooters, for it is student members of the legal academy who moot most often. The majority are undergraduates studying for a law degree, but postgraduates frequently partake, as do students on the Bar Vocational Course (BVC). Indeed, since 1997, students from the various institutions that provide the BVC have competed against each other in an annual moot competition. Meanwhile, the Inns of Court, most notably Lincoln's Inn, continue generously to host student moots every year. Mooting continues to be an intellectually and socially stimulating activity for those who volunteer to participate, be they mooter, clerk or judge.

In its voluntary form mooting is uncontroversial. However, the suggestion that mooting could usefully, and legitimately, appear as a compulsory part of an undergraduate course of study is far more controversial ... it is a moot point! Wishing to test this moot point in a public forum, the authors of this Guide led a workshop on mooting at the Second Annual Learning in Law Initiative (LILI) Conference on 7 January 2000 held at The University of Warwick. We invited delegates to present arguments against the inclusion of mooting in law degrees (following the tradition under which the prosecution speaks first). We then presented the case for the defence. The principal argument advanced against compulsory mooting was that mooting is élitist in as much as it 'trains students to be advocates and judges in appellate courts' and (a related point) that it perpetuates an unhealthy bias in the legal academy towards legal practice, given that it is now the case that less than half of all law graduates progress into legal practice in its traditional forms (solicitor and barrister). Other arguments which could have been raised (but weren't), would have been that the emphasis on oral/aural skills might prejudice students for whom English is not their first language, and students with speech difficulties or impaired hearing , not to mention the merely nervous.

The points we made (or would now make) in response are as follows. First, the accusation of élitism. It must be admitted that the insistence upon smart clothing in moots can give the appearance of élitism and it may be that this insistence might be waived were mooting to be made compulsory. We would argue, however, that, far from creating an élite, smart dress actually creates uniformity (quite literally) between mooters. Of course, the accusation of élitism goes to *substance* and not just to *form* ('uni' or otherwise). What of the suggestion that mooting is only fit for training an élite within legal practice? We consider this argument to be somewhat patronising of those students who may have little hope of entering that practising élite. Why, it might be asked, should they be denied 'élite' education merely because they are unlikely to enter 'élite' practice? If allowed to hold sway, this argument would actually have the perverse effect of reinforcing in legal education that very form of élitism which the accuser was earlier so keen to condemn. But there may be students who, far from lacking the hope to enter the practising élite, actually have no desire to enter it. Compelling these students to moot would indeed be wrong, if mooting really were a mere preparation for legal practice. In fact, as we hope this book has demonstrated, there is much more to mooting than this.

It is now widely accepted that any undergraduate course of study should equip students with transferable skills and subject specific skills. Skills appropriate to a law degree would include, to mention but a few: research (legal writing); handling information technology; communication of ideas; the presentation of reasoned argument; interpretation of documents; analysis of argument; critical analysis of law according to its socio-political context, and team work. If we were to devise an activity from scratch (or from *tabula rasa*, which precedes even the first scratch) to develop these skills in a progressively more sophisticated way throughout a course of undergraduate study in law, we would probably end up with something closely resembling mooting in its modern form. The fact that moots are set in appellate courts is particularly useful in encouraging policy based arguments. Mooting may come with somewhat antiquated baggage, but it is a balanced diet of skills (general as well as legal). It is, in fact, a legal education 'entire of itself'. It is no less valid (far more valid in educational terms) than the usual alternatives of lectures and tutorials (or seminars). The tutorial or seminar, which so often involves consideration of the legal response to hypothetical problem scenarios, is really nothing more than a poor successor to the moot. It is often preferred to mooting because it is perceived to allow a higher student to staff ratio, rather than for any sincere educational reason.

Compulsory mooting in every year of an undergraduate law degree is achievable and desirable. The authors have seen it work. Together with their colleague Cliff Atkins (see Preface) they devised and put in place the following system for compulsory mooting within a law degree at The Nottingham Trent University:

Year one: students watch a two hour exhibition moot and receive a one hour introductory lecture on mooting, they then take part in a one hour, four person moot in which a member of the academic staff acts as moot judge. The module taken as a whole does not, therefore, have an onerous staff to student ratio. In the first year, the moot is designed to put students at their ease, as far as possible, the difficulty of the questions put by the judge are tailored according to the perceived ability of the student to cope. Students are assessed against various categories on a mark sheet (see Appendix 7). Some of the categories award marks for aspects of presentation that are not particularly demanding (for example, maintaining eye-contact). This, together with standard linguistic formulae for commencing the speeches (see the answer to Question 83) are intended to put more nervous students at their ease. Due allowance is made for students for whom English is not their first language (who might otherwise have been penalised in those marking categories that relate to language).

Year two: is like year one, but there is no exhibition moot and no introductory lecture. Therefore, to ensure adequate staff contact with students every member of the tutorial/seminar group attends every moot in order to watch the performance of their colleagues. Usually, these moots will be three or four person moots heard in an hour slot on three successive weeks. In the fourth (and final) week the whole group discusses their experiences in the moot and constructively criticises the performance of its members. To ensure that the skills are being developed year after year, in the second year, students are required to exchange skeleton arguments prior to their moot (in the first year, only authorities are exchanged). Their opponents and the judge will now have an idea of their likely arguments and questioning is consequently more searching than it was in year one. We have used an expanded form of skeleton arguments and written responses to written judicial questions in order to facilitate the participation of deaf students in the mooting exercise in both the first and second years.

Year three: in the final year of the law degree programme, students are allocated to groups and required to draft a workable moot problem, and to keep a group journal in which they describe their meetings and the processes they went through in order to produce the required outcome. The moot problem and journal are handed in to a staff member, in word processed form. The moot is then 'performed' (with a group member acting as judge) and the performance is recorded on video. A group mark is given upon completion of the exercise. We have frequently been pleasantly surprised to witness exceptionally good products, even in groups whose members do not appear to be academically brilliant according to the usual indicators (exams and coursework assessments).

We commend this scheme, or a version of it, for use in any law course. Of course, one can include mooting within a law degree in a more limited form.

Even if one does not wish to 'teach' mooting, one could, at the very least, use it as an alternative form of assessment in some modules, and thereby enrich the student's law school experience.

The future of mooting in legal practice

In the September 1997 edition of the American Bar Association Journal, Dan Schweizer, Supreme Court counsel for the National Association of State Attorney's General, in Washington DC is quoted to have said that 'moot courts are an essential part of the preparation for Supreme Court argument and most certainly improve the caliber of the arguments'. On this side of the Atlantic, we have not heard of moots having been used as a form of rehearsal for appellate court hearings. However, there is no reason to suppose that they might not be used in this way in the future. It is a service one can imagine retired judges and senior academics providing to senior advocates. Already, we have heard of moots being used by practitioners (tax practitioners in fact) in order to test current issues in the law. It would seem a short step to use moots to rehearse 'live' cases, always assuming that client confidentiality and other ethical ordinances are adhered to.

If it is objected that this is to use moots in order to further private interests, there is another way in which moots might be used in practice in order to serve the public interest. Where French and German law is enshrined in the form of code, English law is declared on a case by case basis. The word 'declared' is used because, in theory, English judges do not make law, they simply declare how the existing law applies to the instant case (although modern judges frequently admit to their role as law makers. See, for example, Lord Diplock in *Home Office v Dorset Yacht Co* [1970] AC 1004.) The fact that English judge made (or judge declared) law is reported only on a case by case basis means that English law is perpetually replete with issues which have not yet been decided. These issues will not be aired until a case appears, the facts of which are apt to raise the issues. The issues remain hypothetical or 'moot' until they actually become live (until somebody actually pays to litigate them). The problem is, of course, that some interested parties (for example, insurers and tobacco companies) would rather settle issues out of court than to take the risk of an inconvenient decision appearing in the reports. And, on the other side, some parties who would wish to pursue a point of law might be precluded from doing so on account of financial constraints upon them. The public has an interest in the resolution of such uncertainties in the law. It is no comfort to be told that the truth is out there, waiting to be declared. The public wants an authoritative declaration now. This is where moots could again be of assistance. A moot court comprising senior retired members of the judiciary (and possibly senior academics) could pass moot judgments upon hypothetical sets of facts and thereby create a body of decisions which could be reported in the *Moot Law*

Reports and to which real judges could refer as 'persuasive authority' in the disposal of live cases. It is increasingly the case that judges make reference to academic opinions in their judgments. The reasoning and decisions of a properly constituted moot court should attract no less respect.

Conclusion

It should not be forgotten that mooting originated in the practice of the Inns of Court and made its way from there to the law schools. Even today, moots are frequently one of the few contexts for constructive interaction between legal practitioners (solicitors, barristers, judges) and student and staff members of the legal academy. That mooting has a bright future in the academy and, in practice, is clear and that it is already a bright bridge between the two is clearer still.

Appendix 11

The Human Rights Act 1998 and mooting

The Human Rights Act (HRA) 1998 (which can be accessed on the internet at the following address: http://www.legislation.hmso.gov.uk/acts/acts1998/19980042.htm) is expected to come into force in October 2000. What will be its effect and how should your mooting take it into account?

The effect of the Act

The HRA 1998 does not, as is often thought, *incorporate* the European Convention on Human Rights into English law. It does, however, as the long title to the Act explains: '... give effect to rights and freedoms guaranteed under the European Convention ...' So, in what way does it give effect to those rights? This is a question which, at the time of writing, is very much at the forefront of lawyers' minds.

Judges and magistrates have particular cause to consider the effect of the Act, for at least two reasons. First, they wonder if they will be inundated with arguments brought under the Act. They wonder if the judicial system (which has only recently been rendered more efficient by the Woolf Reforms – see p 5) might soon be clogged up by a plethora of arguments based on the various articles and protocols of the European Convention.[1] Secondly, they are unsure of the impact that the Act will have upon the development of the common law (not to mention potential problems in relation to statutory interpretation). So, for example, there is no general common law tort of infringement of privacy, but will they be obliged to create one as a result of the Convention 'Right to Respect for Private and Family Life' (Art 8)? According to *Hansard*, Lord Wilberforce commented (at the Committee stage of the Human Rights Bill in the House of Lords) that 'the Bill is aimed entirely at public authorities and not at private individuals. It is not meant to introduce a tort of privacy'. Furthermore, 'As regards matters relating to the press, they are to be left to self-regulation and others to the common law'. However, the courts are themselves public

---

1   One of the Civil Procedure Rules (1998) (r 48.7(3)) has already been ruled unlawful on the ground, *inter alia*, that it contravenes the European Convention on Human Rights: see *General Mediterranean Holdings SA v Patel* [1999] 3 All ER 673. In March 2000, the Lord Chancellor's Department published a consultation paper, *Human Rights Act 1998: Rules and Practice Directions*. This invited responses by 23 April 2000 to proposed rules and practice directions for the civil and family courts, up to the Court of Appeal, under the Human Rights Act 1998.

authorities and it is now expected that they might, therefore, be obliged to exercise their judgment in an appropriate case so as to recognise a tort of infringement of privacy where previously there was none. Judgments of the European Court of Human Rights (ECHR) have already observed that public authorities might be obliged, not merely to refrain from interfering in private life, but positively to provide effective protection for private life (for example, *Stjerna v Finland* (1994) 24 EHRR 194).

The likely effect of the Act on the development of case law is still, therefore, a moot point. The effect of the Act in relation to new statutes is much clearer. According to s 19 of the HRA 1998 (which is already in force), a Minister of the Crown in charge of a Bill must do one of two things before the Second Reading of the Bill. Either he must make a written statement to the effect that, in his view, the provisions of the Bill are compatible with convention rights ('a statement of compatibility'), or he must make a statement to the effect that 'although he is unable to make a statement of compatibility the government nevertheless wishes the House to proceed with the Bill': s 19(1)(b)).

An example of a statement of compatibility appears at the top of the Trustee Bill introduced into the House of Lords on 20 January 2000, in relation to which the Lord Chancellor made the necessary statement. It can be accessed on the internet at the following address: http://www.publications.parliament.uk/pa/ld199900/ldbills/020/2000020.htm.

Ironically, the very fact that the Lord Chancellor introduced the Trustee Bill (in his executive capacity) might disqualify him from sitting (in his judicial capacity) on cases brought under the Trustee Act when it comes into force. This (rather unlikely) position might be reached by extension of the judgment of the ECHR in *McGonnell v UK*, 8 February 2000. The ECHR held that a businessman from Guernsey had been denied the right to a fair trial (Art 6) because the judge who heard his planning appeal was also a member of the island's executive and legislature. (See 'The European ruling opens judges to challenge', an article by Frances Gibb (2000) *The Times*, 9 February.) This Guernsey case should not be taken too far. We do not suggest, for instance, that next time you are the respondent in a moot in the House of Lords you should seek to have the appeal dismissed on the ground merely that their Lordships are all members of the Upper House of Parliament.

As regards existing legislation, s 3 of the HRA 1998 requires that, 'so far as it is possible to do so, primary legislation and subordinate legislation must be read and given effect in a way which is compatible with the Convention rights'.

So, what are the Convention rights? Here is not the place to set them out in detail (they can be accessed as an appendix to the Act on the internet, see above). The 'main' ones are the right to life (Art 2), to liberty and security of person (Art 5), to a fair trial (Art 6), to respect for private and family life (Art 8), to freedom of thought, conscience and religion (Art 9) to freedom of expression (Art 10) and assembly (Art 11), the right to marry (Art 12) and the right to an effective remedy (Art 13). The articles also prohibit certain activities, namely, torture (Art 3), slavery (Art 4), punishment without law (Art 7) and discrimination 'on any ground such as sex, race, colour, language, religion, political or other opinion, national or social origin, association with a national minority, property, birth or other status' (Art 14). Then there are the protocols that have been added to the convention since it first appeared in 1950. The first protocol protects the right to peaceful enjoyment of property (Art 1), the right to education (Art 2) and the right to free elections (Art 3). The fourth protocol prohibits imprisonment for debt (Art 1) and restrictions on freedom of movement (Art 2). The sixth protocol abolishes the death penalty (Art 1) except in time of war (Art 2).

Mooting in the light of the Act

The first rule is to carry out detailed research before you attempt to incorporate a human rights argument into your moot. However, if you carry out the necessary research and preparation, you should expect the HRA 1998 to produce a number of moot-winning arguments. You might argue that a particular statute should be construed, where possible, in such a way so as to be compatible with convention rights. You might argue that the Court of Appeal or House of Lords (wherever it is that your moot is imagined to take place) is a public authority and, as such, is bound to exercise its judicial discretions in accordance with convention rights. Nevertheless, however you employ the HRA 1998, bear in mind that very few human rights arguments are as incontrovertible as they sometimes first appear. Very often, one human rights argument can be met head on by another. What to one person is freedom of expression or enjoyment of property might, to another person, be discrimination or restriction of freedom of marriage. An example would be the case of a will that leaves property 'to be divided among my daughters, provided that they are not Muslim or married to a Muslim'. You should also bear in mind that very few convention rights are expressed in absolute terms. The convention rights usually acknowledge that the State must itself be allowed a degree of freedom to perform its tasks. This concession to the State is sometimes called the 'margin of appreciation'. An example appears in Art 1 of the first protocol which provides that 'No one shall be deprived of his possessions except in the public interest' and, later, 'The preceding provisions shall not, however, in any way impair the right of a State to enforce such laws as it deems necessary to control the use of property'.

The fact that this 'margin of appreciation' can vary from one case to another, and from one State to another, may be a ground for distinguishing a case decided against Italy or France or Germany, and so on, from a case brought against the UK. Especially when one bears in mind that the ECHR is not bound by its own decisions. (The Convention is considered to be a 'living instrument', that is, one that may be interpreted differently as social conditions change. Consequently, the decisions of the ECHR do not lay down precedents binding on itself in future cases.)

As far as English domestic courts are concerned, the HRA 1998 does not make the decisions of the ECHR automatically binding upon them. Section 2 of the Act merely provides that every English court or tribunal must take the 'judgment, decision, declaration or advisory opinion' of the ECHR 'into account' to the extent that it may be 'relevant' to the proceedings. This does mean, however, that even the lowest court in the land may choose to consider itself bound to dispose of a case in accordance with a convention right, even if to do so would mean a departure from a pre-HRA 1998 authority of a superior court such as the House of Lords!

In summary, then, you should always consider the use of human rights arguments in your moot, but be careful not to use rights in the wrong way!

Bibliography

The works listed below all contain valuable or interesting information for mooters. The authors have found all of them useful in preparing this Guide.

Books

Anderson, T and Twining, W, *Analysis of Evidence*, 1991, London: Weidenfeld & Nicolson.

Bacon, F, 'Of judicature', in Hawkins, M (ed), *Essays*, 2nd edn, 1973, London: JM Dent.

Bailey, SH and Gunn, MJ, *The Modern English Legal System*, 3rd edn, 1996, London: Sweet & Maxwell.

Ballantine, R, *Some Experiences of a Barrister's Life*, 7th edn, 1883, London: Richard Bentley.

Baker, JH, *The Order of Serjeants at Law: A Chronicle of Creations, With Related Texts and an Historical Introduction*, 1984, London: Selden Society.

Baker, JH (ed), *Readings and Moots at the Inns of Court in the Fifteenth Century*, 1989, London: Selden Society, Vol 2.

Baker, JH, *An Introduction to English Legal History*, 3rd edn, 1990, London: Butterworths.

Bell, J, *Policy Arguments in Judicial Decisions*, 1983, Oxford: Clarendon.

Bell, J and Engle, G (Sir) (eds), *Statutory Interpretation*, 3rd edn, 1995, London: Butterworths.

Bennion, FAR, *Bennion on Statute Law*, 3rd edn, 1990, London: Longman.

Birkenhead (Second Earl), *The Life of FE Smith, First Earl of Birkenhead, By His Son*, 1960, London: Eyre & Spottiswoode.

Birkett, N, *Six Great Advocates*, 1961, London: Penguin.

Boulton, W (Sir), *Conduct and Etiquette at the Bar*, 1975, London: Butterworths

Buckhaven, C, *Barrister By-and-Large*, 1986, London: Pan.

Clinch, P, *Using a Law Library – A Student's Guide to Legal Research Skills*, 1992, London: Blackstone.

Day, R (Sir), *The Grand Inquisitor*, 1990, London: Pan.

Denning (Lord), *The Discipline of Law*, 1979, London: Butterworths.

Denning (Lord), *The Due Process of Law*, 1980, London: Butterworths.

Denning (Lord), *The Family Story*, 1981, London: Butterworths.

Devlin (Lord), *The Judge*, 1979, Oxford: OUP.

Dobson, P and Fitzpatrick, B (eds), *The Observer Book of Moots*, 1986, London: Sweet & Maxwell.

Du Cann, R, *The Art of the Advocate*, 3rd edn, 1982, London: Penguin.

Evans, K, *Advocacy at the Bar – A Beginner's Guide*, 1983, London: Financial Training.

Evans, K, *The Golden Rules of Advocacy*, 1993, London: Blackstone.

Gleitman, H, *Psychology*, 2nd edn, 1986, New York and London: WW Norton.

Goodhart, AL, 'Determining the *ratio decidendi* of a case', in *Essays in Jurisprudence and the Common Law*, 1931, Cambridge: CUP.

Grainger, I and Fealy, M, *An Introduction to the New Civil Procedure Rules*, 1999, London: Cavendish Publishing (see, also, *The Civil Procedure Rules in Action*, 2nd edn, 2000).

Gray, K, *Elements of Land Law*, 2nd edn, 1993, London: Butterworths.

Groves, PJ, *Lecture Notes on European Community Law*, 1995, London: Cavendish Publishing.

Halsbury's Laws of England, 1994, London: Butterworths.

Halsbury's Statutes of England and Wales, 1994, London: Butterworths.

Harris, JW, *Legal Philosophies*, 2nd edn, 1997, London: Butterworths.

Hawkins, H, *The Reminiscences of Sir Henry Hawkins, Baron Brampton*, in Harris, R (ed), 1904, London: Edward Arnold, Vol 1.

Hawkins, M (ed), *Essays*, 2nd edn, 1973, London: JM Dent.

Henry, J (Cardinal Newman), *The Idea of a University*, 1959, New York: Image.

Herbert, AP, *Uncommon Law*, 4th edn, 1942, London: Methuen.

Holdsworth, W (Sir), *A History of English Law*, in Goodhart, AL and Hanbury, HG (eds), 1952, London: Methuen/Sweet & Maxwell, Vol 13.

Kaye, T and Townley, L, *Blackstone Book of Moots*, 1996, London: Blackstone.

Kennedy, H, *Eve Was Framed – Women and British Justice*, 1993, London: Vintage.

The Law Society, *The Guide to the Professional Conduct of Solicitors*, 1999, London: The Law Society.

Lewis, JR, *The Victorian Bar*, 1982, London: Robert Hale.

Llewellyn, KN, *The Bramble Bush – On Our Law and Its Study*, 1930, New York: Oceana.

Lord Chancellor's Department, *Human Rights Act 1998: Rules and Practice Directions*, 2000, London: HMSO.

MacKenzie, J-A and Phillips, M, *A Practical Approach to Land Law*, 6th edn, 1996, London: Blackstone.

Maughan, C and Webb, J, *Lawyering Skills and the Legal Process*, 1995, London: Butterworths.

Montgomery Hyde, H, *Norman Birkett – The Life of Lord Birkett of Ulverston*, 1965, London: The Reprint Society.

Mortimer, J, *Clinging to the Wreckage – A Part of Life*, 1982, London: Weidenfeld & Nicolson.

Mortimer, J, 'Rumpole and the younger generation', in *The Best of Rumpole*, 1993, London: Viking.

Plant, C (ed), *Blackstone's Guide to the Civil Procedure Rules*, 2nd edn, 1999, London: Blackstone.

Pointon, GE (ed), *BBC Pronouncing Dictionary of British Names*, 1983, Oxford: OUP.

Pugh, J, *Goodbye for Ever – The Victim of a System*, 1981, London: Barry Rose.

Rawlins, K, *Presentation and Communication Skills – A Handbook for Practitioners*, 1993, London: Macmillan.

Rozenberg, J, *The Search for Justice*, 1994, London: Hodder & Stoughton.

Savage, N and Watt, G, 'A house of intellect for the profession', in Birks, P (ed), *What are Law Schools For?*, 1996, Oxford: OUP.

Simpson, AWB, *Biographical Dictionary of the Common Law*, 1984, London: Butterworths.

Smith, JC (Sir), *The Law of Theft*, 7th edn, 1993, London: Butterworths.

Stone, J, *Precedent and Law – Dynamics of Common Law Growth*, 1985, London: Butterworths.

Thomas, PA and Cope, C, *How to Use a Law Library: An Introduction to Legal Skills*, 3rd edn, 1996, London: Sweet & Maxwell.

Twining, W, *Blackstone's Tower: The English Law School*, *The Hamlyn Lectures*, 1994, London: Stevens/Sweet & Maxwell.

Wallace, JW, *The Reporters Arranged and Characterised with Incidental Remarks*, 1882, Boston: Soule & Bugbee.

Walker, RJ and Ward, R (eds), *Walker and Walker's English Legal System*, 1994, London: Butterworths.

Weatherill, S and Beaumont, P, *EC Law*, 2nd edn, 1996, London: Penguin.

Williams, G, *Learning The Law*, 11th edn, 1982, London: Stevens.

Wilson, GP, *Frontiers of Legal Scholarship: Twenty Five Years of Warwick Law School*, 1995, Chichester: Wiley.

Wittgenstein, L, *Tractatus Logico-Philosophicus*, Ogden, CK (trans), 1922, London: Routledge.

Articles

Anon, 'Square or round brackets?' (1993) 49 EG 110.

Asquith (Lord), Untitled (1957) 69 LQR 317.

Baker, RW, 'Guest passengers and drunken drivers' (1949) 65 LQR 20.

Bentley, D, 'Mooting in an undergraduate tax program' (1996) 7 Legal Education Rev 1, pp 97–124.

Birkett, N, 'The art of advocacy', in *Six Great Advocates*, 1961, London: Penguin.

Bright, S, 'What, and how, should we be teaching?' (1991) 25 Law Teacher 11.

Brown, C, 'The Jessop Mooting Competition as a vehicle for teaching public international law' (1978) 16 Can Yrbk Intl L 332.

Edwards, HT, 'The growing disjunction between legal education and the legal profession' (1992) 91 Mich L Rev, pp 34–78.

Edwards, HT, 'The role of legal education in shaping the profession' (1988) 38 JLE 3, pp 285–93.

Goodhart, AL, 'Reporting the law' (1939) 55 LQR 29.

Goodhart, AL, 'Contributory negligence and *volenti non fit injuria*' (1939) 55 LQR 184.

Goodhart, AL, 'The *ratio decidendi* of a case' (1959) 22 MLR 117.

Higgs, N, 'Failure is a positive force' (1995) 31 Training Officer 1.

Hyams, R, 'The teaching of skills: rebuilding – not just tinkering around the edges' (1995) 13 J Prof LE 1, pp 63–80.

Keynes, ME and Whincop, MJ, 'The moot reconceived: some theory and evidence on legal skills' (1997) 8 Legal Education Rev 1, pp 1–41.

Kozinski, A, 'In praise of moot court – not!' (1997) Col LR 178.

Lindley, N, 'The history of law reports' (1885) 1 LQR 137.

Lynch, A, 'Why do we moot? Exploring the role of mooting in legal education' (1996) 7 Legal Education Rev 1, pp 67–96.

O'Keeffe, D, 'Sir George Jessel and the union of judicature' (1982) 26 American J of Legal History 227.

Pannick, D, 'American judges behaving badly in the courtroom' (1999) *The Times*, 16 November.

Partington, M, 'Law teachers and legal practice' (1992) 3 Legal Education Rev 75.

Reid (Lord), 'The judge as lawmaker' (1972) 12 JSPTL 22.

Rufford, N, 'Court jargon to suffer GBH' (1999) *The Sunday Times*, 5 December.

Sheppard, S, 'An informal history of how law schools evaluate students, with a predictable emphasis on law school final exams' (1997) 65 UMKCL Rev 657.

Spiegel, M, 'Theory and practice in legal education: an essay on clinical education' (1987) 34 UCLA L Rev 3, pp 577–610.

Telford, A, 'Controlling nervousness in presentations' (1995) 31 Training Officer 1.

Tomain, J and Solimine, M, 'Skills scepticism in the postclinic world' (1990) 40 JLE 307.

Zeeman, WPM, 'Curriculum – a judicial perspective' (1995) 13 J Prof LE 2, pp 215–26.

Lectures

Davies, JW, 'The argument of an appeal', address to the Association of the Bar of the City of New York AQ Ar.

McLaren, I (QC), 'Advocacy before superior appellate courts', lecture given at Nottingham Law School, 23 March 1999.

Pamphlets

Hanstock, T and Donaldson, A 'Electronic information sources in law: a brief guide', The Nottingham Trent University: Library and Information Services.

Unpublished materials

Calder, K and Sacranie, S, 'Is mooting useful in degree level education, and if so, how should it be integrated into a degree programme?', unpublished LLB dissertation, 1996, University of Warwick.

Clinch, P, 'Systems of reporting judicial decision making', unpublished PhD thesis, 1989, University of Sheffield.

Resources on-line

Two former students of the Law School at the University of Warwick, Kevin Calder and Shameer Sacranie, set up Mooting Net in 1997. It is an excellent on-line mooting resource and can be accessed at http://www.mootingnet.org.uk. It also contains a number of links to assist with legal research.

The English-Speaking Union maintains a list of university mooting contacts at http://www.esu.org.uk/educate/centre/mootlist.html.

Index